Appreciation of Masterpiece English Speeches

英语演讲名篇赏析

主　编　林　艳
编　委　陶　勇　胡　兰　应　葳

图书在版编目(CIP)数据

英语演讲名篇赏析/林艳主编. —北京：北京大学出版社,2014.10
（大学英语立体化网络化系列教材·拓展课程教材）
ISBN 978-7-301-24949-9

Ⅰ.①英… Ⅱ.①林… Ⅲ.①英语－演讲－高等学校－教材 Ⅳ.①H311.9

中国版本图书馆 CIP 数据核字(2014)第 231996 号

书　　　名：英语演讲名篇赏析
著作责任者：林　艳　主编
责 任 编 辑：郝妮娜
标 准 书 号：ISBN 978-7-301-24949-9/H·3597
出 版 发 行：北京大学出版社
地　　　址：北京市海淀区成府路 205 号　100871
网　　　址：http://www.pup.cn　　新浪官方微博：@北京大学出版社
电 子 信 箱：zbing@pup.pku.edu.cn
电　　　话：邮购部 62752015　发行部 62750672　编辑部 62759634　出版部 62754962
印 刷 者：北京富生印刷厂
经 销 者：新华书店
　　　　　787 毫米×1092 毫米　16 开本　14.25 印张　360 千字
　　　　　2014 年 10 月第 1 版　2014 年 10 月第 1 次印刷
定　　　价：38.00 元

未经许可，不得以任何方式复制或抄袭本书之部分或全部内容。
版权所有，侵权必究
举报电话：010-62752024　电子信箱：fd@pup.pku.edu.cn

出版前言

英语演讲与辩论是英语语言能力和知识水平、思辨能力、组织能力、心理素质等综合能力的体现。正因如此，各类英语演讲与辩论赛，吸引了越来越多的英语爱好者。很多高校把学生在全国英语竞赛中获得名次当作学校综合实力甚至是知名度的重要指标之一。上海外国语大学梅德明教授曾谈到："全国英语演讲比赛不仅仅是口才的比拼，更是人才的较量，同时也是人才的展示。"

《英语演讲名篇赏析》主要适用于综合性高等院校各学科的本科生。其编写的指导思想是"拓宽学生文化视野，强化学生语言能力"。该书由【政治演讲篇】、【教育演讲篇】、【礼仪演讲篇】三大板块组成，每一版块包含7篇精彩英文演讲名篇。本书以介绍英语演讲名篇为主线，从【教案设计】、【人物简介】、【名篇导读】、【英语原文】、【词汇点拨】、【文化快递】、【参考译文】七个方面将输入与输出结合起来，把阅读、写作、翻译等语言技能与词汇、语法、文化知识等融为一体，确保读者读完该书后不但可以拓宽文化视野，还能快速提高自己的语言能力。

本教材的编写宗旨为注重实用性，强调在英语语言的运用中创新思维、批判思维、反思思维等思维品质的培养，体现了新世纪对人才培养提出的新要求；同时，选材兼顾趣味性和知识性，活动设计循序渐进，内容编排由易到难，由输入到输出。其编写特色具体体现在：

一、教材教案化，主要围绕教学主题设计教案化的口语活动，所有的交际活动设计过程化，最大限度地减轻教师备课、查询资料及设计活动的负担；

二、教材编写强化文化素养教育，融中西文化于大学英语教学之中，在对英语演讲名篇的文化赏析教学中培养学生的审美情趣和文化素养；

三、从思维扩展结合语言能力的角度提高学生对英语演讲名篇的鉴赏能力，强化学生创新思维、外显能力和个性发展；

四、提高学生驾驭不同类型的演讲的实际语言运用能力和学生根据语境要求采用不同组织策略的能力，提高学生查找相关资料、进行英文写作的能力，提高学生的沟通技巧和人际交往的能力等。

这本教材是集体智慧的结晶。陶勇完成了第二章(1—7课)的编写工作；胡兰老师参与了第三章第5课的部分编写工作；应葳老师参与了第一章第4课的部分编写工作。林艳老师完成了其余章节的编写和整部教材的统稿修订工作。北京大学出版社的编辑郝妮娜和有关领导也为本书的出版付出了辛勤的劳动，我们在此表示衷心的感谢。

在本书编写过程中，我们参阅了大量国内外英语演讲相关文字材料，广泛吸收了这些资料的精华，并结合实际进行了新的尝试。特此致谢并恳切希望广大同行、专家、读者的批评和指正。

仅以此书献给热爱英语演讲的广大学子。

编　者
宁波大学杏琴园
2014年8月8日

Contents

Chapter 1 Call of Freedom（政治演讲篇——自由的呼唤） ·· 1
- Lesson 1　I Have A Dream ·· 1
- Lesson 2　Changes Has Come to America ·· 12
- Lesson 3　Blood, Toil, Sweat and Tears ·· 23
- Lesson 4　Inaugural Address ·· 29
- Lesson 5　King's Speech ·· 37
- Lesson 6　Women's Rights Are Human Rights ··· 43
- Lesson 7　Americans Despise Cowards! ··· 54

Chapter 2 Spread of Civilization（教育演讲篇——文明的传递） ······································ 63
- Lesson 1　Commencement Address Delivered on Graduation in Stanford ················ 63
- Lesson 2　The Way Ahead: Innovating Together in China ····································· 74
- Lesson 3　My Story and the Chinese Dream Behind It ·· 82
- Lesson 4　Feelings, Failure and Finding Happiness ·· 95
- Lesson 5　The Fringe Benefits of Failure and the Importance of Imagination ·········· 113
- Lesson 6　Heal the Kids ·· 127
- Lesson 7　Address to Beijing University ··· 148

Chapter 3 Communication of Hearts（礼仪演讲篇——心灵的交流） ································ 164
- Lesson 1　Beautiful Smile and Love ··· 164
- Lesson 2　Unconscious Plagiarism ··· 169
- Lesson 3　Cultural Programs and the 2008 Olympic Games ·································· 174
- Lesson 4　Shall We Choose Death ·· 179
- Lesson 5　Every Home in Scotland Keeps His Fame Bright ·································· 186
- Lesson 6　Oscar Best Actress Speech ··· 193
- Lesson 7　On not Winning the Nobel Prize ··· 198

Chapter 1

Call of Freedom
（政治演讲篇——自由的呼唤）

Lesson 1

I Have a Dream

Task 1 Questions and Answers

Directions: Work in pairs. Read the following speech then take turns to ask and answer the following questions.
1. When was the speech delivered? Where?
2. Who delivered the speech? Who are involved in the speech?
3. What is the theme of the speech?
4. Why is there a need for the request?
5. How can the request be achieved?

Task 2 Group List

Directions: *Work in groups of four. Help each other to activate your prior knowledge about figures of Speech in English with examples. Go through the script of <u>I Have a Dream</u> and locate the main figures of speech used in it. Then make a group list and report your list to class.*

References: Figures of Speech

Figures of speech (修辞) are ways of making our language figurative. When we use words in other than their ordinary or literal sense to lend force to an idea, to heighten effect, or to create suggestive imagery, we are said to be speaking or writing figuratively. Now we are going to talk about some common forms of figures of speech.

1) Simile(明喻): It is a figure of speech which makes a comparison between two unlike elements having at least one quality or characteristic (特性) in

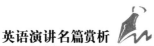

common. To make the comparison, words like **as, as...as, as if** and **like** are used to transfer the quality we associate with one to the other. For example, "As cold waters to a thirsty soul, so is good news from a far country." / "This elephant is like a snake as anybody can see."

2) Metaphor(暗喻): It is like a simile, also makes a comparison between two unlike elements, but unlike a simile, this comparison is implied rather than stated. For example, "The world is a stage." / "The diamond department was the heart and center of the store."

3) Analogy(类比): It is also a form of comparison, but unlike simile or metaphor which usually uses comparison on one point of resemblance, analogy draws a parallel between two unlike things that have several common qualities or points of resemblance.

4) Personification(拟人): It gives human form of feelings to animals, or life and personal attributes to inanimate objects, or to ideas and abstractions. For example, "The wind whistled through the trees."

5) Hyperbole(夸张): It is the deliberate use of overstatement or exaggeration to achieve emphasis. For instance, "He almost died laughing."

6) Understatement(含蓄陈述): It is the opposite of hyperbole, or overstatement. It achieves its effect of emphasizing a fact by deliberately understating it, impressing the listener or the reader more by what is merely implied or left unsaid than by bare statement. For instance, "It is no laughing matter."

7) Euphemism(委婉): It is the substitution of an agreeable or inoffensive expression for one that may offend or suggest something unpleasant. For instance, we refer to "die" as "pass away".

8) Metonymy(转喻): It is a figure of speech that has to do with the substitution of the mane of one thing for that of another. For instance, the pen (words) is mightier than the sword (forces). For instance, "Several years later, word came that Napoleon himself was coming to inspect them." "word" is the substitute for the "news, information". / Al spoke with his eyes".

9) Pun(双关语): It is a play on words, or rather a play on the form and meaning of words. For instance, a cannon-ball took off his legs, so he laid down his arms. (Here "arms" has two meanings: a person's body; weapons carried by a soldier.)/Napoleon was astonished." Either you are mad, or I am," he declared. "Both，sir!" cried the Swede proudly.

10) Irony(反语): It is a figure of speech that achieves emphasis by saying the opposite of what is meant, the intended meaning of the words being the opposite of their usual sense. For instance, "We are lucky, what you said makes me feel real good."

11) Paradox(似非而是的隽语): It is a figure of speech consisting of a statement or proposition which on the face of it seems self-contradictory, absurd or contrary to established fact or practice, but which on further thinking and study may prove to be true, well-founded, and even to contain a succinct point. For example, "More haste, less speed."

12) Oxymoron(矛盾修饰): It is a compressed paradox, formed by the conjoining of two contrasting, contradictory or incongruous terms as in bitter-sweet memories, orderly chaos and proud humility.

13) Antithesis(对照): It is the deliberate arrangement of contrasting words or ideas in balanced structural forms to achieve emphasis. For example, speech is silver; silence is golden.
14) Transferred Epithet(移就): It is a figure of speech where an epithet (an adjective or descriptive phrase) is transferred from the noun it should rightly modify to another to which it does not really apply or belong. For instance, I spent sleepless nights on my project.
15) Alliteration(头韵): It has to do with the sound rather than the sense of words for effect. It is a device that repeats the same sound at frequent intervals and since the sound repeated is usually the initial consonant sound, it is also called "front rhyme". For instance, the fair breeze blew, the white foam flew, the furrow followed free. How and why he had come to Princeton, New Jersey is a story of struggle, success, and sadness.
16) Onomatopoeia(拟声): It is a device that uses words which imitate the sounds made by an object (animate or inanimate), or which are associated with or suggestive of some action rustling of silk, the noises of insects, the creaking of a door, the voice of a loved one.

Task 3 Imitation and Play

Directions: *Watch the authentic video of the speech. Then try to imitate one or two paragraphs with appropriate delivery techniques. First practice by yourself. Then work in groups of four to take turns to deliver the speech.*

Task 4 Dictation

Directions: *Watch the authentic video of the speech. Then fill in the missing words in their appropriate forms. You may watch the video for three times.*

　　We have also come to this hallowed spot to remind America of the fierce _____ of now. This is no time to engage in the _____ of cooling off or to take the tranquilizing drug of gradualism. Now is the time to rise from the dark and _____ valley of segregation to the _____ path of racial justice. Now is the time to open the doors of _____ to all of God's children. Now is the time to lift our nation from the _____ of racial injustice to the solid rock of _____.

Task 5 Speaking Practice

Directions: *Give a speech to the class for 2-3 minutes on a topic which you are interested in. You may choose from the following:*
1. My Dream
2. Dreams Enlighten Reality
3. American Dreams & Chinese Dreams

I Have a Dream
我有一个梦
Lincoln Memorial Address on August 28, 1963
By Martin Luther King

人物简介

马丁·路德·金（Martin Luther King Jr.，1929年1月15日—1968年4月4日），著名的美国民权运动领袖，诞生于美国东南部的佐治亚州的亚特兰大市。1948年他大学毕业，担任教会的牧师。1948年到1951年间，马丁·路德·金在美国东海岸的费城继续深造。1963年，马丁·路德·金晋见了肯尼迪总统，要求通过新的民权法，给黑人以平等的权利。1963年8月28日在林肯纪念堂前发表《我有一个梦想》的演说。1964年度诺贝尔和平奖获得者，有金牧师之称。1968年4月，马丁·路德·金前往孟菲斯市领导工人罢工被人谋杀，年仅39岁。1986年起美国政府将每年一月的第三个星期一定为马丁·路德·金全国纪念日。

名篇导读

在美国，曾经有这样一个黑人，他是一个奴隶的后代，他把毕生的精力都投入到为了黑人的平等和自由而进行的民权运动中。在他风华正茂的时候，却在"砰"的一声枪响中结束了年轻的生命。他的鲜血在地上画出了一个大大的惊叹号！后来，美国人为了纪念他，用他的生日命名了一个节日。今天，他的著名的演说《我有一个梦想》仍就被人们广泛地传诵着。他，就是美国著名的民权运动的领导人——马丁·路德·金。

《我有一个梦想》是马丁·路德·金于1963年8月28日在华盛顿林肯纪念堂发表的著

名演讲，内容主要是关于种族平等。《我有一个梦想》自问世以来就一直为世人所传诵，被视为演讲词的典范。其精彩之处不仅在于演讲者的美好理想与坚忍不拔的人格力量，更在于这篇演讲词所散发出的语言魅力。该演讲气势恢宏，文采飞扬，几乎每一句话都运用了一种或多种修辞手法而被喻为"一座修辞的富矿"，堪称字字珠玑，句句富彩。马丁·路德·金的演讲造诣十分高，通篇绝无错漏，善于运用循序渐进的排比句。他更善于运用情感而不激进，他的个人魅力和亲和力更能争取更广泛的中间团体的支持（如女权运动组织，宗教团体，自由主义者等）。《我有一个梦》被很多英语爱好者奉为经典演讲之冠，与那场浩浩荡荡的民权运动一起载入史册。

他的经典演讲还包括《攀越巅峰》和反对越战的《打破沉默》。他的演讲，不论是风格还是遣词造句，不论是语调还是情感运用，方方面面都值得学习和借鉴。

马丁·路德·金去世后，人们把他的尸体运回了他的故乡。在他的墓碑上，雕刻着这样一句话："Free at last, free at last, thank God Almighty, I'm free at last！"今天，美国无数的黑人和白人一样，过着自由自在的生活，享受着美国的民主和自由，追求着自己的美国梦。而他的"I have a dream"精彩的演说已经融化到了美国梦之中。

英文原文

Five score years ago, a great American, in whose symbolic shadow we stand today, signed the **Emancipation Proclamation**[1]. This momentous **decree**[2] came as a great beacon light of hope to millions of Negro slaves who had been **seared**[3] in the flames of **withering**[4] injustice. It came as a joyous daybreak to end the long night of bad **captivity**[5].

But one hundred years later, the Negro still is not free. One hundred years later, the life of the Negro is still sadly crippled by the **manacles**[6] of **segregation**[7] and the chains of discrimination. One hundred years later, the Negro lives on a lonely island of poverty in midst of a vast ocean of material prosperity. One hundred years later, the Negro is still **languished**[8] in the corners of American society and finds himself an exile in his own land. So we've come here today to dramatize a shameful condition.

In a sense we have come to our nation's capital to cash a check. When the architects of our republic wrote the magnificent words of *the Constitution* and *the Declaration of Independence*, they were signing a promissory note to which every American was to fall heir. This note was a promise that all men would be guaranteed the **inalienable**[9] rights of life, liberty, and the pursuit

---

1　Emancipation Proclamation 解放宣言
2　decree 法令
3　sear 烧焦
4　withering 令人无地自容的
5　captivity 囚禁
6　manacles 手铐
7　segregation 隔离
8　languish 冷落
9　inalienable 不可分割的

of happiness. It is obvious today that America has **defaulted**[1] on this promissory note insofar as her citizens of color are concerned. Instead of honoring this sacred obligation, America has given the Negro people a bad check which has come back marked "insufficient funds".

But we refuse to believe that the bank of justice is bankrupt. We refuse to believe that there are insufficient funds in the great **vaults**[2] of opportunity of this nation. So we have come to cash this check—a check that will give us upon demand the riches of freedom and the security of justice.

We have also come to this hallowed spot to remind America of the fierce urgency of now. This is no time to engage in the luxury of cooling off or to take the **tranquilizing**[3] drug of gradualism. Now is the time to rise from the dark and desolate valley of segregation to the sunlit path of racial justice. Now is the time to open the doors of opportunity to all of God's children. Now is the time to lift our nation from the quicksands of racial injustice to the solid rock of brotherhood. Now is the time to make justice a reality for all of God's children.

It would be fatal for the nation to overlook the urgency of the moment and to underestimate the determination of the Negro. This sweltering summer of the Negro's legitimate discontent will not pass until there is an **invigorating**[4] autumn of freedom and equality. Nineteen sixty-three is not an end, but a beginning. Those who hope that the Negro needed to blow off steam and will now be content will have a rude awakening if the nation returns to business as usual. There will be neither rest nor tranquility in America until the Negro is granted his citizenship rights. The whirlwinds of revolt will continue to shake the foundations of our nation until the bright day of justice emerges.

But there is something that I must say to my people who stand on the warm **threshold**[5] which leads into the palace of justice. In the process of gaining our rightful place we must not be guilty of wrongful deeds. Let us not seek to satisfy our thirst for freedom by drinking from the cup of bitterness and hatred. We must forever conduct our struggle on the high plane of dignity and discipline. We must not allow our creative protest to degenerate into physical violence. Again and again we must rise to the majestic heights of meeting physical force with soul force.

The marvelous new militancy which has **engulfed**[6] the Negro community must not lead us to distrust of all white people, for many of our white brothers, as evidenced by their presence here today, have come to realize that their destiny is tied up with our destiny and their freedom is **inextricably**[7] bound to our freedom.

We cannot walk alone.

And as we walk, we must make the pledge that we shall march ahead.

---

1 default 拖欠债务
2 vault 地下室；银行的金库
3 tranquilize 使安静，使平静，使镇静
4 invigorating 爽快的
5 threshold 门槛
6 engulf 吞没
7 inextricably 无法解救地

We cannot turn back.

There are those who are asking the devotees of civil rights, "When will you be satisfied?" We can never be satisfied as long as the Negro is the victim of the unspeakable horrors of police brutality. We can never be satisfied as long as our bodies, heavy with the fatigue of travel, cannot gain lodging in the motels of the highways and the hotels of the cities. We cannot be satisfied as long as the Negro's basic mobility is from a smaller ghetto to a larger one. We can never be satisfied as long as a Negro in Mississippi cannot vote and a Negro in New York believes he has nothing for which to vote. No, no, we are not satisfied, and we will not be satisfied until justice rolls down like waters and righteousness like a mighty stream. I am not unmindful that some of you have come here out of great trials and **tribulations**[1]. Some of you have come fresh from narrow jail cells. Some of you have come from areas where your quest for freedom left you battered by the storms of persecution and staggered by the winds of police brutality. You have been the veterans of creative suffering. Continue to work with the faith that unearned suffering is **redemptive**.[2] Go back to Mississippi, go back to Alabama, go back to South Carolina, go back to Georgia, go back to Louisiana, go back to the slums and **ghettos**[3] of our northern cities, knowing that somehow this situation can and will be changed.

Let us not **wallow**[4] in the valley of despair. I say to you today, my friends.

So even though, we face the difficulties of today and tomorrow, I still have a dream. It is a dream deeply rooted in the American dream.

I have a dream that one day this nation will rise up, live up to the true meaning of its creed: "We hold these truths to be self-evident; that all men are created equal."

I have a dream that one day on the red hills of Georgia the sons of former slaves and the sons of former slaver-owners will be able to sit down together at the table of brotherhood.

I have a dream that one day even the state of Mississippi, a state **sweltering**[5] with the heat of injustice, sweltering with the heat of oppression, will be transformed into an **oasis**[6] of freedom and justice.

I have a dream that my four little children will one day live in a nation where they will not be judged by the color of their skin but by the content of their character.

I have a dream today!

I have a dream that one day, down in Alabama, with its governor, having his lips dripping with the words of **interposition**[7] and **nullification**[8], one day right down in Alabama little black boys and black girls will be able to join hands with little white boys and white girls as sisters and brothers.

I have a dream today!

1　tribulation 苦难
2　redemptive 赎回的, 拯救的
3　ghettos 贫民区, 少数民族聚居区
4　wallow 沉迷；纵乐
5　sweltering 闷热的
6　oasis 绿洲
7　interposition 干涉
8　nullification 无效

I have a dream that one day every valley shall be exalted, every hill and mountain shall be made low, the rough places will be made plain, and the crooked places will be made straight, and the glory of the Lord shall be revealed, and all flesh shall see it together.

This is our hope. This is the faith that I go back to the South with.

With this faith we will be able to hew out of the mountain of despair a stone of hope. With this faith we will be able to transform the **jangling**[1] discords of our nation into a beautiful symphony of brotherhood. With this faith we will be able to work together, to pray together, to struggle together, to go to jail together, to stand up for freedom together, knowing that we will be free one day.

This will be the day when all of God's children will be able to sing with new meaning.

My country, 'tis of thee, sweet land of liberty, of thee I sing.

Land where my fathers died, land of the pilgrims' pride,

From every mountainside, let freedom ring!

And if America is to be a great nation this must become true.

So let freedom ring from the **prodigious**[2] hilltops of New Hampshire.

Let freedom ring from the mighty mountains of New York!

Let freedom ring from the heightening **Alleghenies**[3] of Pennsylvania!

Let freedom ring from the snowcapped Rockies of Colorado!

Let freedom ring from the curvaceous slopes of California!

But not only that:

Let freedom ring from Stone Mountain of Georgia!

Let freedom ring from Lookout Mountain of Tennessee!

Let freedom ring from every hill and **molehill**[4] of Mississippi!

From every mountainside, let freedom ring!

When we let freedom ring, when we let it ring from every village and every hamlet, from every state and every city, we will be able to speed up that day when all of God's children, black men and white men, Jews and **Gentiles**[5], **Protestants**[6] and Catholics, will be able to join hands and sing in the words of the old Negro spiritual,

"Free at last! Free at last!

Thank God **almighty**[7], we are free at last!"

文化快递

1. Emancipation Proclamation（解放宣言）

熟悉有关美国南北战争的历史背景知识的读者会知道此处的"a great man"指的是

---

1 jangling 烦扰人的
2 prodigious 巨大的
3 Alleghenies 阿勒格尼山脉
4 molehill 鼹鼠丘
5 Gentiles 非犹太人
6 Protestant 新教教徒
7 almighty 全能的

Abraham Lincoln，"the Emancipation Proclamation"便是指林肯总统在1863年签署的《解放奴隶宣言》。演说首句的"in whose symbolic shadow we stand today"为一语双关，一方面指发表演说的地点是在华盛顿林肯纪念堂，在林肯塑像之前，一方面是指林肯开创的民主运动影响了马丁·路德·金和他的同行者不畏强权、奋勇前行。

2. Protestants（新教徒）

新教，Protestantism，在文艺复兴时期的宗教改革中产生的，首倡者是马丁路德和加尔文，它的本质是革罗马天主教廷的命，提出了"《圣经》的权威高于教皇"的主张。信奉新教的人被称为新教徒。新教逐渐发展出了6大教派：

Lutheran Church，是宗教改革后出现的新教主要宗派之一，是对以马丁·路德的宗教思想为依据的各教会的统称。

Calvinists，是以加尔文的宗教思想为依据的各教会的统称。

Anglican Communion，欧洲宗教改革时期产生于英国。

Wesleyans，是以创始人约翰·卫斯理宗教思想为依据的各教会统称，于18世纪产生于英国。

Congregationalists，16世纪后期产生于英国。

Baptists，于17世纪初产生于英国和流亡于荷兰的英国人当中。

▶ 参考译文

一百年前，一位伟大的美国人——我们现在正站立在他的灵魂的安息处——签署了《解放黑奴宣言》。这条重要法令的颁发，在一直忍受着不义与暴虐的火焰烧灼的百万黑人奴隶的心中，竖起一座光明与希望的灯塔。《宣言》似令人欢愉的黎明，即将结束种族奴役的漫漫长夜。

但从那时至今，已经有一百年历史了，可黑人仍无自由可言。一百年后的今天，黑人的生活仍旧悲惨地为隔离的桎梏和歧视的锁链所捆缚。一百年后的今天，在浩瀚的物质财富海洋之中，黑人仍旧在贫困的孤岛上生活。一百年后的今天，黑人仍旧在美国社会的一隅受苦受难，并且发现自己竟然是自己所在国土上的流放者。因此，我们今天来到这里，把这种不体面的身份戏剧性地表演一下。

就某种意义而言，我们是来首都兑现期票的。当我们共和国的"建筑师"们撰写《宪法》和《独立宣言》中富丽堂皇的篇章时，他们是在签写一张"期票"，每个美国人都是这张期票的合法继承人。这张期票是一项允诺，即所有的美国人都保证拥有不容剥夺的生活的权利、享受自由的权利和追求幸福的权利。但是现在，很显然，就有色公民而论，美国却一直拒付这张期票。美国没有承担如期兑现这张期票的神圣义务。黑人满怀期望地得到的是一张空头期票，这张期票被签上"资金不足"的字样。

然而我们绝不相信，正义的银行会破产。我们绝不相信，在美国，储存机遇的巨大金库竟会"资金不足"!

所以,我们来兑现这张期票来了,来兑现一张将给予我们堪称最高财富——自由和正义的保障的——期票。

我们来到这个尊为神圣的地点,其又一目的是提醒美国政府,现在是最为紧迫的时刻。现在既不是享用缓和激动情绪的奢侈品的时刻,也不是服用渐进主义麻醉剂的时刻。现在是从黑暗荒凉的深渊中崛起,向阳光普照的种族平等的道路奋进的时刻。现在是把我们的国家从种族歧视的流沙中拯救出来,重建在兄弟情谊般的坚石之上的时刻。现在是为上帝的子孙实现平等的时刻!

如果再继续无视时机的紧迫,就将导致我们国家的不幸。不实现自由与平等,黑人的完全合法的不满情绪就不会平息;令人心旷神怡的金秋就不会降临;炎炎酷暑就不会消逝。1963年不是尾声,仅是序曲。如果美国政府继续一意孤行,就会使那些幻想黑人只要发泄一下不满情绪就会满足的人猛醒。在未授予黑人以公民权之前,美国既不会安宁,也不会平静。反叛的飓风将会不断地撼动这个国家的根基,直到迎来光辉灿烂的正义的黎明。

可是我必须对站在通往正义之宫的温暖入口处的人们进一言,我们在争取合法地位的进程中,决不能轻举妄动。我们决不能为了满足对自由的渴望,就啜饮敌意和仇恨。我们必须永远在自尊和教规的最高水平上继续我们的抗争。我们必须不断地升华到用精神的力量来迎接暴力的高尚顶峰。

已经吞没了黑人共同体的新的敌对状态令人不解,但它决不应该导致我们对所有白人的不信任——因为有许多白人兄弟参加了今天这个集会。这就告诉我们,他们已经逐渐认识到他们自己的命运和自由是与我们的命运和自由休戚相关的。

我们不能独自前进,而当我们前进的时候,我们必须宣誓永远向前,义无反顾。

有些人向我们这些热衷于获得公民权的人发问:你们何时才会满足?答案是明确的:只要黑人还是警察的骇人听闻的恐怖手段和野蛮行为的牺牲品,我们是不会满足的。只要我们因旅途劳顿而疲惫不堪,想在路旁的游客旅馆里歇息,或在市内的旅馆投宿却不被允许,我们就不会满足的。只要黑人的基本活动范围还是局限于从一个较小的黑人区到一个稍大的黑人区,我们就不会满足的。只要密西西比的黑人不能参加选举,而纽约黑人的选票还无实际意义,我们就不会满足的。不会的,不会的!除非平等泻如飞瀑,除非正义涌入湍流,我们是不会满足的。我并非没有留意到,你们之中有些人是从巨大的痛苦与磨难中来到这里的。有些人来自狭小的牢房,还有些人来自那对自由的要求竟会招致迫害的风暴接二连三的打击,竟会招致警察兽行般地反复摧残的地区。而你们却一直富于创造性地、坚韧地忍耐着。那么,就怀着一定能获得拯救的信念坚持下去吧!回到密西西比去吧!回到阿拉巴马去吧!回到南卡罗来纳去吧!回到佐治亚去吧!回到路易丝安那去吧!既然知道这种境况能够而且必定改变,那么就回到我们北方城市中的陋巷和贫民窟去吧!

今天,我对大家说,我的朋友们,我们决不可以在绝望的深渊中纵乐。

纵使我们面临着今天与明天的种种艰难困苦，我仍然有个梦想，这是一个深深植根于美国之梦的梦想。

我梦想着，有那么一天，我们这个民族将会奋起反抗，并且一直坚持实现它的信条的真谛——"我们认为所有的人生来平等是不言自明的真理"。

我梦想着，有那么一天，在佐治亚的红山上，昔日奴隶的儿子将能够和昔日奴隶主的儿子坐在一直，共叙兄弟情谊。

我梦想着，有那么一天，甚至现在仍为不平等的灼热和压迫的高温所炙烤着的密西西比，也能变为自由与平等的绿洲。

我梦想着，有那么一天，我的四个孩子，能够生活在一个不是以他们的肤色，而是以他们的品性来判断他们的价值的国度里。

我今天有一个梦想。

我梦想着，有那么一天，就在邪恶的种族主义者仍然对黑人活动横加干涉的阿拉巴马州，就在其统治者拒不取消种族歧视政策的阿拉巴马州，黑人儿童将能够与白人儿童如兄弟姐妹一般携起手来。

我梦想着，有那么一天，沟壑填满，山岭削平，崎岖地带铲为平川，坎坷地段夷为平地，上帝的灵光大放光彩，芸芸众生共睹光华！

这就是我们的希望！这是我返回南方时所怀的信念！

怀着这个信念，我们就能从绝望的群山中辟出一颗希望的宝石。怀着这个信念，我们就能变我们祖国的嘈杂喧嚣为一曲优美和谐的兄弟交响乐。有了这个信念，我们就能一同工作，一同祈祷，一同斗争，一同入狱，一同维护自由，因为我们知道，我们终有一天会获得自由。

到了这一天，上帝的所有孩子都能以新的含义高唱这首歌：

我的祖国，可爱的自由之邦，我为您歌唱。

这是我祖先终老的地方，这是早期移民自豪的地方，让自由之声，响彻每一座山岗。

如果美国要成为伟大的国家，这一点必须实现。

因此，让自由之声响彻新罕布什尔州的巍峨高峰！

让自由之声响彻纽约州的崇山峻岭！

让自由之声响彻宾夕法尼亚州的阿勒格尼高峰！

让自由之声响彻科罗拉多州冰雪皑皑的洛基山！

让自由之声响彻加利福尼亚州的婀娜群峰！

不，不仅如此：

让自由之声响彻佐治亚州的石山！

让自由之声响彻田纳西州的望山！

让自由之声响彻密西西比州的一座座山峰，一个个土丘！

让自由之声响彻每一个山岗!

当我们让自由之声轰响,当我们让自由之声响彻每一个大村小庄,每一个州府城镇,我们就能加速这一天的到来。那时,上帝的所有孩子,黑人和白人,犹太教徒和非犹太教徒,耶稣教徒和天主教徒,将能携手同唱那首古老的黑人灵歌:"终于自由了!终于自由了!感谢全能的上帝,我们终于自由了!"

Lesson 2

Changes Has Come to America

Task 1 Questions and Answers

Directions: Work in pairs. Read the following speech then take turns to ask and answer the following questions.
1. When was the speech delivered? Where?
2. Who delivered the speech? Who are involved in the speech?
3. What is the theme of the speech?
4. Why is there a need for the request?
5. How can the request be achieved?

Task 2 Read, Comprehend and Imitation

Directions: *Read the whole passage until you understand every word of it. Then watch the authentic video of the speech, try to imitate one or two paragraphs you like with appropriate delivery techniques. First practice by yourself. Then work in groups of four to take turns to deliver the speech.*

Task 3 Group Discussion

Directions: *Work in groups of four and discuss the following questions. You may locate some useful information from the script.*
1. Who is Ann Nixon Cooper?
2. How old is she?
3. What changes has she witnessed?

Task 4 Role Play

Directions: *Work in pairs. Suppose one of you were Senator McCain, the other were Barack Obama. Role play the situation where McCain gave Obama a gracious call on his victory and Obama replied with due courtesy.*

Task 5 Writing Practice

Directions: *Is Barack Obama a good speaker? What techniques does he use when he speaks. What impressed you most? Write a passage on these topics for about 200 words. You may use the following format to start your writing:*

One thing I like about the speaker/ speech/ their presentation is…

I also enjoy…

As for suggestions, I think they/ he/she may…

If… could be improved, it would be even better.

Changes Has Come to America
变革已然降临美利坚

Election Victory Speech on November 5, 2008
By Barack Obama

▶ 人物简介

贝拉克·侯赛因·奥巴马（Barack Hussein Obama）1961年8月4日出生，美国民主党

英语演讲名篇赏析
Appreciation of Masterpiece English Speeches

政治家，第44任美国总统。童年和青少年时期分别在印尼和夏威夷度过。1991年，奥巴马以优等生荣誉从哈佛法学院毕业。2007年2月10日，宣布参加2008年美国总统选举。2008年11月4日正式当选美国总统。2009年10月9日，获得诺贝尔委员会颁发的诺贝尔和平奖。2012年11月6日，第45届总统大选中，奥巴马击败共和党候选人罗姆尼，成功连任。

▶ 名篇导读

成功赢得美国总统大选的奥巴马于2008年11月5日在早先已经安排的芝加哥格兰特公园举行的百万民众"竞选之夜"集会上，在拥趸的欢呼声中，走上半个篮球场大的舞台发表获胜演说。奥巴马成为美国历史上第一位非洲裔总统，反映了选民思变的心态，是对共和党尤其是布什政府八年内外政策改变的具体体现。这是美国选举史上一次历史性的选举。它将对美国国内政治和对外政策产生深远影响。这篇演说词激情洋溢，辞章华美，听之令人动容，读之使人振奋。奥巴马在演说中感谢自己的家庭和竞选团队，并对对手麦凯恩表示敬意。他提到美国未来将充满了挑战和险阻，承诺将会带领美国走出重重危机。他表示将会听取不同的意见以重建美国。奥巴马用非常感性的话语说出"美国已开始改变"。

▶ 英文原文

Hello, Chicago.

If there is anyone out there who still doubts that America is a place where all things are possible; who still wonders if the dream of our founders is alive in our time; who still questions the power of our democracy, tonight is your answer. It's the answer told by lines that stretched around schools and churches in numbers this nation has never seen; by people who waited three hours and four hours, many for the very first time in their lives, because they believed that this time must be different; that their voice could be that difference.

It's the answer spoken by young and old, rich and poor, Democrat and Republican, black, white, Latino, Asian, Native American, gay, straight, disabled and not disabled—Americans who sent a message to the world that we have never been a collection of **Red States and Blue States**: we are, and always will be, the United States of America.

It's the answer that led those who have been told for so long by so many to be **cynical**[1], and fearful, and doubtful of what we can achieve to put their hands on the arc of history and bend it once more toward the hope of a better day.

It's been a long time coming, but tonight, because of what we did on this day, in this election, at this defining moment, change has come to America.

1　cynical 愤世嫉俗的

I just received a very **gracious**[1] call from Senator McCain. He fought long and hard in this campaign, and he's fought even longer and harder for the country he loves. He has endured sacrifices for America that most of us cannot begin to imagine, and we are better off for the service rendered by this brave and selfless leader. I congratulate him and Governor Palin for all they have achieved, and I look forward to working with them to renew this nation's promise in the months ahead.

I want to thank my partner in this journey, a man who campaigned from his heart and spoke for the men and women he grew up with on the streets of Scranton and rode with on that train home to Delaware, the Vice President-elect of the United States, Joe Biden.

I would not be standing here tonight without the unyielding support of my best friend for the last sixteen years, the rock of our family and the love of my life, our nation's next First Lady, Michelle Obama. Sasha and Malia, I love you both so much, and you have earned the new puppy that's coming with us to the White House. And while she's no longer with us, I know my grandmother is watching, along with the family that made me who I am. I miss them tonight, and know that my debt to them is beyond measure.

To my campaign manager David Plouffe, my chief strategist David Axelrod, and the best campaign team ever assembled in the history of politics—you made this happen, and I am forever grateful for what you've sacrificed to get it done.

But above all, I will never forget who this victory truly belongs to—it belongs to you.

I was never the likeliest candidate for this office. We didn't start with much money or many endorsements. Our campaign was not **hatched**[2] in the halls of Washington—it began in the backyards of Des Moines and the living rooms of Concord and the front porches of Charleston.

It was built by working men and women who dug into what little savings they had to give five dollars and ten dollars and twenty dollars to this cause. It grew strength from the young people who rejected the myth of their generation's **apathy**[3]; who left their homes and their families for jobs that offered little pay and less sleep; from the not-so-young people who braved the bitter cold and scorching heat to knock on the doors of perfect strangers; from the millions of Americans who volunteered, and organized, and proved that more than two centuries later, a government of the people, by the people and for the people has not perished from this Earth. This is your victory.

I know you didn't do this just to win an election and I know you didn't do it for me. You did it because you understand the enormity of the task that lies ahead. For even as we celebrate tonight, we know the challenges that tomorrow will bring are the greatest of our lifetime—two wars, a planet in **peril**[4], the worst financial crisis in a century. Even as we stand here tonight, we know there are brave Americans waking up in the deserts of Iraq and the mountains of

---

1 gracious 亲切的，和蔼的；谦和的；雅致的
2 hatch 孵化、策划
3 apathy 无动于衷
4 peril 极大危险

Afghanistan to risk their lives for us. There are mothers and fathers who will lie awake after their children fall asleep and wonder how they'll make the mortgage, or pay their doctor's bills, or save enough for college. There is new energy to **harness**[1] and new jobs to be created; new schools to build and threats to meet and alliances to repair.

The road ahead will be long. Our climb will be steep. We may not get there in one year or even one term, but America—I have never been more hopeful than I am tonight that we will get there. I promise you—we as a people will get there.

There will be setbacks and false starts. There are many who won't agree with every decision or policy I make as President, and we know that government can't solve every problem. But I will always be honest with you about the challenges we face. I will listen to you, especially when we disagree. And above all, I will ask you join in the work of remaking this nation the only way it's been done in America for two-hundred and twenty-one years—block by block, brick by brick, **calloused**[2] hand by calloused hand.

What began twenty-one months ago in the depths of winter must not end on this autumn night. This victory alone is not the change we seek—it is only the chance for us to make that change. And that cannot happen if we go back to the way things were. It cannot happen without you.

So let us summon a new spirit of patriotism; of service and responsibility where each of us resolves to pitch in and work harder and look after not only ourselves, but each other. Let us remember that if this financial crisis taught us anything, it's that we cannot have a thriving Wall Street while Main Street suffers—in this country, we rise or fall as one nation; as one people.

Let us resist the temptation to fall back on the same partisanship and **pettiness**[3] and immaturity that has poisoned our politics for so long. Let us remember that it was a man from this state who first carried the banner of the Republican Party to the White House—a party founded on the values of self-reliance, individual liberty, and national unity. Those are values we all share, and while the Democratic Party has won a great victory tonight, we do so with a measure of humility and determination to heal the divides that have held back our progress. As Lincoln said to a nation far more divided than ours, "We are not enemies, but friends…though passion may have strained it must not break our bonds of affection." And to those Americans whose support I have yet to earn—I may not have won your vote, but I hear your voices, I need your help, and I will be your President too.

And to all those watching tonight from beyond our shores, from parliaments and palaces to those who are **huddled**[4] around radios in the forgotten corners of our world—our stories are singular, but our destiny is shared, and a new dawn of American leadership is at hand. To those who would tear this world down—we will defeat you. To those who seek peace and security—we

---

1 harness 利用
2 calloused 起老茧的
3 pettiness 琐碎
4 huddle 聚在一团

support you. And to all those who have wondered if America's beacon still burns as bright—tonight we proved once more that the true strength of our nation comes not from the might of our arms or the scale of our wealth, but from the enduring power of our ideals: democracy, liberty, opportunity, and unyielding hope.

For that is the true genius of America—that America can change. Our union can be perfected. And what we have already achieved gives us hope for what we can and must achieve tomorrow.

This election had many firsts and many stories that will be told for generations. But one that's on my mind tonight is about a woman who cast her **ballot**[1] in Atlanta. She's a lot like the millions of others who stood in line to make their voice heard in this election except for one thing—*Ann Nixon Cooper* is 106 years old.

She was born just a generation past slavery; a time when there were no cars on the road or planes in the sky; when someone like her couldn't vote for two reasons—because she was a woman and because of the color of her skin.

And tonight, I think about all that she's seen throughout her century in America—the heartache and the hope; the struggle and the progress; the times we were told that we can't, and the people who pressed on with that American creed: Yes we can.

At a time when women's voices were silenced and their hopes dismissed, she lived to see them stand up and speak out and reach for the ballot. Yes we can.

When there was despair in the dust bowl and depression across the land, she saw a nation conquer fear itself with a New Deal, new jobs and a new sense of common purpose. Yes we can.

When the bombs fell on our harbor and **tyranny**[2] threatened the world, she was there to witness a generation rise to greatness and a democracy was saved. Yes we can.

She was there for the **buses in Montgomery, the hoses in Birmingham, a bridge in Selma**, and a preacher from Atlanta who told a people that **"We Shall Overcome."** Yes we can.

A man touched down on the moon, a wall came down in Berlin, a world was connected by our own science and imagination. And this year, in this election, she touched her finger to a screen, and cast her vote, because after 106 years in America, through the best of times and the darkest of hours, she knows how America can change. Yes we can.

America, we have come so far. We have seen so much. But there is so much more to do. So tonight, let us ask ourselves—if our children should live to see the next century; if my daughters should be so lucky to live as long as Ann Nixon Cooper, what change will they see? What progress will we have made?

This is our chance to answer that call. This is our moment. This is our time—to put our people back to work and open doors of opportunity for our kids; to restore prosperity and promote the cause of peace; to reclaim the American Dream and reaffirm that fundamental truth—that out of many, we are one; that while we breathe, we hope, and where we are met with cynicism, and

---

1 ballot 选票
2 tyranny 暴虐；暴政

doubt, and those who tell us that we can't, we will respond with that timeless creed that sums up the spirit of a people: Yes We Can.

Thank you, God bless you, and may God Bless the United States of America.

文化快递

1. Red States and Blue States（红州和蓝州）

美国的总统选举并不是由选民直接选举，而是由选举团的成员来选举。其大致程序为：宣布候选人身份、党内初选、党内提名、大选（也称普选）、选举人选举（也称选举团选举）和宣誓就职。美国自2000年小布什和戈尔的那场旷日持久的竞选战较量后，美国各州被标上"红州"和"蓝州"的不同标签。前者指共和党占据优势的州，后者指民主党占据优势的州。奥巴马在2008年的大选一开始就强调不分"蓝州""红州"，只有一个联合起来的"美利坚"，而这种放眼五十个州又充满调和色彩的政治态度早在2004年就被奥巴马提出来了。

2004年7月27日，在美国民主党全国代表大会上，奥巴马发表"基调演讲"。演讲的题目就是《无畏的希望》，奥巴马充满激情地宣示："不存在一个自由主义的美国和一个保守主义的美国，而只有一个美利坚合众国。不存在黑人的美国和白人的美国、拉丁族裔的美国和亚洲人的美国，而只有美利坚合众国。"正是这场演讲让名不见经传的奥巴马开始声名鹊起。一个弥合两党党派纷争的希望开始在美国出现。奥巴马的当选，有助于最终打破美国政界近十年来的两党分裂形势，重新整合"红州""蓝州"政治版图，使美国重现团结。

2. Wall Street and Main Street（华尔街与主街）

奥巴马提到了Wall Street和Main Street两个概念。Wall Street的直接含义是指位于纽约金融区的一条名叫"华尔街"的街道，泛指包括金融、投资银行在内的美国的巨型企业，也指美国的富人阶层及他们的生活。Main Street的直接含义是指小城镇的主街，是小城镇商业和社交活动的街道通用名称，人们在那里购物，喝咖啡聊天，参加一些庆典活动，泛指小企业、小作坊和平民百姓，也指平民阶层及他们的生活。2004年总统竞选时，约翰·爱德华兹（John Edwards）以平民主义的思想提出他的竞选纲领，主要提出了Wall Street和Main Street的两元经济论。所以自2004年开始，Wall Street和Main Street的含义基本就定位在：Wall Street指包括金融、投资在内的美国的巨型企业和富人阶层，即表征富有阶层的利益或是少数富人的利益，Main Street是指小企业、小作坊和平民阶层，即表征平民阶层的利益，或社会主要群体的利益。

3. The buses in Montgomery（蒙哥马利的公共汽车）

1955年12月1日，黑人派克斯（Parks）女士搭乘2857号公车回家，选择第十一排靠走道的座位坐下。根据当时阿拉巴马州蒙哥马利市的种族隔离法，前十排是写有"white only"的白人座位，黑人只能坐在第十一排以后，而且如果前十排坐满，只要有白人站着，后面黑人就必须让位。当天公车很挤，后来上来了几位白人，司机要求坐在第十一排的四名黑人乘客让位。其他三名黑人站起来，但派克斯坐着不动。司机叫警察前来处理。两名警察上车后。问她为什么不让位。她对警察说："我不认为我应该让位，我付的车资跟这名男子一样多。为什么我要受不平等待遇？"警察回答说："我不知道，我只知道执行法律。你被逮捕了。"派克斯被逮捕的消息立刻传遍全市。蒙哥马利17000名黑人被激怒了，他们在著名黑人民权运动领导人马丁·路德·金博士的带领下（演讲词中所称 a preacher from Athmta），采取非暴力的形式联合抵制公交公司并向最高法院提起上诉。1956年11月13日，最高法院宣判种族隔离法违宪，下令蒙市取消黑白分坐及黑人必须让位的规定。

4. Bridge in Selma （塞尔马的桥）

在1965年的亚拉巴马州塞尔马地区，适龄投票的黑人只有20.1%获得了投票权。而且受到诸多限制，例如每月只设两天给他们登记投票，到时却安排警察在街上殴打他们。有时还要求他们答一些莫名其妙的问题，例如"一块肥皂有多少个泡"。3月7日，塞尔马的黑人不满政府无理剥夺他们的投票权，决定游行到州首府蒙哥马利，但在经过埃蒙德佩图斯桥时，警察向游行队伍施放催泪弹，又用木棍殴打游行人士，结果造成100人浴血的"埃盟德佩图斯桥"（Edmund Pettus Bridge）惨剧，史称"血腥星期天"。两星期后，约翰逊将国民警卫队置于联邦政府管辖下，向金亲自率领的和平游行队伍提供保护。25000人冒着清晨的蒙蒙细雨在塞尔马集合，步行52英里来到蒙哥马利，金在那里向群众发表了讲话。

5. We shall overcome （我们能成功）

这是马丁·路德·金博士在民权运动中号召黑人传唱的一首歌曲。它本来是一首福音歌曲，在1959年成为了美国黑人民权运动的非官方主题歌。

参考译文

芝加哥的市民们，你们好！

如果还有人对在美国是否凡事皆有可能这一点存疑，还有人怀疑美国奠基者的梦想在我们所处的时代是否依然鲜活，还有人质疑我们的民主制度的力量，那么今晚，这些问题都有了答案。这是设在学校和教堂的投票站前排起的前所未见的长队给出的答案；是等了三四个小时的选民所给出的答案，其中许多人都是有生以来第一次投票，因为他们认定这一次肯定会不一样，认为自己的声音会是这次大选有别于以往之所在。

这是所有美国人民共同给出的答案——无论老少贫富，无论是民主党还是共和党，无论是黑人、白人、拉美裔、亚裔、原住民，是同性恋者还是异性恋者、残疾人还是健全人——我们从来不是"红州"和"蓝州"的对立阵营,我们是美利坚合众国这个整体,永远都是。

长久以来,很多人一再受到告诫,要对我们所能取得的成绩极尽讽刺、担忧和怀疑之能事,但这个答案让这些人伸出手来把握历史,再次让它朝向美好明天的希望延伸。

已经过去了这么长时间,但今晚,由于我们在今天、在这场大选中、在这个具有决定性的时刻所做的,美国已经迎来了变革。

我刚刚接到了麦凯恩参议员极具风度的致电。他在这场大选中经过了长时间的努力奋斗,而他为自己所深爱的这个国家奋斗的时间更长、过程更艰辛。他为美国做出了我们大多数人难以想象的牺牲,我们的生活也因这位勇敢无私的领袖所做出的贡献而变得更美好。我向他和佩林州长所取得的成绩表示祝贺,我也期待着与他们一起在未来的岁月中为复兴这个国家的希望而共同努力。

我要感谢我在这次旅程中的伙伴——已当选美国副总统的拜登。他全心参与竞选活动,为普通民众代言,他们是他在斯克兰顿从小到大的伙伴,也是在他回特拉华的火车上遇到的男男女女。

如果没有一个人的坚决支持,我今晚就不会站在这里,她是我过去16年来最好的朋友、是我们一家人的中坚和我一生的挚爱,更是我们国家的下一位第一夫人:米歇尔·奥巴马。萨莎和玛丽亚,我太爱你们两个了,你们已经得到了一条新的小狗,它将与我们一起入驻白宫。虽然我的外祖母已经不在了,但我知道她与我的亲人肯定都在看着我,因为他们,我才能拥有今天的成就。今晚,我想念他们,我知道自己欠他们的无可计量。

我的竞选经理大卫·普劳夫、首席策略师大卫·艾克斯罗德以及政治史上最好的竞选团队——是你们成就了今天,我永远感激你们为实现今天的成就所做出的牺牲。

但最重要的是,我永远不会忘记这场胜利真正的归属——它属于你们。

我从来不是最有希望的候选人。一开始,我们没有太多资金,也没有得到太多人的支持。我们的竞选活动并非诞生于华盛顿的高门华第之内,而是始于得梅因、康科德、查尔斯顿这些地方的普通民众家中。

我们的竞选活动能有今天的规模,是因为辛勤工作的人们从自己的微薄积蓄中拿出钱来,捐出一笔又一笔5美元、10美元、20美元。而竞选活动的声势越来越大则是源自那些年轻人,他们拒绝接受认为他们这代人冷漠的荒诞说法;他们离开家、离开亲人,从事报酬微薄、极其辛苦的工作;同时也源自那些已经不算年轻的人们,他们冒着严寒酷暑,敲开陌生人的家门进行竞选宣传;更源自数百万的美国民众,他们自发地组织起来,证明了在两百多年以后,民有、民治、民享的政府并未从地球上消失。这是你们的胜利。

我知道你们的所作所为并不只是为了赢得大选,我也知道你们做这一切并不是为了我。你们这样做是因为你们明白摆在面前的任务有多艰巨。因为即便我们今晚欢呼庆祝,我们也知道明天将面临我们一生之中最为艰巨的挑战——两场战争、一个面临危险的星球，还有百年来最严重的金融危机。今晚站在此地，我们知道伊拉克的沙漠里和阿富汗的群山中还有勇敢的美国士兵醒来，甘冒生命危险保护着我们。会有在孩子熟睡后仍难以入眠的父母，担心如何偿还按揭月供、付医药费或是存够钱送孩子上大学。我们亟待开发新能源、创造新的工作机会；我们需要修建新学校，还要应对众多威胁、修复与许多盟国的关系。

前方的道路会十分漫长艰辛。我们可能无法在一年甚至一届任期之内实现上述目标，但我从未像今晚这样满怀希望，相信我们会实现。我向你们承诺——我们作为一个整体将会达成目标。

我们会遭遇挫折和不成功的开端。对于我作为总统所做的每项决定和政策，会有许多人持有异议，我们也知道政府并不能解决所有问题。但我会向你们坦陈我们所面临的挑战。我会聆听你们的意见，尤其是在我们意见相左之时。最重要的是，我会请求你们参与重建这个国家，以美国221年来从未改变的唯一方式——一砖一瓦而成、胼手胝足相续。

21个月前那个寒冬所开始的一切不应该在今天这个秋夜结束。今天的选举胜利并不是我们所寻求的改变——这只是我们进行改变的机会。而且如果我们仍然按照旧有方式行事，我们所寻求的改变不可能出现。没有你们，也不可能有这种改变。

因此，让我们发扬新的爱国精神，树立新的服务意识和责任感，让我们每个人下定决心全情投入、更加努力地工作，并彼此关爱。让我们铭记这场金融危机带来的教训：我们不可能在金融以外的领域备受煎熬的同时拥有繁荣兴旺的华尔街——在这个国家，我们患难与共。

让我们抵制重走老路的诱惑，避免重新回到令美国政治长期深受毒害的党派纷争和由此引发的遗憾和不成熟表现。让我们牢记，正是伊利诺伊州的一名男子首次将共和党的大旗扛到了白宫。共和党是建立在自强自立、个人自由以及全民团结的价值观上，这也是我们所有人都珍视的价值。虽然民主党今天晚上赢得了巨大的胜利，但我们是以谦卑的态度和弥合阻碍我们进步的分歧的决心赢得这场胜利的。林肯在向远比我们眼下分歧更大的国家发表讲话时说，"我们不是敌人，而是朋友——虽然激情可能褪去，但是这不会割断我们感情上的联系。"对于那些现在并不支持我的美国人，我想说，或许我没有赢得你们的选票，但是我听到了你们的声音，我需要你们的帮助，而且我也将是你们的总统。

那些彻夜关注美国大选的海外人士，从国会到皇宫，以及在这个世界被遗忘的角落里挤在收音机旁的人们，我们的经历虽然各有不同，但是我们的命运是相通的，新的美国领袖诞生了。那些想要颠覆这个世界的人们，我们必将击败你们。那些追求和平和安全的人们，我们支持你们。那些所有怀疑美国能否继续照亮世界发展前景的人们，今天晚上我们再次证明，我们国家真正的力量并非来自我们武器的威力或财富的规模，而是来自我们理

想的持久力量：民主、自由、机会和不屈的希望。

这才是美国真正的精华——美国能够改变。我们的联邦会日臻完善。我们取得的成就为我们将来能够取得的以及必须取得的成就增添了希望。

这次大选创造了多项"第一"，也诞生了很多将世代流传的故事。但是今天晚上令我难忘的却是在亚特兰大投票的一名妇女：安·尼克松·库波尔。她和其他数百万排队等待投票的选民没有什么差别，除了一点：她已是106岁的高龄。

她出生的那个时代奴隶制度刚刚结束；那时路上没有汽车，天上也没有飞机；当时像她这样的人由于两个原因不能投票——一个原因是她是女性，另一个原因是她的肤色。

今天晚上，我想到了她在美国过去一百年间所经历的种种：心痛和希望；挣扎和进步；那些我们被告知我们办不到的世代，以及那些坚信美国信条——是的，我们能做到——的人们。

曾几何时，妇女没有发言权，她们的希望化作泡影，但是安·尼克松·库波尔活了下来，看到妇女们站了起来，看到她们大声发表自己的见解，看到她们去参加大选投票。是的，我们能做到。

当30年代的沙尘暴和大萧条引发人们的绝望之情时，她看到一个国家用罗斯福新政、新就业机会以及对新目标的共同追求战胜恐慌。是的，我们能做到。

当炸弹袭击了我们的海港、独裁专制威胁到全世界，她见证了美国一代人的伟大崛起，见证了一个民主国家被拯救。是的，我们能做到。

她看到蒙哥马利通了公共汽车、伯明翰接上了水管、塞尔马建了桥，一位来自亚特兰大的传教士告诉人们：我们能成功。是的，我们能做到。

人类登上月球、柏林墙倒下，世界因我们的科学和想象被连接在一起。今年，就在这次选举中，她用手指触碰屏幕投下自己的选票，因为在美国生活了106年之后，经历了最好的时光和最黑暗的时刻之后，她知道美国如何能够发生变革。是的，我们能做到。

美国，我们已经走过漫漫长路。我们已经历了很多。但是我们仍有很多事情要做。因此今夜，让我们自问——如果我们的孩子能够活到下个世纪；如果我们的女儿有幸活得和安一样长，他们将会看到怎样的改变？我们将会取得怎样的进步？

现在是我们回答这个问题的机会。这是我们的时刻。这是我们的时代——让我们的人民重新就业，为我们的后代敞开机会的大门；恢复繁荣发展，推进和平事业；让"美国梦"重新焕发光芒，再次证明这样一个基本的真理：我们是一家人；一息尚存，我们就有希望；当我们遇到嘲讽和怀疑，当有人说我们办不到的时候，我们要以这个永恒的信条来回应他们：是的，我们能做到。

感谢你们。上帝保佑你们。愿上帝保佑美利坚合众国。

Lesson 3

Blood, Toil, Sweat and Tears

Task 1 Questions and Answers

Directions: *Work in pairs. Read the following speech then take turns to ask and answer the following questions.*

1. When was the speech delivered? Where?
2. Who delivered the speech? Who are involved in the speech?
3. What is the theme of the speech?
4. Why is there a need for the request?
5. How can the request be achieved?

Task 2 Brainstorming and Paper Talk

Directions: *Work in groups of six. Each group selects one topic among the three words "blood, toil, sweat and tears". Put the word in the middle of a piece of paper, then each member brainstorms and puts any ideas, questions, answers or comments on the topic using a mind map. Then one representative from the group summarizes and reports to the class.*

Task 3 Dictation

Directions: *Watch the authentic video of the speech. Then fill in the missing words in their appropriate forms. You may watch the video for three times.*

　　To form an administration of this scale and complexity is a serious undertaking in itself. But we are in the preliminary _____ of one of the greatest battles in history. We are in _____ at any other points—in Norway and in Holland—and we have to be prepared in the Mediterranean. The air battle is continuing, and many _____ have to be made here at home.

　　In this _____ I think I may be pardoned if I do not _____ the House at any length today, and I hope that any of my friends and colleagues or former colleagues who are affected by the political _____ will make all allowances for any _____ of ceremony with which it has been necessary to act.

Task 4 Discussion

Directions: Work in groups of four and discuss the following questions. You may locate some useful information from the script.

1. What is "our aim"? What is "our policy"?
2. What difficulties was U.K. faced with at that time?
3. Was Churchill trustworthy to his people? How do you know?

Task 5 Speaking Practice

Directions: Give a speech to the class for 2-3 minutes on the topic "Hardships Make Heroes".

Blood, Toil, Sweat and Tears
热血、辛劳、汗水和眼泪
By Winston Churchill
May 13, 1940

人物简介

温斯顿·丘吉尔，政治家、画家、演说家、作家以及记者，1953年诺贝尔文学奖得主（获奖作品《第二次世界大战回忆录》），曾于1940—1945年及1951—1955年期间两度任英国首相，带领英国获得第二次世界大战的胜利，被认为是20世纪最重要的政治领袖之一。据传为历史上掌握英语单词词汇量最多的人之一（十二万多）。被美国杂志《展示》

列为近百年来世界最有说服力的八大演说家之一。2002年，BBC举行了一个名为"最伟大的100名英国人"的调查，结果丘吉尔获选为有史以来最伟大的英国人。

名篇导读

《热血、辛劳、汗水和眼泪》是丘吉尔出任英国首相时发表的著名演说。二战期间，英法联军惨败，当希特勒的铁蹄跨过比利时、丹麦、荷兰、法国、直扑英吉利海峡的时候，英伦三岛上空顿时阴云弥漫。首相张伯伦因绥靖政策失败而引咎辞职，整个英国民众陷入了恐慌之中。英国泰晤士报头版发表了文章《谁来拯救大英帝国》，此刻的帝国急需一个铁腕人物。

1940年5月，丘吉尔出任英国首相，并发表了这篇演说，一扫英伦三岛的低迷之气，极大的鼓舞和唤起了英国民众战胜法西斯的勇气和信心。而事实也证明，丘吉尔的精彩演讲，给当时处于巨大恐惧和不安的英国人带来了勇气，所以后人是如此评价丘吉尔的演讲："丘吉尔的演讲，豪不夸张地说，拯救了世界。"赢得战争不仅靠的是子弹和炸弹，关键是信仰。这信仰是丘吉尔那动人心魄的演讲灌输给每个英国人的。它证明了文字的力量可以影响整个国家并最终取得胜利。语言的力量有时候比武器更强大。

英文原文

On last Friday evening I received from **His Majesty** the mission to form a new administration.

It was the evident will of **Parliament** and the nation that this should be **conceived**[1] on the broadest possible basis and that it should include all parties.

I have already completed the most important part of this task. A war cabinet has been formed of five members, representing, with the **Labor, Opposition and Liberals**, the unity of the nation.

It was necessary that this should be done in one single day on account of the extreme urgency and **rigor**[2] of events. Other key positions were filled yesterday. I am submitting a further list to the King tonight. I hope to complete the appointment of principal Ministers during tomorrow.

The appointment of other Ministers usually takes a little longer. I trust when Parliament meets again this part of my task will be completed and that the administration will be complete in all respects.

I considered it in the public interest to suggest to the Speaker that the House should be **summoned**[3] today. At the end of today's proceedings, the **adjournment**[4] of the House will be

---

1 conceive 构思；持有
2 rigor 严酷，艰苦
3 summon 召集
4 adjournment 休会期间

proposed until May 21 with **provision**¹ for earlier meeting if need be. Business for that will be notified to **M. P.'s**² at the earliest opportunity.

I now invite the House by a **resolution**³ to record its approval of the steps taken and declare its confidence in the new government. The resolution:

"That this House welcomes the formation of a government representing the united and inflexible resolve of the nation to **prosecute**⁴ the war with Germany to a victorious conclusion."

To form an administration of this scale and complexity is a serious undertaking in itself. But we are in the preliminary phase of one of the greatest battles in history. We are in action at any other points—in Norway and in Holland—and we have to be prepared in the **Mediterranean**⁵. The air battle is continuing, and many preparations have to be made here at home.

In this crisis I think I may be pardoned if I do not address the House at any length today, and I hope that any of my friends and colleagues or former colleagues who are affected by the political reconstruction will make all allowances for any lack of ceremony with which it has been necessary to act.

I say to the House as I said to Ministers who have joined this government, I have nothing to offer but blood, toil, tears and sweat. We have before us an **ordeal**⁶ of the most grievous kind. We have before us many, many months of struggle and suffering.

You ask, what is our policy? I say it is to wage war by land, sea and air. War with all our might and with all the strength God has given us, and to wage war against a monstrous tyranny never surpassed in the dark and **lamentable**⁷ catalogue of human crime. That is our policy.

You ask, what is our aim? I can answer in one word. It is victory. Victory at all costs—victory in spite of all terrors—victory, however long and hard the road may be, for without victory there is no survival.

Let that be realized. No survival for the British Empire, no survival for all that the British Empire has stood for, no survival for the urge, the impulse of the ages, that mankind shall move forward toward his goal.

I take up my task in **buoyancy**⁸ and hope. I feel sure that our cause will not be suffered to fail among men.

I feel **entitled**⁹ at this **juncture**¹⁰, at this time, to claim the aid of all and to say, "Come then, let us go forward together with our united strength."

---

1 provision 预备
2 M.P.'s 国会议员，其全写为Members of Parliament
3 resolution 决议
4 prosecute 彻底进行
5 Mediterranean 地中海
6 ordeal 严酷的考验
7 lamentable 可悲的
8 buoyancy 心情愉快
9 entitled 有资格的
10 juncture 时刻，关头

文化快递

1. His Majesty（国王陛下）

英国是一个君主立宪的议会民主国家，国王或女皇为国家象征性元首，没有实权。与大多数别的国家不同，英国的宪法不是单独的文本，而由成文法、不成文法和惯例组成。惯例指的是那些不是法定的但对于政府工作来说又是必不可少的规则和做法。英国君主与其近亲的关系由其名号可知。王室成员虽然没有严格的法律或者正式的定义，并且不同的名单会有不同的成员，不过拥有国王/女王陛下（HM）（His/Her Majesty）或者王子/公主殿下头衔（HRH）（His/Her Royal Highness）的一般都被视为王室成员。

文中所指His Majesty，即二战爆发时的英国国家元首乔治六世（Geroge VI）。现任英国国家元首为伊丽莎白二世（Elizabeth II）。

2. Parliament（议会）

议会（Parliament）是英国政治的中心舞台，是英国的最高立法机关。政府从议会中产生，并对其负责。英国的国会为两院制，由上议院和下议院组成。

英国上议院（Upper House）又称贵族院（House of Lords），主要由王室后裔、世袭贵族、新封贵族、上诉法院法官和教会的重要人物组成。上议院议员不由选举产生，部分是世袭贵族。上议院是英国最高司法机关，议长由大法官兼任。和下议院相比，上议院的权力相对有限，保留着历史上遗留下来的司法权，有权审查下议院通过的法案，并通过必要的修正案，还可以要求推迟它不赞成的立法，最长可达一年。

下议院（Lower House）又称平民院或众议院（House of Commons），其议员由直接选举产生，任期5年。下议院的主要职权是立法、监督财政和政府。英国全国被划分为多个选民人数基本相同的选区（选区的划分由一个独立的委员会决定），每个选区选举一名下议院议员。大多数选区议员是一个政党的成员，但是没有政党背景的人士也可以参加选举。通常情况下，下议院总有一个拥有绝对多数的政党，该党领袖被国王任命为首相。下议院第二大党的领袖则成为反对党领袖。

3. Labor, Opposition and Liberals（工党、反对党和自由党）

英国工党（Labour Party，Great Britain），英国两大执政党之一。1900年2月27日建立于伦敦，称劳工代表委员会。1906年称工党。其宗旨是在议会里实现独立的劳工代表权。

英国自由党The Freedom Party of the United Kingdom，英国资产阶级政党。前身是1679年成立的辉格党。1832年议会改革后（见英国议会君主制），辉格党逐渐转向自由主义，要求自由贸易和自由政治。

参考译文

上星期五晚上，我奉陛下之命，组织新的一届政府。

按国会和国民的意愿，新政府显然应该考虑建立在尽可能广泛的基础上，应该兼容所有的党派。

我已经完成了这项任务的最主要的部分。战时内阁已由五人组成,包括工党、反对党和自由党,这体现了举国团结一致。

由于事态的极端紧急和严峻,新内阁政府须于一天之内组成,其他的关键岗位也于昨日安排就绪。今晚还要向国王呈报一份名单。我希望明天就能完成几位主要大臣的任命。

其余大臣们的任命照例得晚一些。我相信,在国会下一次召开时,任命将告完成,臻于完善。

为公众利益着想,我建议议长今天就召开国会。今天的议程结束时,建议休会到5月21日,并准备在必要时提前开会。有关事项当会及早通知各位议员。

现在我请求国会作出决议,批准我所采取的各项步骤,启示记录在案,并且声明信任新政府。决议如下:

"本国会欢迎新政府的组成,她体现了举国一致的坚定不移的决心:对德作战,直到最后胜利。"

组织如此规模和如此复杂的政府原本是一项重大的任务。但是我们正处于历史上罕见的一场大战的初始阶段。我们在许多地点作战——在挪威,在荷兰,我们还必须在地中海做好准备。空战正在继续,而且在本土也必须做好许多准备工作。

值此危急关头,我想,即使我今天向国会的报告过于简略,也当能见谅。我还希望所有在这次改组中受到影响的朋友、同僚和旧日的同僚们对必要的礼仪方面的任何不周之处能毫不介意。

我向国会表明,一如我向入阁的大臣们所表明的,我所能奉献的唯有热血、辛劳、眼泪和汗水。我们所面临的将是一场极其严酷的考验,将是旷日持久的斗争和苦难。

若问我们的政策是什么?我的回答是:在陆上、海上、空中作战。尽我们的全力,尽上帝赋予我们的全部力量去作战,对人类黑暗、可悲的罪恶史上空前凶残的暴政作战。这就是我们的政策。

若问我们的目标是什么?我可以用一个词来回答,那就是胜利。不惜一切代价,去夺取胜利——不惧一切恐怖,去夺取胜利——不论前路如何漫长、如何艰苦,去夺取胜利。因为没有胜利就不能生存。

我们务必认识到,没有胜利就不复有大英帝国,没有胜利就不复有大英帝国所象征的一切,没有胜利就不复有多少世纪以来的强烈要求和冲动:人类应当向自己的目标迈进。

我精神振奋、满怀信心地承担起我的任务。我确信,大家联合起来,我们的事业就不会遭到挫败。

在此时此刻的危急关头,我觉得我有权要求各方面的支持。我要说:"来吧,让我们群策群力,并肩前进!"

Lesson 4

Inaugural Address

Task 1 Questions and Answers

Directions: Work in pairs. Read the following speech then take turns to ask and answer the following questions.

1. When was the speech delivered? Where?
2. Who delivered the speech? Who are involved in the speech?
3. What is the theme of the speech?
4. Why is there a need for the request?
5. How can the request be achieved?

Task 2 Think-Pair-Share

Directions: Work individually first. Go through the script and underline the lines that impress you most. Then share your list with a partner. Explain to each other why these lines talk. Learn some famous lines by heart.

E.g.

1. "ask not what your country can do for you—ask what you can do for your country".
2. ...

Task 3 Imitation and Play

Directions: Watch the authentic video of the speech. Then try to imitate one or two paragraphs you like with appropriate delivery techniques. First practice by yourself. Then work in groups of four to take turns to deliver the speech.

Task 4 Dictation

Directions: Watch the authentic video of the speech. Then fill in the missing words in their appropriate forms. You may watch the video for three times.

　　In the long history of the world, only a few generations have been _____ the role of defending freedom in its hour of _____ danger. I do not _____ from this responsibility—I welcome it. I do not believe that any of us would

_____ places with any other people or any other generation. The energy, the faith, the _____ which we bring to this _____ will light our country and all who serve it—and the _____ from that fire can truly light the world.

Task 5 Speaking Practice

Directions: *Suppose you were elected Monitor of your class or chair of Students' Union. Please deliver a speech to your fellow students for 2—3 minutes. You may focus on the following:*

1. Greet the audience
2. Give thanks for trust
3. Your plans for future development of the class/ Students' Union
4. End the speech in a creative and impressive way

Inaugural Address
就职演说

By John F. Kennedy

▶ 人物简介

约翰·菲茨杰拉德·肯尼迪（John Fitzgerald Kennedy），美国第35任总统，美国著名的肯尼迪家族成员，执政时间从1961年1月20日开始到1963年11月22日在达拉斯遇刺身亡为止。肯尼迪在1946年—1960年期间曾先后任众议员和参议员，并于1960年当选为美国总统，成为美国历史上最年轻的当选总统，他朝气蓬勃，是美国口才最好的总统之一，也是美国历史上唯一信奉罗马天主教的总统和唯一获得普利策奖的总统。

名篇导读

肯尼迪的就职演讲被认为是美国总统就职演讲中最为精彩的篇章之一，其语言简明、结构巧妙，内容也反映了当时的政治、文化、社会背景，值得我们探究学习。

肯尼迪在就职演讲词中，呼吁以果断与牺牲的精神来应付当前的许多挑战。

他的就职演说50年后听起来仍然掷地有声。有评论认为，肯尼迪的这篇就职演说是第一篇为媒体而设计的就职演说，当电视开始进入千家万户时，话题有针对性作为演讲准备的第一要素就变得尤为重要。虽然在演说的开头和结尾，肯尼迪都提到了美国人，特别是那几句非常著名的排比"不要问"中，但他比以往任何美国总统都清楚，他要针对的不再只是美国人。全球化大众媒体的时代已经到来，他的话会被传播到世界的每一个角落。

在冷战正酣之际，肯尼迪要把他的外交政策宣告给全世界。所以他演讲中的不同段落分别针对不同的人群：

"Let every nation know, whether it wishes us well or ill."
让所有国家知道，不管他们是敌是友。

"To those new nations whom we welcome to the ranks of the free,"
对于那些刚刚加入自由国度行列的国家，

"To those in the huts and villages of half the globe,"
对于占全世界一半面积的农村，

"To our sister republics south of the border,"
对于我们边界南边的那些邻国，

"To that world assembly of sovereign states, the United Nations,"
对于主权国际的世界联盟，也就是联合国，

"Finally, to those nations who would make themselves our adversary."
最后，对那些与我们为敌的国家。

英文原文

Vice President Johnson, Mr. Speaker, Mr. Chief Justice, President Eisenhower, Vice President Nixon, President Truman, reverend clergy, fellow citizens, we observe today not a victory of party, but a celebration of freedom—symbolizing an end, as well as a beginning—signifying renewal, as well as change. For I have sworn before you and Almighty God the same solemn oath our forebears prescribed nearly a century and three quarters ago.

The world is very different now. For man holds in his **mortal**[1] hands the power to abolish all forms of human poverty and all forms of human life. And yet the same revolutionary beliefs for which our forebears fought are still at issue around the globe—the belief that the rights of man come not from the generosity of the state, but from the hand of God.

We dare not forget today that we are the heirs of that first revolution. Let the word go forth from this time and place, to friend and **foe**[2] alike, that the torch has been passed to a new generation of Americans—born in this century, tempered by war, disciplined by a hard and bitter peace, proud of our ancient heritage—and unwilling to witness or permit the slow undoing of those human rights to which this Nation has always been committed, and to which we are committed today at home and around the world.

Let every nation know, whether it wishes us well or ill, that we shall pay any price, bear any burden, meet any hardship, support any friend, oppose any foe, in order to assure the survival and the success of liberty.

This much we pledge—and more.

To those old allies whose cultural and spiritual origins we share, we pledge the loyalty of faithful friends. United, there is little we cannot do in a host of cooperative ventures. Divided, there is little we can do—for we dare not meet a powerful challenge at odds and split **asunder**[3].

To those new States whom we welcome to the ranks of the free, we pledge our word that one form of colonial control shall not have passed away merely to be replaced by a far more iron tyranny. We shall not always expect to find them supporting our view. But we shall always hope to find them strongly supporting their own freedom—and to remember that, in the past, those who foolishly sought power by riding the back of the tiger ended up inside.

To those peoples in the huts and villages across the globe struggling to break the bonds of mass misery, we pledge our best efforts to help them help themselves, for whatever period is required—not because the Communists may be doing it, not because we seek their votes, but because it is right. If a free society cannot help the many who are poor, it cannot save the few who are rich.

To our sister republics south of our border, we offer a special pledge—to convert our good words into good deeds—in a new alliance for progress—to assist free men and free governments in casting off the chains of poverty. But this peaceful revolution of hope cannot become the prey of hostile powers. Let all our neighbors know that we shall join with them to oppose aggression or subversion anywhere in the Americas. And let every other power know that this Hemisphere intends to remain the master of its own house.

To that world assembly of sovereign states, the United Nations, our last best hope in an age where the instruments of war have far outpaced the instruments of peace, we renew our pledge of

---

1 mortal 凡人的；致死的；终有一死的；不共戴天的
2 foe 敌人
3 asunder 分开地；分离地；化为碎片

support—to prevent it from becoming merely a forum for **invective**[1]—to strengthen its shield of the new and the weak—and to enlarge the area in which its **writ**[2] may run.

Finally, to those nations who would make themselves our **adversary**[3], we offer not a pledge but a request: that both sides begin anew the quest for peace, before the dark powers of destruction **unleashed**[4] by science **engulf**[5] all humanity in planned or accidental self-destruction.

We dare not tempt them with weakness. For only when our arms are sufficient beyond doubt can we be certain beyond doubt that they will never be employed.

But neither can two great and powerful groups of nations take comfort from our present course—both sides overburdened by the cost of modern weapons, both rightly alarmed by the steady spread of the deadly atom, yet both racing to alter that uncertain balance of terror that stays the hand of mankind's final war.

So let us begin anew—remembering on both sides that **civility**[6] is not a sign of weakness, and sincerity is always subject to proof. Let us never negotiate out of fear. But let us never fear to negotiate.

Let both sides explore what problems unite us instead of **belaboring**[7] those problems which divide us.

Let both sides, for the first time, formulate serious and precise proposals for the inspection and control of arms—and bring the absolute power to destroy other nations under the absolute control of all nations.

Let both sides seek to invoke the wonders of science instead of its terrors. Together let us explore the stars, conquer the deserts, **eradicate**[8] disease, tap the ocean depths, and encourage the arts and commerce.

Let both sides unite to **heed**[9] in all corners of the earth the command of Isaiah—to "undo the heavy burdens ... and to let the oppressed go free."

And if a **beachhead**[10] of cooperation may push back the jungle of suspicion, let both sides join in creating a new endeavor, not a new balance of power, but a new world of law, where the strong are just and the weak secure and the peace preserved.

All this will not be finished in the first 100 days. Nor will it be finished in the first 1,000 days, nor in the life of this Administration, nor even perhaps in our lifetime on this planet. But let us begin.

In your hands, my fellow citizens, more than in mine, will rest the final success or failure of our course. Since this country was founded, each generation of Americans has been summoned to

---

1 invective 恶言谩骂
2 writ 法令
3 adversary 对手，敌手
4 unleash 释放
5 engulf 吞噬
6 civility 礼貌
7 belabor 抨击
8 eradicate 根除，消灭
9 heed 注意，留心
10 beachhead 滩头阵地

give testimony to its national loyalty. The graves of young Americans who answered the call to service surround the globe.

Now the trumpet summons us again—not as a call to bear arms, though arms we need; not as a call to battle, though embattled we are—but a call to bear the burden of a long twilight struggle, year in and year out, "rejoicing in hope, patient in tribulation"—a struggle against the common enemies of man: tyranny, poverty, disease, and war itself.

Can we forge against these enemies a grand and global alliance, North and South, East and West, that can assure a more fruitful life for all mankind? Will you join in that historic effort?

In the long history of the world, only a few generations have been granted the role of defending freedom in its hour of maximum danger. I do not shank from this responsibility—I welcome it. I do not believe that any of us would exchange places with any other people or any other generation. The energy, the faith, the devotion which we bring to this endeavor will light our country and all who serve it—and the glow from that fire can truly light the world.

And so, my fellow Americans: ask not what your country can do for you—ask what you can do for your country.

My fellow citizens of the world: ask not what America will do for you, but what together we can do for the freedom of man.

Finally, whether you are citizens of America or citizens of the world, ask of us the same high standards of strength and sacrifice which we ask of you. With a good **conscience**[1] our only sure reward, with history the final judge of our deeds, let us go forth to lead the land we love, asking His blessing and His help, but knowing that here on earth God's work must truly be our own.

▶ 文化快递

1. Inaugural address（就职演说）

自1937年，美国总统就职演说日改为每年的1月20日，从此每隔四年的1月20日，新任美国总统首次与民众见面，举行总统的就职宣誓，并发表就职演说。

2. Solemn oath（庄严的誓言）

总统誓言，在《美国宪法》第1章第2条中有所描述："I do solemnly swear（or affirm）that I will faithfully execute the Office of President of the United States, and will to the best of my Ability, preserve, protect and defend the Constitution of the United States.我庄严宣誓，我会履行美利坚合众国总统的职务，并尽我所能，维护，保护美利坚合众国宪法。"

▶ 参考译文

首席法官先生、艾森豪威尔总统、尼克松副总统、杜鲁门总统、尊敬的牧师、各位公民：

今天我们庆祝的不是政党的胜利，而是自由的胜利。这象征着一个结束，也象征着一

---

1 conscience 良心；道德心

个开端，表示了一种更新，也表示了一种变革。因为我已在你们和全能的上帝面前，宣读了我们的先辈在170多年前拟定的庄严誓言。

现在的世界已大不相同了，人类的巨手掌握着既能消灭人间的各种贫困，又能毁灭人间的各种生活的力量。但我们的先辈为之奋斗的那些革命信念，在世界各地仍然有着争论。这个信念就是：人的权利并非来自国家的慷慨，而是来自上帝恩赐。

今天，我们不敢忘记我们是第一次革命的继承者。让我们的朋友和敌人同样听见我此时此地的讲话：火炬已经传给新一代美国人。这一代人在本世纪诞生，在战争中受过锻炼，在艰难困苦的和平时期受过陶冶，他们为我国悠久的传统感到自豪——他们不愿目睹或听任我国一向保证的、今天仍在国内外做出保证的人权渐趋毁灭。

让每个国家都知道——不论它希望我们繁荣还是希望我们衰落——为确保自由的存在和自由的胜利，我们将付出任何代价，承受任何负担，应付任何艰难，支持任何朋友，反抗任何敌人。

这些就是我们的保证——而且还有更多的保证。

对那些和我们有着共同文化和精神渊源的老盟友，我们保证待以诚实朋友那样的忠诚。我们如果团结一致，就能在许多合作事业中无往而不胜；我们如果分歧对立，就会一事无成——因为我们不敢在争吵不休、四分五裂时迎接强大的挑战。

对那些我们欢迎其加入到自由行列中来的新国家，我们恪守我们的誓言：决不让一种更为残酷的暴政来取代一种消失的殖民统治。我们并不总是指望他们会支持我们的观点。但我们始终希望看到他们坚强地维护自己的自由——而且要记住，在历史上，凡愚蠢地骑在虎背上谋求权力的人，都是以葬身虎口而告终。

对世界各地身居茅舍和乡村，为摆脱贫困而斗争的人们，我们保证尽最大努力帮助他们自立，不管需要花多长时间——之所以这样做，并不是因为共产党可能正在这样做，也不是因为我们需要他们的选票，而是因为这样做是正确的，自由社会如果不能帮助众多的穷人，也就无法保全少数富人。

对我国南面的姐妹共和国，我们提出一项特殊的保证——在争取进步的新同盟中，把我们善意的话变为善意的行动，帮助自由的人们和自由的政府摆脱贫困的枷锁。但是，这种充满希望的和平革命决不可以成为敌对国家的牺牲品。我们要让所有邻国都知道，我们将和他们在一起，反对在美洲任何地区进行侵略和颠覆活动。让所有其他国家都知道，本半球的人仍然想做自己家园的主人。

联合国是主权国家的世界性议事机构，是我们在战争手段大大超过和平手段的时代里最后的、最美好的希望所在。因此，我们重申予以支持；防止它仅仅成为谩骂的场所；加强它对新生国家和弱小国家的保护；扩大它的行使法令的管束范围。

最后，对那些想与我们作对的国家，我们提出一个要求而不是一项保证：在科学释放出可怕的破坏力量，把全人类卷入到预谋的或意外的自我毁灭的深渊之前，让我们双方重

新开始寻求和平。

我们不敢以怯弱来引诱他们。因为只有当我们毫无疑问地拥有足够的军备,我们才能毫无疑问地确信永远不会使用这些军备。

但是,这两个强大的国家集团都无法从目前所走的道路中得到安慰——发展现代武器所需的费用使双方负担过重,致命的原子武器的不断扩散理所当然使双方忧心忡忡,但是,双方却在争着改变那制止人类发动最后战争的不确定的恐怖均势。

因此,让我们双方重新开始——双方都要牢记。礼貌并不意味着怯弱,诚意永远有待于验证。让我们决不要由于畏惧而谈判。但我们决不能畏惧谈判。

让双方都来探讨使我们团结起来的问题,而不要操劳那些使我们分裂的问题。

让双方首次为军备检查和军备控制制订认真而又明确的提案,把毁灭他国的绝对力量置于所有国家的绝对控制之下。

让双方寻求利用科学的奇迹,而不是乞灵于科学造成的恐怖。让我们一起探索星球,征服沙漠,根除疾患,开发深海,并鼓励艺术和商业的发展。

让双方团结起来,在全世界各个角落倾听以赛亚的训令——"解下轭上的索,使被欺压的得自由。"

如果合作的滩头阵地可以逼退猜忌的丛林,那么就让双方共同作一次新的努力:不是建立一种新的均势,而是创造一个新的法治世界,在这个世界中,强者公正,弱者安全,和平将得到维护。

所有这一切不可能在第一个一百天内完成,也不可能在第一个一千天或者在本届政府任期内完成,甚至不可能在我们居住在这个星球上的有生之年内完成。但是,让我们开始吧。

公民们,我们方针的最终成败与其说掌握在我手中,不如说掌握在你们手中。自从合众国建立以来,每一代美国人都曾受到召唤去证明他们对国家的忠诚。响应召唤而献身的美国青年的坟墓遍及全球。

现在,号角已再次吹响——不是召唤我们拿起武器,虽然我们需要武器,不是召唤我们去作战,虽然我们严阵以待。它召唤我们为迎接黎明而肩负起漫长斗争的重任,年复一年,"从希望中得到欢乐,在苦难中保持坚韧",去反对人类共同的敌人——专制、贫困、疾病和战争本身。

为反对这些敌人,确保人类更为丰裕的生活,我们能够组成一个包括东西南北各方的全球大联盟吗?你们愿意参加这一历史性的努力吗?

在漫长的世界历史中,只有少数几代人在自由处于最危急的时刻被赋予保卫自由的责任。我不会推卸这一责任,我欢迎这一责任。我不相信我们中间有人想同其他人或其他时代的人交换位置。我们为这一努力所奉献的精力、信念和忠诚,将照亮我们的国家和所有为国效劳的人,而这火焰发出的光芒定能照亮全世界。

因此，美国同胞们，不要问国家能为你们做些什么，而要问你们能为国家做些什么。

全世界的公民们，不要问美国将为你们做些什么，而要问我们共同能为人类的自由做些什么。

最后，不论你们是美国公民还是其他国家的公民，你们应该要求我们献出我们同样要求于你们的高度力量和牺牲。问心无愧是我们唯一可靠的奖赏，历史是我们行动的最终裁判，让我们走向前去，引导我们所珍爱的国家。我们祈求上帝的福佑和帮助，但我们知道，确切地说，上帝在尘世的工作必定是我们自己的工作。

Lesson 5

King's Speech

Task 1 Questions and Answers

Directions: *Work in pairs. Read the following speech then take turns to ask and answer the following questions.*

1. To whom was the speech delivered? Where?
2. What is the background of the speech delivered?
3. Which style does the speech belong to according to the text?
4. Does the style of speech match the identity of the speaker?

Task 2 Brainstorming and Paper Talk

Directions: *Work in groups of six. Put the phrase "stage fright" in the middle of a piece of paper, then each member brainstorms and puts any ideas, questions, answers or comments on the topic using a mind map. Each group may focus on a different aspect, such as reasons, symptoms and ways to conquer Stage Fright. Then one representative from the group summarizes and reports to the class.*

Task 3 Imitation and Play

Directions: *Watch the authentic video of the speech. Then try to imitate the whole speech with appropriate delivery techniques. First practice by yourself. Then work in groups of four to take turns to deliver the speech.*

Task 4 Discussion

Directions: *Work in groups of four and discuss the following questions. You may locate some useful information from the script.*

1. What is your definition of "courage"?
2. How to become a courageous man/woman?
3. A bank accountant was reported to be killed by gangsters with Arms, as a result of refusing to give out the code of bank strongbox. What would you do in the same situation?

Task 5 Writing Practice

Directions: *Do a research on King George VI. You may watch the movie* **King's Speech** *or read his biographies. Write a passage for about 300 words, with a title of* **From a Stammer to a Speaker: How King George VI Overcame his Stage Fright.**

King's Speech
国王的演讲
Britain Declared War on Germany, 1939
By King George VI

人物简介

乔治六世（King George VI，1895年12月14日—1952年2月6日），全名艾伯特·弗雷德里克·阿瑟·乔治·温莎（"Albert Frederick Arthur George Windsor"）英国国王，1936年12月11日至1952年2月6日在位。他是乔治五世（原为约克公爵）和玛丽王后（原为玛丽公爵夫人）的第二个儿子。艾伯特十分害羞，终身都患有严重的口吃。1937年5月12日，因为爱德华八世最终决定为了婚姻问题而退位，艾伯特在威斯敏斯特大教堂登基，并改名为乔治六世。

两年后，第二次世界大战爆发，当时名望很低的王室希望能够成为带领国家迈向胜利的楷模，而他们确实是在二战中保持英国人民的斗志的重要因素。战争初期国王的圣诞节讲话鼓舞了士气。

名篇导读

演讲在西方是政治家的一项基本功，乔治六世的父亲乔治五世就非常重视演讲，他是历史上第一位通过广播发表演讲的英国国王。一次，老国王做完广播演讲后，让儿子乔治六世也尝试一下，口吃的王子紧张地说："父亲……我……我恐怕……做不来……"。老国王开导他说："以前的国王都要穿上军装骑在马上对众人演讲，现在我们只需要坐在家里说就可以了，没有比这更容易的了。"

1936年，老国王乔治五世逝世，长子爱德华八世继位，爱德华八世不爱美人不爱江山，与一位交际广泛、信仰天主教而不是英国国教、而且还离过婚的辛普森夫人结婚。他违背英国王室惯例，被不堪忍受他的内阁逼下台。因此，爱德华八世在执政325天便被迫退位了，烂摊子留给了弟弟艾伯特王子，即乔治六世。乔治六世自幼性格内向，还口吃，处处比不上聪明英俊的哥哥。乔治六世不是长子，正常情况下没有继承王位的可能，也从来没想过要当国王。但是，历史和命运偏偏选择了他。

1937年12月11日，爱德华八世退位，乔治六世面色苍白地出现在群臣面前，语气迟缓地宣读即位演说："事已至此，我决心倾尽全力，我的妻子将与我共渡难关，希望所有的国民也能支持我。"乔治六世实践了诺言，也许是自身的缺陷令他格外勤奋并怀有更强烈的责任感，他很快就用自己的行动赢得了人们的信任和尊重。

首先，作为政治家和公众人物，乔治六世要克服口吃。事实上，在登基之前的几年里，乔治六世就一直在接受澳大利亚藉语言治疗师莱昂纳尔·朗格的治疗。据白金汉宫工作人员回忆，乔治六世在莱昂纳尔面前就像一个刻苦学习的小学生。

1939年9月1日，纳粹德国闪击波兰，两天后，英国就向德国宣战。当天，乔治六世拒绝了内阁提出的王室撤离伦敦的请求，他宣布全家将留守伦敦直到战争结束。乔治六世知

道战争无法逃避，他必须挺身而出鼓舞人心。为此，他发表了练习多次的演讲鼓舞人们的士气，这就是电影《国王的演讲》的高潮部分："在这个庄严的时刻，也许是我国历史上最生死攸关的时刻……为了捍卫我们珍视的一切，我们必须接受这个挑战。"

1940年5月，乔治六世召见主战派大臣温斯顿·丘吉尔，任命他为首相，这对性格截然相反的君臣开始默契合作，乔治六世温和包容，丘吉尔却是火爆脾气，但乔治六世竭力支持他战时首相的地位。乔治六世在英国社会各界的支持下力挽狂澜，以战时演讲作为转折点，终于获取大多数国人的拥戴，鼓舞英国反抗法西斯的士气。乔治六世还冒着敌机轰炸的危险，每天访问部队、工厂。1940年11月，他赶到刚被纳粹德军空袭过的考文垂，面对麦克风，久经考验的国王不再局促，他说："我知道，对于那些失去了所有穷苦民众们来说，语言是不足以表达感情的。"国王诚恳朴实的一句话，唤起雷鸣般的掌声。1943年，乔治六世不顾丘吉尔和军方的反对，来到欧洲战略要塞马耳他战场，慰问军队。

二战中，白金汉宫一共遭遇9次空袭，供暖系统被炸毁，所有房间都伤痕累累。乔治六世一直坚守王宫，和伦敦市民一样，过着缺吃少穿的日子。美国驻英国大使约瑟夫·肯尼迪到访王宫时，国王只有两道菜让他选择。

战争结束后，乔治六世身体状况急剧恶化，他从小体弱，不像哥哥那样精力充沛、聪明敏捷，但他毫不退缩地履行着国王的义务，工作的压力和害羞的性格最终弄垮他的身体。1952年乔治六世去世，时年57岁，丘吉尔亲笔写下拉丁文悼词：勇者无敌。乔治六世没有儿子，他的女儿伊丽莎白二世在他去世后继位，伊丽莎白二世也就是现在的英国女王。

▶ 英文原文

In this grave hour, perhaps the most fateful in history, I send to every household of my peoples, both at home and overseas, this message, spoken with the same depth of feeling for each one of you as if I were able to cross your threshold and speak to you myself.

For the second time in the lives of most of us, we are at war.

Over and over again, we have tried to find a peaceful way out of the differences between ourselves and those who are now our enemies; but it has been in vain.

We have been forced into a conflict, for which we are called, with our allies to meet the challenge of a principle which, if it were to **prevail**[1], would be fatal to any civilized order in the world.

It is a principle which permits a state in the selfish pursuit of power to disregard its

---

1 prevail 流行，盛行；获胜，占优势

treaties[1] and its solemn pledges, which **sanctions**[2] the use of force or threat of force against the **sovereignty**[3] and independence of other states.

Such a principle, **stripped**[4] of all disguise, is surely the mere primitive **doctrine**[5] that might is right, and if this principle were established through the world, the freedom of our own country and of the whole British **Commonwealth**[6] of nations would be in danger.

But far more than this, the peoples of the world would be kept in **bondage**[7] of fear, and all hopes of settled peace and of security, of justice and liberty, among nations, would be ended.

This is the ultimate issue which confronts us. For the sake of all that we ourselves hold dear, and of the world order and peace, it is unthinkable that we should refuse to meet the challenge.

It is to this high purpose that I now call my people at home and my peoples across the seas, who will make our cause their own.

I ask them to stand calm and firm and united in this time of trial.

The task will be hard. There may be dark days ahead, and war can no longer be confined to the battlefield, but we can only do the right as we see the right, and **reverently**[8] commit our cause to God. If one and all we keep resolutely faithful to it, ready for whatever service or sacrifice it may demand, then with God's help, we shall prevail.

May He bless and keep us all.

文化快递

1. World War II（第二次世界大战）

1939年9月1日—1945年9月2日，以德国、意大利、日本法西斯等轴心国（及芬兰、伊拉克、伪满洲国等国）为一方，以反法西斯同盟和全世界反法西斯力量为另一方进行的第二次全球规模的战争。从欧洲到亚洲，从大西洋到太平洋，先后有61个国家和地区、20亿以上的人口被卷入战争，作战区域面积2200万平方千米。据不完全统计，战争中军民共伤亡9000余万人，4万多亿美元付诸流水。第二次世界大战最后以美国、苏联、中国、英国等反法西斯国家和世界人民战胜法西斯侵略者赢得世界和平与进步而告终。

2. Allies & Axis（同盟国与轴心国）

同盟国又称反法西斯同盟，第二次世界大战时期建立的国家联盟。参与该联盟的国家主要有美国、英国、法国、苏联、中国、加拿大、朝鲜、澳大利亚、埃塞俄比亚等数十个国家。同盟国集团最终打败了轴心国集团，取得了胜利。意大利、芬兰、匈牙利、罗马尼

1　treaty 条约，协定
2　sanction 批准；鼓励，容忍
3　sovereignty 主权，统治权
4　strip 剥去
5　doctrine 信条
6　Commonwealth 共和国；联邦；团体；协会
7　bondage 奴役，束缚
8　reverently 恭敬地；虔诚地

亚和保加利亚在退出轴心国阵营之后也加入了同盟国。

轴心国（Axis），指在第二次世界大战中结成的战争联盟，包括纳粹德国、意大利和日本等国家。1936年10月25日，德国和意大利达成协调外交政策的同盟条约，建立柏林—罗马轴心。1939年5月22日，两国又签订了《德意同盟条约》（又被称为"钢铁条约"）。此前日本已经在1936年11月25日同德国签署反共产国际协定（意大利于1937年11月6日加入）。1940年9月27日，德国、日本和意大利三国外交代表在柏林签署《德意日三国同盟条约》（三国公约），成立以柏林—罗马—东京轴心为核心的军事集团。这个军事集团的成员被称为"轴心国"。1945年5月8日德国投降后，日本于5月25日宣布废除三国公约。同年8月15日日本向同盟国投降，轴心国集团灭亡。

◎ 参考译文

在这样严峻的时刻，可能是国家存亡的紧要关头，我向领土上的所有子民，不论是国内或是海外，传达这份消息，我和你们一样，百感交集，只希望我能挨家挨户亲自向你们诉说。

我们大部分人，都是第二次经历战争的洗礼。

不止一次，我们尝试过寻求和平之道，求同存异，化敌为友，然而徒劳无功。

我们被迫卷入了一场战争，我们所面临的，是一个邪恶信念的挑战，如果敌方取胜，世界的文明秩序将毁于一旦。

在一种信念的驱使下,一个国家追逐私权,不惜违背自己条约和自己庄严的承诺,背信弃义,滥用武力或用武力威胁其他国家的主权和独立地位。

这样的信念，剥去伪装的外衣，只是赤裸裸的强权既是公理的野蛮信条。如果这一信条成为世界准则，我们的国家，整个英联邦所有国家的自由都将受到威胁。

但远远不止这些。世界人民都将终日惶惶不安。国与国之间已经建立起来的所有和平、安全、正义和自由都将化为乌有。

这就是我们面临的最终问题。为了捍卫我们所珍视的一切，为了捍卫这个世界已经有的秩序和和平，我们必须接受这个挑战。

为此崇高目标，我呼吁国内的民众，海外的子民们，万众一心。

我希望你们能冷静坚定，在时间的历练中团结向前。

任务将会困难重重，前路可能乌云密布，战场将不再局限于前线阵地。只有心怀正义才能正确行事，在此我们虔诚地向上帝承诺。只要每个人坚定信念，在上帝的帮助下，我们必将获胜。

愿上帝永远保佑我们每个人。

Lesson 6

Women's Rights Are Human Rights

Task 1 Questions and Answers

Directions: *Work in pairs. Read the following speech then take turns to ask and answer the following questions.*
1. When was the speech delivered? Where?
2. Who delivered the speech? Who are involved in the speech?
3. What is the theme of the speech?
4. Why is there a need for the request?
5. How can the request be achieved?

Task 2 Co-Operative Study

Directions: *Work in pairs. Go through the script and locate the lines that confuse you. Underline these places. Then discuss with your partner to seek for their understanding of these lines. Then bring the unsolved questions to a larger group of six, and finally to the whole class.*

Task 3 Imitation and Play

Directions: *Watch the authentic video of the speech. Then try to imitate one or two paragraphs you like with appropriate delivery techniques. First practice by yourself. Then work in groups of four to take turns to deliver the speech.*

Task 4 Discussion

Directions: *Work in groups of four and discuss the following questions. You may locate some useful information from the script.*
1. According to the speaker, have women acquired equal rights as men now?
2. Can you cite some examples to illustrate women's status in nowadays world?
3. What are the reasons that contribute to the women's current problems?
4. Are women's right human rights, in your point of view?

Task 5　Speaking Practice

Directions: *Give a speech to the class for 2-3 minutes on a topic which you are interested in. You may choose from the following:*

1. Highly Educated Women Don't Make Good Wives
2. Marrying Well is Better than Working Well
3. Real Men Only Weep in Deep Grief

Women's Rights Are Human Rights
女权也是人权
Remarks to the United Nations Fourth World Conference on Women Plenary Session
By Hillary Clinton

▶ 人物简介

希拉里·克林顿（1947年——　），美国第67任国务卿，前联邦参议员，美国著名律师、政治家，美国第42届总统比尔·克林顿的妻子，美国前第一夫人。

比尔·克林顿卸任后，她参加了2008年美国总统选举，并曾在民主党总统候选人初选中大幅度领先，但最终败给了伊利诺伊州的联邦参议员贝拉克·奥巴马。奥巴马成功当选后，提名她出任国务卿，并最终成为美国历史上的第3位女性国务卿。

她的政治立场偏向自由主义，在政界的影响力也不俗。舆论普遍认为她是美国历史上最有实权的第一夫人。

名篇导读

《女权也是人权》是希拉里1995年在联合国第四届妇女大会上的演讲,该演讲至今仍是世界妇女人权的重要篇章。

1975年,希拉里与比尔·克林顿结婚初时,希拉里拒绝改从丈夫姓氏,仍坚持自称"希拉里·罗德姆"。在当时普遍保守的阿肯色州,此举明显过于激进,被认为是缺乏传统家庭观念的表现,也对比尔·克林顿的政治前途产生了负面影响。权衡利弊之后,希拉里最终让步,从此真正成为了"希拉里·克林顿"。

1998年莱温斯基事件揭露后,希拉里与比尔·克林顿的婚姻状态一度成为全美关注的焦点。不少支持者敦促希拉里同克林顿离婚,但她最后选择妥协。她的决定保护了她自己和比尔·克林顿的政治前途,但也在很大程度上背离了她一向提倡的女权主义理想。

英文原文

Thank you very much, Gertrude Mongella, for your **dedicated**[1] work that has brought us to this point. Distinguished delegates, and guests:

I would like to thank the Secretary General of the United Nations for inviting me to be a part of the United Nations Fourth World Conference of Women. This is truly a celebration—a celebration of the contributions women make in every aspect of life: in the home, on the job, in their communities, as mothers, wives, sisters, daughters, learners, workers, citizens and leaders.

It is also a coming together, much of the way women come together ever day in every country. We come together in fields and in factories. We come together in village markets and supermarkets. We come together in living rooms and board rooms. Whether it is while playing with our children in the park, or washing clothes in a river, or taking a break at the office water cooler, we come together and talk about our **aspirations**[2] and concern. And time and again, our talk turns to our children and our families. However different we may be, there is far more that unites us than divides us. We share a common future, and are here to find common ground so that we may help bring new dignity and respect to women and girls all over the world. By doing this, we bring new strength and stability to families as well.

By gathering in Beijing, we are focusing world attention on issues that matter most in the lives of women and their families: access to education, health care, jobs and credit, the chance to enjoy basic legal and human rights and participate fully in the political life of their countries.

There are some who question the reason for this conference. Let them listen to the voices of women in their homes, neighborhoods, and workplaces. There are some who wonder whether the lives of women and girls matter to economic and political progress around the globe. Let them

---

1 dedicated 专注的,投入的;献身的;专用的
2 aspiration 强烈的愿望;吸气,吸入

look at the women gathered here and at *Huairou*—the homemakers, nurses, teachers, lawyers, policymakers, and women who run their own businesses. It is conferences like this that compel governments and people everywhere to listen, look and face the world's most pressing problems. Wasn't it after the women's conference in Nairobi ten years ago that the world focused for the first time on the crisis of domestic violence?

Earlier today, I participated in a World Health Organization forum, where government officials, NGOs, and individual citizens are working on ways to address the health problems of women and girls. Tomorrow, I will attend a gathering of the United Nations Development Fund for Women. There, the discussion will focus on local—and highly successful—programs that give hard-working women access to credit so they can improve their own lives and the lives of their families.

What we are learning around the world is that if women are healthy and educated, their families will flourish. If women are free from violence, their families will flourish. If women have a chance to work and earn as full and equal partners in society, their families will flourish. And when families flourish, communities and nations will flourish. That is why every woman, every man, every child, every family, and every nation on our planet has a stake in the discussion that takes place here.

Over the past 25 years, I have worked persistently on issues relating to women, children, and families. Over the past two-and-a half years, I have had the opportunity to learn more about the challenges facing women in my own country and around the world.

I have met new mothers in Jojakarta and Indonesia, who come together regularly in their village to discuss nutrition, family planning, and baby care. I have met working parents in Denmark who talk about the comfort they feel in knowing that their children can be cared for in creative, safe, and nurturing after-school centers. I have met women in South Africa who helped lead the struggle to end **apartheid**[1] and are now helping build a new democracy. I have met with the leading women of the Western Hemisphere who are working every day to promote literacy and better health care for the children of their countries. I have met women in India and Bangladesh who are taking out small loans to buy milk cows, **rickshaws**[2], thread and other materials to create a **livelihood**[3] for themselves and their families. I have met doctors and nurses in Belarus and Ukraine who are trying to keep children alive in the **aftermath**[4] of *Chernobyl*.

The great challenge of this Conference is to give voice to women everywhere whose experiences go unnoticed, whose words go unheard. Women comprise more than half the word's population. Women are 70% of the world's poor, and two-thirds of those are not taught to read and write. Women are the primary caretakers for most of the world's children and elderly. Yet

---

1 apartheid（以往南非的）种族隔离制度；分离，隔离；孤傲
2 rickshaw 黄包车；人力车
3 livelihood 生活，生计；谋生之道；营生
4 aftermath 后果；余波；再生草

much of the work we do is not valued—not by economists, not by historians, not by popular culture, not by government leaders.

At this very moment, as we sit here, women around the world are giving birth, raising children, cooking meals, washing clothes, cleaning houses, planting crops, working on assembly lines, running companies, and running countries. Women also are dying from diseases that should have been prevented or treated. They are watching their children **succumb**[1] to malnutrition caused by poverty and economic deprivation. They are being denied the right to go to school by their own fathers and brothers. They are being forced into prostitution, and they are being barred from the band lending office and banned from the ballot box.

Those of us who have the opportunity to be here have the responsibility to speak for those who could not. As an American, I want to speak up for those women in my own country women who are raising children on the minimum wage, women who can't afford health care or child care, women whose lives are threatened by violence, including violence in their own homes.

I want to speak up for mothers who are fighting for good schools, safe neighborhoods, clean air, and clean **airwaves**[2]; for older women, some of them widows, who have raised their families and now find their skills and life experiences are not valued in the workplace; for women who are working all night as nurses, hotel clerks, and fast food cooks so that they can be at home during the day with their kids; and for women everywhere who simply don't have time to do everything they are called upon to do each day.

Speaking to you today, I speak for them, just as each of us speaks for women around the world who are denied the chance to go to school, or see a doctor, or own property, or have a say about the direction of their lives, simply because they are women. The truth is that most women around the world work both inside and outside the home, usually by necessity.

We need to understand that there is no formula for how women should lead their lives. That is why we must respect the choices that each woman makes for herself and her family. Every woman deserves the chance to realize her own God-given potential. We also must recognize that women will never gain full dignity until their human rights are respected and protected.

Our goals for this Conference, to strengthen families and societies by **empowering**[3] women to take greater control over their destinies, cannot be fully achieved unless all governments—here and around the world—accept their responsibility to protect and promote internationally recognized human rights. The international community has long acknowledged—and recently affirmed at Vienna—that both women and men are entitled to a range of protections and personal freedoms, from the right of personal security to the right to determine freely the number and spacing of the children they bear. No one should be forced to remain silent for fear of religious or political persecution, arrest, abuse or torture.

1　succumb 屈服；死亡
2　airwaves 广播；电视；〔电子〕空中电波
3　empowering 授权，允许

Tragically[1], women are most often the ones whose human rights are violated. Even in the late 20th century, the rape of women continues to be used as an instrument of armed conflict. Women and children make up a large majority of the world's refugees. When women are excluded from the political process, they become even more vulnerable to abuse. I believe that, on the eve of a new **millennium**[2], it is time to break our silence. It is time for us to say here in Bejing, and the world to hear, that it is no longer acceptable to discuss women's rights as separate from human rights.

These abuses have continued because, for too long, the history of women has been a history of silence. Even today, there are those who are trying to silence our words. The voices of this conference and of the women at Huairou must be heard loud and clear:

It is a violation of human rights when babies are denied food, or drowned, or **suffocated**[3], or their **spines**[4] broken, simply because they are born girls.

It is a violation of human rights when woman and girls are sold into the slavery of prostitution for human greed—and the kinds of reasons that are used to justify this practice should no longer be tolerated.

It is a violation of human rights when women are **doused**[5] with gasoline, set on fire and burned to death because their marriage **dowries**[6] are deemed too small.

It is a violation of human rights when individual women are raped in their own communities and when thousands of women are subjected to rape as a tactic or prize of war.

It is a violation of human rights when a leading cause of death worldwide along women ages 14 to 44 is the violence they are subjected to in their own homes by their own relatives.

It is a violation of human rights when young girls are brutalized by the painful and degrading practice of genital mutilation.

It is a violation of human rights when women are denied the right to plan their own families, and that includes being forced to have abortions or being **sterilized**[7] against their will.

If there is one message that echoes forth from this conference, it is that human rights are women's rights—and women's rights are human rights. Let us not forget that among those rights are the right to speak freely—and the right to be heard.

Women must enjoy the right to participate fully in the social and political lives of their countries if we want freedom and democracy to thrive and endure. It is indefensible that many women in nongovernmental organizations who wished to participate in this conference have not been able to attend—or have been prohibited from fully taking part.

Let me be clear. Freedom means the right of people to assemble, organize and debate openly.

---

1 tragically 悲剧地，悲惨地
2 millennium 一千年；千年期；千禧年；全人类未来的幸福时代
3 suffocate （使某人）窒息而死；（将某人）闷死；让人感觉闷热；憋气
4 spine 脊椎；（动植物的）刺；书脊
5 douse 浇水在……上；浸泡
6 dowry 嫁妆
7 sterilize 消毒；使无菌；使失去生育能力；使绝育

It means respecting the views of those who may disagree with the views of their governments. It means not taking citizens away from their loved ones and jailing they, mistreating them, or denying them their freedom or dignity because of the peaceful expression of their ideas and opinions.

In my country, we recently celebrated the 75th anniversary of women's **suffrage**[1]. It took 150 years after the signing of our Declaration of Independence for women to win the right to vote. It took 72 years of organized struggle on the part of many courageous women and men. It was one of America's most **divisive**[2] philosophical wars. But it was also a bloodless war. Suffrage was achieved without a shot being fired.

We have also been reminded, in V-J Day observances last weekend, of the good that comes when men and women join together to combat the forces of tyranny and build a better world. We have seen peace prevail in most places for a half century. We have avoided another world war. But we have not solved older, deeply-rooted problems that continue to diminish the potential of half the world's population.

Now it is time to act on behalf of women everywhere. If we take bold steps to better the lives of women, we will be taking bold steps to better the lives of children and families too. Families rely on mothers and wives for emotional support and care; families rely on women for labor in the home; and increasingly, families rely on women for income needed to raise healthy children and care for other relatives.

As long as discrimination and inequities remain so commonplace around the world—as long as girls and women are valued less, red less, fed last, overworked, underpaid, not schooled and subjected to violence in and out of their homes—the potential of the human family to create a peaceful, prosperous world will not be realized.

Let this Conference be our—and the world's—call to action. And let us heed the call so that we can create a world in which every woman is treated with respect and dignity, every boy and girl is loved and cared for equally, and every family has the hope of a strong and stable future.

That is the work before you. That is the work before all of us who have a vision of the world we want to see—for our children and our grandchildren.

The time is now. We must move beyond rhetoric. We must move beyond recognition of problems to working together, to have the comment efforts to build that common ground we hope to see.

God's blessing on you, your work, and all who will benefit from it.

Thank you very much.

1　suffrage（政治性选举的）选举权，投票权
2　divisive 离间的；造成不合的；制造分裂的

英语演讲名篇赏析
Appreciation of Masterpiece English Speeches

▶ 文化快递

1. Huairou（怀柔）

怀柔是北京市的郊区县。北依燕山山脉，南偎华北平原，土地面积2128.7平方公里。

怀柔具有悠久的历史，春秋战国时期，著名的渔阳郡即在怀柔；隋唐时期，怀柔始见立名，1368年开始，正式有了现今怀柔县的建制。2001年国务院批准成立北京市怀柔区。1995年9月，联合国第四次世界妇女大会NGO分会在怀柔举行。

2. Chernobyl（切尔诺贝利）

切尔诺贝利是乌克兰北部基辅州城市，地处白俄罗斯边境，邻近另一个被废弃的城市普里皮亚季。切尔诺贝利在1986年因切尔诺贝利核事故而被废弃。

切尔诺贝利核电站是苏联时期在乌克兰境内修建的第一座核电站，曾被认为是世界上最安全、最可靠的核电站。但1986年4月26日，核电站的第4号核反应堆在进行半烘烤实验中突然失火，引起爆炸，核泄漏事故后产生的放射污染相当于日本广岛原子弹爆炸产生的放射污染的100倍。爆炸使机组完全损坏，8吨多强辐射物质泄露，尘埃随风飘散，致使俄罗斯、白俄罗斯和乌克兰许多地区遭到核辐射的污染。2013年4月26日是切尔诺贝利核电站核泄漏事故27周年纪念日。

▶ 参考译文

十分感谢格特鲁德·蒙盖拉的工作，把我们聚到一起。各位代表，各位来宾：

我十分感谢秘书长邀请我成为联合国第四次世界妇女大会这一重要会议的成员。这是一个真正的庆祝活动，庆祝妇女在生活的各个方面：在家里、工作、社区中作为母亲、妻子、姐妹、女儿、学生、工人、市民和领导人的贡献。

这也是每天任何国家的妇女走到一起的方式。我们从农场和工厂、从农村市场和超市、从客厅和会议室走到一起。无论是在与我们的孩子在公园里玩，或在河边洗衣服，或在办公室饮水机旁休息，我们走到一起，谈论我们的愿望和关注的事情。无数次，我们都在谈我们的孩子和我们的家庭。不管我们的外表差异有多大，始终都有一些东西能够把我们团结起来，而不是割裂开来。我们有着共同的未来，我们在这里为了找到共同点，以便给世界各地的妇女和女孩带来新的尊严和尊重，这样做同样可以给我们的家庭注入新的活力和带来稳定性。

通过齐聚在北京，我们把世界的目光聚焦在严重困扰我们生活的问题上——妇女及其家人的生活：受教育机会、医疗保健、就业和信贷、享受基本的法律和人权的机会以及充分参与我们国家的政治生活。

有些人怀疑此次会议的原因。让他们听听他们家中、邻居、和工作场所中妇女的声音。有些人怀疑妇女和女孩问题对于世界经济和政治进展的影响力。让他们看看聚集在这里和怀柔的妇女——家庭主妇和护士、教师和律师、决策者和经营自己的企业女性。这是一个迫使任何地方的政府和人们倾听、注视、和面对世界上最紧迫问题的会议。毕竟，这是十年前在内罗毕的聚焦世界目光的第一次家庭暴力危机的妇女会议后的又一次会议。

今天早上，我参加了世界卫生组织论坛。在论坛上，我们讨论了关于政府官员、非政府组织、和公民个人着手处理妇女和女孩健康问题的方法。明天，我将出席联合国妇女发展基金会议。那个会议将聚焦于非常成功的地方给予辛勤工作的妇女获得信贷的措施，以便使他们能够改善自己及其家庭的生活。

我们现在在世界各地学习的是，如果妇女身体健康并接受过教育，那么她们的家庭将繁荣昌盛。如果妇女免受暴力，他们的家庭会欣欣向荣。如果妇女有机会工作和赚钱，作为社会充分和平等的伙伴，那么她们的家庭将蓬勃发展。并且，当家庭蓬勃发展，社区和国家也将繁荣。这就是为什么每一个妇女、每个人、每个儿童、每一个家庭、及这个星球上的每个国家在这里有责任讨论此事。

在过去的25年里，我坚持做关于妇女、孩子和家庭的工作。在过去的两年半时间里，我有机会了解在我自己的国家和世界各地妇女所面临的挑战。

我在印度尼西亚会见了刚做母亲的妇女，她们在村里经常聚在一起讨论营养、家庭计划以及婴儿护理。我在丹麦会见了双薪夫妇，他们谈论在知道自己的孩子在课余中心被安全的照顾和喂养后的放心感觉。我在南非会见了领导结束种族隔离斗争，并正在帮助建立一个新的民主国家的妇女。我会见了每天都在为提高本国儿童识字率和更好的卫生保健而工作的西半球妇女。我会见了印度和孟加拉国正在为维持自己和家人生计而用小额贷款购买奶牛、或人力车、或纱线的妇女。我会见了白俄罗斯和乌克兰正在尝试让切尔诺贝利事件中的儿童活下来的医生和护士。

这次会议的巨大挑战是给予世界各地那些被忽视的、默默无闻的妇女一些发言权。妇女占世界人口的一半多，占世界贫困人口的70%，其中三分之二的人不会阅读和写作。我们是照顾世界小孩和老人的主力军。然而我们的很多工作没有被足够的评价——不被经济学家、历史学家、流行文化、政府领导人的评价。

此时此刻，就在我们坐在这里时，世界各地的妇女正在生孩子、抚养孩子、做饭、洗衣服、打扫房间、种植作物、在流水线上工作、经营公司、管理国家。妇女也同样正在遭受本来可以预防和治疗的疾病所带来的死亡。她们眼看着自己的孩子因贫困和经济匮乏而营养不良。他们被自己的父亲和兄弟剥夺了上学的权利。他们被迫卖淫，他们被禁止在银行贷款办事处和投票箱之外。

我们当中有机会在这里的人有责任为那些没有机会的人说话。作为一个美国人，我想为这些妇女发言，为我自己国家的妇女，为用很低薪水抚养孩子的妇女，为负担不起医疗保健和幼儿保健的妇女，为遭受暴力（包括在她们自己家中的暴力）威胁的

妇女。

我想为这些母亲发言,为争取好学校、安全社区、清洁空气、和干净天空(没有电磁波)的妇女;为在养育了家庭后发现自己的技能和生活经历不被市场重视的老年妇女(其中一些是寡妇);为整夜做护理、酒店职员、或者快餐厨师工作,以便她们能够在白天与自己的孩子团圆的妇女;以及为世界各地每天根本没有时间去做完其尽其所能的事情的女人。

今天和你们说话,我为她们发言,就像我们每个人为世界各地、仅仅因为他们是女人就没有机会上学、或者看病、或者有财产、或者决定自己生活方向的女性而呐喊。事实上是大多数的妇女都同时兼顾工作与家庭。

我们必须理解,没有一个固定模式能够回答妇女到底该如何引领我们的生活。这就是为什么我们必须尊重每个妇女对于她自己和她的家庭所做的选择。每个女性都应该有机会去实现自己的天赋。但是,我们必须认识到除非他们的人权受到保护和尊重,否则女性永远不会赢得充分的尊重。

我们这次会议的目标是通过赋予女性足够控制她们自己命运的权利来加强家庭和社会。实现这个目标除非世界各国政府接受他们保护和提升国际公认的人权的责任,否则不能够充分实现。国际社会长期以来一直承认,并且最近在维也纳重申妇女和男子享有同等的保护和个人自由,从个体自由权力到自由决定生孩子的数量和间隔。任何人都不应该因对宗教和政治迫害、逮捕、虐待或酷刑的恐惧而被迫保持沉默。

可悲的是妇女们往往是人权被侵犯的群体。即便是现在,在20世纪末,强奸妇女仍然被继续作为军事冲突的工具。妇女和儿童是世界上难民的绝大组成部分。并且,当妇女被排除参与政治活动时,她们更加容易遭受虐待。在新千年到来之际,我认为是打破沉默的时候了。在北京,我们是时候发言给世界听了,就是把妇女权利的讨论排除在人权讨论之外不再被接受了。

这种虐待长久以来都在继续,因为妇女的历史遗址都是沉默的。即使在今天,仍然存在试图使我们的话沉默的人。但是,这次会议和怀柔妇女的声音必须大声清楚地被听到。

只因是女孩,婴儿就被剥夺食品、或淹死、或闷死、或刺死,此种行为是对人权的侵犯。

妇女和女孩由于人类的贪婪和其它各种原因而被拐卖为妓女奴隶的、在过去被合法化的行为不应该再被容忍,这是对人权的侵犯。

妇女因他们的嫁妆太少而被浇上汽油放火烧死,这是对人权的侵犯。

个别妇女在自己的社区被强奸,成千上万的妇女被作为战争的手段或奖励而被强奸,这是对人权的侵犯。

当世界上14至44岁的妇女死亡的首要原因是遭受自己家中亲人的暴力行为时,这是对人权的侵犯。

当年轻的女孩遭受痛苦的切割生殖器官的侮辱人格的兽行时，这是对人权的侵犯。

当妇女被剥夺规划自己的家庭的权利，包括违反她们意愿被强迫堕胎或绝育时，这是对人权的侵犯。

如果未来此次会议能够发出一个信号，请让它永远是"人权就是妇女权利和妇女权利就是人权"。让我们不要忘记，在这些权利中包含言论自由权和发表意见权。

如果我们想让自由和民主繁荣昌盛并持久，那么在她们国家的社会和政治生活中，妇女就必须享有充分参与的权利。在非政府组织中的很多妇女希望参与本次会议但没能够出席或者被完全禁止参与的行为是站不住脚的。

我要明确。自由意味着人民享有集会、组织和公开辩论的权利。这意味着尊重与政府意见不同的人的意见。这意味着不能因为和平表达他们的观点和意见就把他们强行从他们亲人身边拉走、关押他们、虐待他们、或者剥夺他们的自由或尊严。

在我的国家，我们最近庆祝妇女选举权75周年。妇女获得投票权发生在签署独立宣言150年后。在此事发生之前，有勇气的妇女和男子进行了72年有组织的抗争。它是美国最具分裂的哲学战争之一。但是它是一场不流血的战争。妇女选举权的成功没有经过一枪一弹就达成了。

但是，在上周末的南军日纪念活动上，我们同样回想起当男子和妇女齐心协力打击暴政军队和建立一个美好世界所带来的好处。我们见证了世界大部分地区半个世纪的和平。我们避免了新的世界大战。但是，我们没有解决旧的、根深蒂固的问题，这个问题将继续减少潜在的世界另一半人口。

现在，是世界另一半妇女行动的时候了。如果我们采取大胆的措施来改善妇女的生活，那么，我们也就能采取大胆的步骤改善儿童和家庭的生活了。家庭依赖于母亲和妻子精神上的支持和照顾。家庭依靠妇女在家中的劳动。以及越来越多的世界各地的家庭依赖于妇女的收入来抚养健康的儿童和照顾其他亲属。

只要世界上歧视和不平等现象仍然很普遍，只要女孩和妇女仍然不被重视、喂得少、最后喂、过度劳累，报酬过低，未受教育，遭受家里家外的暴力——创造一个和平繁荣世界的人类家园便无法实现。

让本次会议成为我们和世界行动的呐喊。让我们响应这一呼吁，以便我们能够建立一个的世界，其中每个女人都被尊重和有尊严，每个男孩和女孩都被平等的关心和爱护，和每个家庭都期待有一个强大和稳定的未来。这就是摆在你面前的工作。这就是摆在我们面前的工作——希望看到所期望的世界——为我们的子孙后代。

现在是时候了。我们必须超越言辞。我们必须超越对于共同合作、对于努力建立我们愿意看到的共同立场的评论问题的认识。

愿上帝保佑你、你的工作和所有从此次会议获得益处的人。

祝您平安，十分感谢。

Lesson 7

Americans Despise Cowards!

Task 1 Questions and Answers

Directions: Work in pairs. Read the following speech then take turns to ask and answer the following questions.

1. When was the speech delivered? Where?
2. Who delivered the speech? Who are involved in the speech?
3. What is the theme of the speech?
4. Why is there a need for the request?
5. How can the request be achieved?

Task 2 Vocabulary Learning

Directions: Translate the following phrases into Chinese. Then try to learn by heart the cultural connotations of these color-related phrases.

yellow cowards _____   green-eyed _____
be in the red _____   blue blood _____
black lie _____   black sheep _____
white lie _____   gray market _____
blue film _____   white night _____

Task 3 Imitation and Play

Directions: Watch the authentic video of the speech. Then try to imitate one or two paragraphs you like with appropriate delivery techniques. First practice by yourself. Then work in groups of four to take turns to deliver the speech.

Task 4 Discussion

Directions: Work in groups of four and discuss the following questions. You may locate some useful information from the script.

1. What are the reasons why " You are here today" (Line3, Paragraph 2)? What do words "you", "here" and "today" refer to specifically?

2. Do you agree to the statement that "The real hero is the man who fights even though he is scared (Line 5, Paragraph 3)."? Why or why not?
3. Can you use specific details or examples to share your understanding of the statement that "Every man serves the whole" (Line 8, Paragraph 7)?
4. What does foxhole indicate in the sentence "My men don't dig foxholes" (Line 2, Paragraph 13)?

Task 5 **Speaking Practice**

Directions: *Give a speech to the class for 2-3 minutes on the topic "A Person I Admire Most".*

Americans Despise Cowards (adapted)
美国人瞧不起胆小鬼（改编）
General Patton's Address to the Troops
By George Patton

🔊 背景知识

乔治·巴顿（George Smith Patton），第二世界大战中一颗耀眼军事明星。

乔治·巴顿1885年11月11日生于美国加利福尼亚豪门，1909年毕业于美国西点军校。巴顿是一位美国陆军四星上将，是第二次世界大战中著名的美国军事统帅。乔治·巴顿一个为战争而生，视和平为地狱的男人。他是一个天才的军事领袖，在战斗中勇猛而残酷。乔治·巴顿作战重视坦克作用，强调快速进攻，有"热血铁胆""血胆老将"之称。巴顿

英语演讲名篇赏析
Appreciation of Masterpiece English Speeches

不仅是将军也是文人；是一个具有政治、军事、哲学头脑的人；更是一个最具个性和人性的人。有文记载，1945年4月14日，巴顿上将应邀参加莱茵河大桥落成典礼。剪彩仪式上，普兰克少将递过一把剪刀请他剪彩。巴顿十分不满意："你把我当成什么人了。裁缝师傅吗？他妈的，给我拿把刺刀来！"随从参谋立即递上一把刺刀。将军用刺刀完成了剪彩仪式。

名篇导读

本文是二战中诺曼底登陆前夜，乔治·巴顿对第三军的军事动员演讲。

巴顿在演讲中满嘴脏话，就像一个老兵油子，而且在提到他自己时，也称之为"fucking-bitch patton"（狗娘养的巴顿）。很显然，巴顿并没有顾及作为一个将军的尊严，也没有高高在上的大摆架子，而是把自己当成了普通士兵。这样的低姿态，反而加强了士兵的认同感，让士兵在心理上觉得巴顿永远和他们在一起，激励他们一直向前。这篇动员讲话，里面不乏粗辞糙语，但也不时闪烁着他的军事思想。他的演讲语言粗俗，却极富特性，最能激发士兵的斗志，勇建奇功。

本文对部分过于粗俗的字句做了删减。

英文原文

Be seated.

Men, this stuff that some sources **sling around**[1] about America wanting out of this war, not wanting to fight, is a crock of bullshit. Americans love to fight, traditionally. All real Americans love the sting and clash of battle. <u>You are here today for three reasons</u>. First, because you are here to defend your homes and your loved ones. Second, you are here for your own self respect, because you would not want to be anywhere else. Third, you are here because you are real men and all real men like to fight. When you, here, every one of you, were kids, you all admired the champion **marble**[2] player, the fastest runner, the toughest boxer, the big league ball players, and the All-American football players. Americans love a winner. Americans will not tolerate a loser. Americans despise cowards. Americans play to win all of the time. I wouldn't **give a hoot**[3] in hell for a man who lost and laughed. That's why Americans have never lost nor will ever lose a war; for the very idea of losing is hateful to an American.

You are not all going to die. Only two percent of you right here today would die in a major battle. Death must not be feared. Death, in time, comes to all men. Yes, every man is scared in his first battle. If he says he's not, he's a liar. Some men are cowards but they fight the same as the brave men or they get the hell slammed out of them watching men fight who are just as scared

---

1 sling around 宣传，造势
2 marble 大理石；大理石制品；弹子游戏
3 give a hoot 介意（计较）

as they are. <u>The real hero is the man who fights even though he is scared</u>. Some men get over their fright in a minute under fire. For some, it takes an hour. For some, it takes days. But a real man will never let his fear of death **overpower**[1] his honor, his sense of duty to his country, and his **innate**[2] manhood. Battle is the most magnificent competition in which a human being can **indulge**[3]. It brings out all that is best and it removes all that is base. Americans pride themselves on being *He Men* and they ARE He Men. Remember that the enemy is just as frightened as you are, and probably more so. They are not supermen.

All through your Army careers, you men have bitched about what you call "chicken shit drilling". That, like everything else in this Army, has a definite purpose. That purpose is alertness. Alertness must be bred into every soldier. You men are veterans or you wouldn't be here. You are ready for what's to come. A man must be alert at all times if he expects to stay alive. If you're not alert, sometime, a German is going to **sneak**[4] up behind you and beat you to death with a sockful of shit!" (The men roared in agreement.)

There are four hundred neatly marked graves somewhere in *Sicily*. All because one man went to sleep on the job. But they are German graves, because we caught the **bastard**[5] asleep before they did. An Army is a team. It lives, sleeps, eats, and fights as a team. This individual heroic stuff is pure horse shit.

We have the finest food, the finest equipment, the best spirit, and the best men in the world. Why, by God, I actually pity those poor sons-of-bitches we're going up against. By God, I do. My men don't surrender. I don't want to hear of any soldier under my command being captured unless he has been hit. Even if you are hit, you can still fight back. That's not just bull shit either. The kind of man that I want in my command is just like the lieutenant in Libya, who, with a Luger against his chest, **jerked**[6] off his helmet, swept the gun aside with one hand, and busted the hell out of the Kraut with his helmet. Then he jumped on the gun and went out and killed another German before they knew what the hell was coming off. And, all of that time, this man had a bullet through a lung. There was a real man!

All of the real heroes are not storybook combat fighters, either. Every single man in this Army plays a vital role. Don't ever **let up**[7]. Don't ever think that your job is unimportant. Every man has a job to do and he must do it. Every man is a vital link in the great chain. What if every truck driver suddenly decided that he didn't like the **whine**[8] of those shells overhead, turned yellow, and jumped **headlong**[9] into a ditch? The cowardly bastard could say, "Hell, they won't miss me, just one man in thousands." But, what if every man thought that way? Where in the hell

---

1 overpower 制服；压倒；使无法忍受
2 innate 天生的；特有的，固有的；内在的，直觉的
3 indulge 迁就，纵容；(使)满足；(使)快乐
4 sneak 潜行；偷偷溜走；打小报告；告状
5 bastard 私生子，杂种
6 jerk 猛甩
7 let up 让（某人）上到某处；放松警惕
8 whine 哀诉，诉怨
9 headlong 头向前地；急速地；轻率地

would we be now? What would our country, our loved ones, our homes, even the world, be like? No, God damn it, Americans don't think like that. Every man does his job. <u>Every man serves the whole</u>. Every department, every unit, is important in the vast scheme of this war. The **ordnance**[1] men are needed to supply the guns and machinery of war to keep us rolling. The Quartermaster is needed to bring up food and clothes because where we are going there isn't a hell of a lot to steal. Every last man on K.P. has a job to do, even the one who heats our water to keep us from getting the 'G.I. Shits'."

Each man must not think only of himself, but also of his buddy fighting beside him. We don't want yellow cowards in this Army. They should be killed off like rats. If not, they will go home after this war and breed more cowards. The brave men will breed more brave men. Kill off the Goddamned cowards and we will have a nation of brave men. One of the bravest men that I ever saw was a fellow on top of a telegraph pole in the midst of a furious fire fight in Tunisia. I stopped and asked what the hell he was doing up there at a time like that. He answered, "Fixing the wire, Sir." I asked, "Isn't that a little unhealthy right about now?" He answered, "Yes Sir, but the Goddamned wire has to be fixed." I asked, "Don't those planes **strafing**[2] the road bother you?" And he answered, "No, Sir, but you sure as hell do!" Now, there was a real man. A real soldier. There was a man who devoted all he had to his duty, no matter how seemingly insignificant his duty might appear at the time, no matter how great the odds.

And you should have seen those trucks on the road to Tunisia. Those drivers were magnificent. All day and all night they rolled over those son-of-a-bitching roads, never stopping, never **faltering**[3] from their course, with shells bursting all around them all of the time. We got through on good old American guts. Many of those men drove for over forty **consecutive**[4] hours. These men weren't combat men, but they were soldiers with a job to do. They did it, and in one hell of a way they did it. They were part of a team. Without team effort, without them, the fight would have been lost. All of the links in the chain pulled together and the chain became unbreakable.

Don't forget, you men don't know that I'm here. No mention of that fact is to be made in any letters. The world is not supposed to know what the hell happened to me. I'm not supposed to be commanding this Army. I'm not even supposed to be here in England. Let the first bastards to find out be the Goddamned Germans. Some day I want to see them raise up on their piss-soaked hind legs and howl, 'Jesus Christ, it's the Goddamned Third Army again and that son-of-a-fucking-bitch Patton'."

"We want to get the hell over there, the quicker we clean up this Goddamned mess, the quicker we can take a little **jaunt**[5] against the purple pissing Japs and clean out their nest, too. Before the Goddamned Marines get all of the credit.

1　ordnance 军械（如弹药、军车等）；军用品，军需品
2　strafe 用机枪扫射，猛烈炮轰，惩罚
3　falter（嗓音）颤抖；支吾其词；蹒跚，摇晃
4　consecutive 连续的，连贯的
5　jaunt 游览

Sure, we want to go home. We want this war over with. The quickest way to get it over with is to go get the bastards who started it. The quicker they are whipped, the quicker we can go home. The shortest way home is through Berlin and Tokyo. And when we get to Berlin, I am personally going to shoot that paper hanging son-of-a-bitch Hitler. Just like I'd shoot a snake!

　　When a man is lying in a shell hole, if he just stays there all day, a German will get to him eventually. The hell with that idea. The hell with taking it. My men don't dig foxholes. I don't want them to. Foxholes only slow up an offensive. Keep moving. And don't give the enemy time to dig one either. We'll win this war, but we'll win it only by fighting and by showing the Germans that we've got more guts than they have; or ever will have. We're not going to just shoot the sons-of-bitches, we're going to rip out their living goddamned guts and use them to **grease**[1] the **treads**[2] of our tanks. War is a bloody, killing business. You've got to spill their blood, or they will spill yours. Rip them up the belly. Shoot them in the guts. When shells are hitting all around you and you wipe the dirt off your face and realize that instead of dirt it's the blood and guts of what once was your best friend beside you, you'll know what to do!

　　From time to time there will be some complaints that we are pushing our people too hard. I don't give a good Goddamn about such complaints. I believe in the old and sound rule that an ounce of sweat will save a gallon of blood. The harder WE push, the more Germans we will kill. The more Germans we kill, the fewer of our men will be killed. Pushing means fewer **casualties**[3]. I want you all to remember that.

　　There is one great thing that you men will all be able to say after this war is over and you are home once again. You may be thankful that twenty years from now when you are sitting by the fireplace with your grandson on your knee and he asks you what you did in the great World War II, you WON'T have to cough, shift him to the other knee and say, "Well, your Granddaddy **shoveled**[4] shit in Louisiana." No, Sir, you can look him straight in the eye and say, "Son, your Granddaddy rode with the Great Third Army and a Son-of-a-Goddamned-Bitch named George Patton."

文化快递

1. He Men（爷们，男子汉）

He Men，美国俚语，意思是"有男人味、有气概的男人"。与之对应的是She Men，意思是"娘娘腔的男人"

2. Sicily（西西里岛）

西西里岛是地中海最大和人口最稠密的岛。它属于意大利，位于亚平宁半岛的西南，东与亚平宁半岛仅隔宽3公里的墨西拿海峡。

1　grease 涂油脂于，用油脂润滑；贿赂
2　tread 轮胎接触地面的部分；（楼梯的）踏板
3　casualty 伤亡者；牺牲品；受害者；毁坏物
4　shovel 铲，铲出；用铲子挖；把……胡乱投入

参考译文

坐下。

兄弟们,最近有些小道消息,说我们美国人对这场战争缺乏斗志,想置身事外。那都是一些混账话!美国人天生爱打仗,真正的美国人喜欢的是战场上的刀光剑影。你们今天来此有三个原因:一、为了保卫家乡和亲人的安全;二、为了荣誉,因为此时你不想去别的任何地方;三、因为你们是真正的男子汉,而真正的男子汉都喜欢打仗。当在场的各位都还是孩子的时候,你们都崇拜弹球冠军、短跑健将、拳击高手和职业球员。美国人只热爱胜利者,对失败者决不宽容。美国人瞧不起懦弱的胆小鬼。美国国人参赛只有一个目标,那就是夺取胜利。对那些失败了还笑得出来的人,我向来都嗤之以鼻。这就是美国人能一直取胜并将永远取胜的原因。对一个真正的美国人来说,动一下失败的念头都令人恨之入骨。

你们不会全部牺牲。每次大战下来,你们当中只有百分之二可能会牺牲。死并不可怕,而且,谁都难逃一死。不错,每个人在第一次上战场时,都难免会胆怯。如果有人说他不害怕,那他就是骗子。有的人虽然胆小,但他们仍能像勇士一样战斗,因为如果他们看到其他同样对战争感到恐惧的战友能够奋勇作战,而他们却袖手旁观的话,他们就会感到羞愧。真正的英雄,是那些即使害怕,也能照样勇敢作战的男子汉。有的战士在火线上不到一分钟,便能克服恐惧,而有的则需要一小时,还有的,大概要几天才能适应。但是,真正的男子汉,是不会让死亡的恐惧战胜荣誉感、责任感和一个男人应有的雄风的。战斗是想出人头地的男子汉表现自己胆量的最好的竞争方式。战斗能逼出伟大,剔除渺小。美国人以能成为雄中之雄而自豪,而他们正是雄中之雄。大家记住,敌人和你们一样害怕,很可能更害怕。他们并非刀枪不入。

在大家的军旅生涯中,你们把演习训练称为"鸡屎",经常怨声载道。这些训练演习,像军中其他条条框框一样,自有它们的目的。训练演习的目的,就是培养大家的警惕性。警惕性必须渗透到每个战士的血液中去。对放松警惕的人,我决不手软。大家都是枪林弹雨里冲杀出来的,不然你们今天也不会战在这儿。你们对将要到来的厮杀,想必已有所准备。谁要是想活着回来,就必须时刻保持警惕。哪怕你有一点点疏忽,就会有个混账的德国鬼子悄悄溜到你的背后,用一坨屎置你于死地!

在西西里的某个地方,有一块墓碑码得整整齐齐的墓地,里面埋了四百具尸体。那四百人丧生,只因一名哨兵打了个盹。一个战队是个集体。大家在那集体里一起吃饭,一起睡觉,一起战斗。所谓个人英雄主义是一堆马粪。

我们有世界上最好的给养、最好的武器设备、最旺盛的斗志和最棒的战士。说实在地,我真可怜那些将和我们作战的狗杂种们。真的,我麾下的将士从不投降。我不想听到我手下任何战士被俘的消息,除非他们先受了伤。即便受了伤,你同样可以还击。这不是吹牛。我愿我的部下,都像在利比亚作战时的一位我军少尉。当时一个德国鬼子用手枪顶着他胸膛，他甩下钢盔，一只手拔开手枪，另一只手抓住钢盔，把那鬼子打得七窍流血。然后，他拾起手枪，在其他鬼子反应过来之前，击毙了另一个鬼子。在此之前，他的一侧肺叶已被一颗子弹洞穿。这，才是一个真正的男子汉！

不是所有的英雄都像传奇故事里描述的那样。军中每个战士都扮演一个重要的角色。千万不要吊儿郎当，以为自己的任务无足轻重。每个人都有自己的任务，而且必须做好。每个人都是一条长链上的必不可少的环节。大家可经设想一下，如果每个卡车司机都突然决定，不愿再忍受头顶呼啸的炮弹威胁，胆怯起来，跳下车去，一头栽到路旁的水沟中躲起来，那会产生什么样的后果。这个懦弱的混蛋可以给自己找借口："管他娘的，没我地球照样转，我不过是千万分之一。"但如果每个人都这样想呢？到那时，我们怎么办？我们的国家、亲人甚至世界会是一个什么样子？不，美国人不那样想。每个人都能完成他的任务。每个人都应对集体负责。每个部门，每个战队，对整个战争的宏伟篇章，都是重要的。弹药武器人员保证我们的枪支弹药的供应。没有后勤人员给我们送衣做饭，我们就会饥寒交迫，因为在我们要去作战的地方，已经没有任何东西值得偷抢。指挥部的所有人员，都各有所用，即使是个只管烧水给我们洗澡的勤务兵。

每个战士不能只顾自己，还要想着身边一起出生入死的战友。我们军队容不下胆小鬼。所有的懦夫都应当像耗子一样地被斩尽杀绝。否则，战后他们就会回家生出更多的懦夫来。英雄创造英雄，懦夫制造软蛋。干掉所有的胆小鬼，我们的国家将是勇士的天下。我所见过最勇敢的好汉，是在突尼斯一次激烈的战斗中，爬到电线杆上的一个通讯兵。当时我正好路过，便停下来问他，在这么危险的时候爬到那么高的地方瞎折腾什么？他答道："在修理线路，将军。"我问："现在修不是太危险了吗？"他答道："是危险，将军，但线路不修不行啊。"我问："敌机低空扫射，不影响你吗？"他答："敌机不怎么影响，将军，你倒是影响得一塌糊涂。"弟兄们，那才是真正的男子汉，真正的战士。他全心全意地履行自己的职责，不管那职责当时看起来多么不起眼，不管情况多危险。

还有那些通往突尼斯路上的卡车司机们，他们真了不起。他们没日没夜，行驶在那狗娘养的破路上，从不停歇，从不偏向，把四处开花的炮弹当成伴奏。我们能顺利前进，全靠这些天不怕地不怕的美国硬汉。这些司机中，有人连续开车已超过四十小时。他们不属战斗部队，但他们同样是军人，有重要的任务要完成。他们不仅完成了任务，而且完成的真他娘的棒！他们是大集体的一部分。如果没有大家的共同努力，没有他们，那场战斗很可能就输掉了。只因为所有环节都各司其职，各尽其责，整个链条才坚不可破。

大家要记住，就当我没来过这里。千万不要在信件里提及我。按理说，我是死是活，对外界要保密，我既不统率第三集团军，更不在英国。让那狗日的德国佬第一个发现吧！我希望有一天看到，那些狗杂种们屁滚尿流，哀鸣道："我的天哪！又是那个挨千刀的第三集团军！又是那狗娘养的巴顿！"我们已经迫不及待了。

早一日收拾掉该死的德国鬼子，我们就能早一日掉转枪口，去端掉日本鬼子的老巢。

如果我们不抓紧，功劳就会全让可恶的海军陆战队抢去了。

是的，我们想早日回家，想让这场战争早日结束。最快的办法，就是干掉燃起这场战争的混蛋们。早一日把他们消灭干净，我们就可以早一日凯旋。回家的捷径，要通过柏林和东京。到了柏林，我要亲手干掉那个纸老虎、混账的希特勒，就像干掉一条蛇！

如果谁想在炮弹坑里蹲上一天，那就让他见鬼去吧！德国鬼子早晚会找到他头上。我的手下从不挖猫耳洞，我也不希望他们挖。猫耳洞只会延缓进攻的速度。我们要连续不断地进攻，不给敌人挖猫耳洞的时间。我们迟早会胜利，但我们只有不停战斗，比敌人勇敢，胜利才会到来。我们不仅要击毙那些狗杂种们，而且要把他们的五脏六腑掏出来润滑我们的坦克履带。战争本来就是血腥野蛮残酷的。你不让敌人流血，敌人就会让你流血。挑开他们的肚子，冲着他们的胸膛来上一枪。如果一颗炮弹在你身旁爆炸，炸了你一脸灰土，你一抹，发现那竟是你最好伙伴的模糊血肉时，你就知道该怎么办了！

有时免不了会听到有人抱怨，说我们对战士要求太严，太不近情理。让那些抱怨见鬼去吧！我坚信一条金玉良言，那就是"一杯汗水，挽救一桶鲜血。"我们的进攻越坚决，消灭的德国鬼子就越多。我们消灭的德国鬼子越多，我们自己人死得就会越少。进攻意味着更少的伤亡。我希望大家牢牢记住这一点。

凯旋回家后，今天在场的弟兄们都将获得一种值得夸耀的资格。二十年后，你会庆幸自己参加了这次世界大战。到那时，当你坐在壁炉边，你的孙子坐在你的膝盖上问你："爷爷，第二次世界大战中，你是干什么的？"你不用尴尬地干咳一声，把孙子移到另一个膝盖上，支支吾吾地说："啊……爷爷我当时在路易斯安那铲粪。"相反，弟兄们，你可以直盯着他的眼睛，理直气壮地说："孙子，爷爷我当年在伟大的第三集团军和那个狗娘养的乔治·巴顿并肩作战！"

Chapter 2

Spread of Civilization
（教育演讲篇——文明的传递）

Lesson 1

Commencement Address Delivered on Graduation in Stanford

Task 1 Questions and Answers

Directions: *Work in pairs. Read the following speech then take turns to ask and answer the following questions.*

1. When was the speech delivered? Where?
2. Who delivered the speech? Who are involved in the speech?
3. What is the theme of the speech?
4. Why is there a need for the request?
5. How can the request be achieved?

Task 2 Dictation

Directions: *Watch the authentic video of the speech. Then fill in the missing words in their appropriate forms. You may watch the video for three times.*

It started before I was born. My _____ mother was a young, _____ college graduate student, and she decided to put me up for _____. She felt very strongly that I should be adopted by college graduates, so everything was all set for me to be adopted at _____ by a lawyer and his wife. Except that when I _____ out they decided at the last minute that they really wanted a girl. So my parents, who were on a waiting _____, got a call in the middle of the night asking, "We have an _____ baby boy; do you want him?" They said, "Of course."

Task 3 Imitation and Play

Directions: *Watch the authentic video of the speech. Then try to imitate one or two paragraphs you like with appropriate delivery techniques. First practice by yourself. Then work in groups of four to take turns to deliver the speech.*

Task 4 Paraphrasing

Directions: *Work in groups of four and paraphrase the following sentences into simple English. Use specific details and examples to support yourself. You may locate some useful information from the script.*

1. Again, you can't connect the dots looking forward; you can only connect them looking backwards.
2. It was awful tasting medicine, but I guess the patient needed it.
3. If you live each day as if it was your last, someday you'll most certainly be right.
4. Stay hungry. Stay foolish.

Task 5 Writing Practice

Directions: *Write a speech for about 300 words on the topic of* **I Believe I Can Fly / The Significance of Choice.**

Commencement Address Delivered on Graduation in Stanford
斯坦福毕业典礼上的讲话

By Steve Jobs
June 12, 2005

人物简介

史蒂夫·乔布斯（Steven Paul Jobs，1955年2月24日—2011年10月5日），苹果公司的首席执行官兼创办人之一。1976年，时年21岁的乔布斯和26岁的沃兹尼艾克在乔布斯家的车库里成立了苹果电脑公司；1985年获得了由里根总统授予的国家级技术勋章；1996年，苹果公司重新雇用乔布斯作为其兼职顾问；1997年9月，乔布斯重返该公司任首席执行官。1997年成为《时代周刊》的封面人物；2009年被财富杂志评选为这十年美国最佳CEO，同年当选时代周刊年度风云人物之一。乔布斯被认为是计算机业界与娱乐业界的标志性人物。他始终倾听消费者的需求、以极大的热忱贯彻"在一般人与高深的计算机之间搭起桥梁"的初衷。不论是在苹果以艺术创造科技，或是在Pixar以科技创造艺术，乔布斯都孜孜不倦地设法使他的梦想变成现实。他用计算机作工具，协助填补科技与艺术之间的鸿沟。

名篇导读

毕业典礼上的演讲大都轻松愉快，而且容易被遗忘。然而，史蒂夫·乔布斯2005年6月在斯坦福大学的演讲让很多人记忆犹新，至今常常被人提及。这位苹果电脑公司（Apple Computer）和皮克斯动画公司（Pixar Animation Studios）首席执行官在演讲中谈到了他生活中的三次体验，这三次体验不仅在斯坦福大学的毕业生、也在硅谷乃至其他地方的技术同行中引起了巨大反响。经历了多年的工作以后，乔布斯说："太多的事情令人感到遗憾，但最大的遗憾莫过于那些你没去做的事。如果我早点明白现在才明白的道理，我可以把事情做得更好些，但这又怎么样呢？关键是要把握好现在。生命是短暂的，不久以后我们都将走到尽头，这就是现实。"乔布斯的演讲结束隽语，"好学若饥、谦卑若愚"，在此次演讲之后，成为很多人的座右铭。

英文原文

I am honored to be with you today at your **commencement**[1] from one of the finest universities in the world. I never graduated from college. Truth be told, this is the closest I've ever gotten to a college graduation. Today I want to tell you three stories from my life. That's it. No big deal. Just three stories.

The first story is about connecting the **dots**[2].

I dropped out of Reed College after the first 6 months, but then stayed around as a **drop-in**[3] for another 18 months or so before I really quit. So why did I drop out?

---

1 commencement 毕业典礼
2 dots 小事
3 drop-in 不速之客

It started before I was born. My biological mother was a young, **unwed**¹ college graduate student, and she decided to put me up for adoption. She felt very strongly that I should be adopted by college graduates, so everything was all set for me to be adopted at birth by a lawyer and his wife. Except that when I popped out they decided at the last minute that they really wanted a girl. So my parents, who were on a waiting list, got a call in the middle of the night asking, "We have an unexpected baby boy; do you want him?" They said, "Of course." My **biological**² mother later found out that my mother had never graduated from college and that my father had never graduated from high school. She refused to sign the final adoption papers. She only **relented**³ a few months later when my parents promised that I would someday go to college.

And 17 years later I did go to college. But I naively chose a college that was almost as expensive as Stanford, and all of my working-class parents' savings were being spent on my college tuition. After six months, I couldn't see the value in it. I had no idea what I wanted to do with my life and no idea how college was going to help me figure it out. And here I was spending all of the money my parents had saved their entire life. So I decided to drop out and trust that it would all work out OK. It was pretty **scary**⁴ at the time, but looking back it was one of the best decisions I ever made. The minute I dropped out I could stop taking the required classes that didn't interest me, and begin dropping in on the ones that looked far more interesting.

It wasn't all romantic. I didn't have a dorm room, so I slept on the floor in friends' rooms, I returned coke bottles for the 5 cents deposits to buy food with, and I would walk the 7 miles across town every Sunday night to get one good meal a week at the Hare Krishna temple. I loved it. And much of what I **stumbled**⁵ into by following my curiosity and intuition turned out to be priceless later on. Let me give you one example:

Reed College at that time offered perhaps the best calligraphy instruction in the country. Throughout the campus every poster, every label on every drawer, was beautifully hand **calligraphy**⁶. Because I had dropped out and didn't have to take the normal classes, I decided to take a calligraphy class to learn how to do this. I learned about *serif and san serif typefaces*, about varying the amount of space between different letter combinations, about what makes great **typography**⁷ great. It was beautiful, historical, artistically subtle in a way that science can't capture, and I found it fascinating.

None of this had even a hope of any practical application in my life. But ten years later, when we were designing the first Macintosh computer, it all came back to me. And we designed it all into the Mac. It was the first computer with beautiful typography. If I had never dropped in on that single course in college, the Mac would have never had multiple typefaces or proportionally

---

1 unwed 未婚的
2 biological 生物的；有血亲关系的
3 relent 软化
4 scary 胆小的
5 stumble 跨踏，蹒跚
6 calligraphy 书法
7 typography 排印，印刷

spaced **fonts**[1]. And since C, its likely that no personal computer would have them. If I had never dropped out, I would have never dropped in on this calligraphy class, and personal computers might not have the wonderful typography that they do. Of course it was impossible to connect the dots looking forward when I was in college. But it was very, very clear looking backwards ten years later.

<u>Again, you can't connect the dots looking forward; you can only connect them looking backwards.</u> So you have to trust that the dots will somehow connect in your future. You have to trust in something—your **gut**[2], destiny, life, **karma**[3], whatever. This approach has never let me down, and it has made all the difference in my life.

My second story is about love and loss.

I was lucky—I found what I loved to do early in life. Woz and I started Apple in my parents garage when I was 20. We worked hard, and in 10 years Apple had grown from just the two of us in a garage into a $2 billion company with over 4000 employees. We had just released our finest creation—the Macintosh—a year earlier, and I had just turned 30. And then I got fired. How can you get fired from a company you started? Well, as Apple grew we hired someone who I thought was very talented to run the company with me, and for the first year or so things went well. But then our visions of the future began to **diverge**[4] and eventually we had a falling out. When we did, our Board of Directors sided with him. So at 30 I was out. And very publicly out. What had been the focus of my entire adult life was gone, and it was **devastating**[5].

I really didn't know what to do for a few months. I felt that I had let the previous generation of entrepreneurs down—that I had dropped the **baton**[6] as it was being passed to me. I met with David Packard and Bob Noyce and tried to apologize for **screwing up**[7] so badly. I was a very public failure, and I even thought about running away from the valley. But something slowly began to dawn on me—I still loved what I did. The turn of events at Apple had not changed that one bit. I had been rejected, but I was still in love. And so I decided to start over.

<u>I didn't see it then, but it turned out that getting fired from Apple was the best thing that could have ever happened to me.</u> The heaviness of being successful was replaced by the lightness of being a beginner again, less sure about everything. It freed me to enter one of the most creative periods of my life.

During the next five years, I started a company named NeXT, another company named Pixar, and fell in love with an amazing woman who would become my wife. Pixar went on to create the worlds first computer **animated**[8] feature film, *Toy Story*, and is now the most successful animation studio in the world. In a remarkable turn of events, Apple bought NeXT, I returned to

---

1　fonts 字体
2　gut 胆量
3　karma 因果
4　diverge 使分离
5　devastating 毁灭性的
6　baton 接力棒
7　screw up 糟蹋；搞砸
8　animated 活生生的；愉快的；动画（片）的

Apple, and the technology we developed at NeXT is at the heart of Apple's current renaissance. And Laurene and I have a wonderful family together.

I'm pretty sure none of this would have happened if I hadn't been fired from Apple. It was awful tasting medicine, but I guess the patient needed it. Sometimes life hits you in the head with a brick. Don't lose faith. I'm convinced that the only thing that kept me going was that I loved what I did. You've got to find what you love. And that is as true for your work as it is for your lovers. Your work is going to fill a large part of your life, and the only way to be truly satisfied is to do what you believe is great work. And the only way to do great work is to love what you do. If you haven't found it yet, keep looking. Don't settle. As with all matters of the heart, you'll know when you find it. And, like any great relationship, it just gets better and better as the years roll on. So keep looking until you find it. Don't settle.

My third story is about death.

When I was 17, I read a quote that went something like: "If you live each day as if it was your last, someday you'll most certainly be right." It made an impression on me, and since then, for the past 33 years, I have looked in the mirror every morning and asked myself: "If today were the last day of my life, would I want to do what I am about to do today?" And whenever the answer has been "No" for too many days in a row, I know I need to change something.

Remembering that I'll be dead soon is the most important tool I've ever encountered to help me make the big choices in life. Because almost everything—all external expectations, all pride, all fear of embarrassment or failure—these things just fall away in the face of death, leaving only what is truly important. Remembering that you are going to die is the best way I know to avoid the trap of thinking you have something to lose. You are already naked. There is no reason not to follow your heart.

About a year ago I was diagnosed with cancer. I had a scan at 7:30 in the morning, and it clearly showed a **tumor**[1] on my **pancreas**[2]. I didn't even know what a pancreas was. The doctors told me this was almost certainly a type of cancer that is incurable, and that I should expect to live no longer than three to six months. My doctor advised me to go home and get my affairs in order, which is doctor's code for prepare to die. It means to try to tell your kids everything you thought you'd have the next 10 years to tell them in just a few months. It means to make sure everything is buttoned up so that it will be as easy as possible for your family. It means to say your goodbyes.

I lived with that **diagnosis**[3] all day. Later that evening I had a **biopsy**[4], where they stuck an **endoscope**[5] down my throat, through my stomach and into my **intestines**[6], put a needle into my

---

1. tumor 肿瘤
2. pancreas 胰腺
3. diagnosis 诊断
4. biopsy 活性
5. endoscope 内窥镜
6. intestine 肠

pancreas and got a few cells from the tumor. I was **sedated**¹, but my wife, who was there, told me that when they viewed the cells under a microscope the doctors started crying because it turned out to be a very rare form of pancreatic cancer that is curable with surgery. I had the surgery and thankfully I'm fine now.

This was the closest I've been to facing death, and I hope its the closest I get for a few more decades. Having lived through it, I can now say this to you with a bit more certainty than when death was a useful but purely intellectual concept:

No one wants to die. Even people who want to go to heaven don't want to die to get there. And yet death is the destination we all share. No one has ever escaped it. And that is as it should be, because Death is very likely the single best invention of Life. It is Life's change agent. It clears out the old to make way for the new. Right now the new is you, but someday not too long from now, you will gradually become the old and be cleared away. Sorry to be so dramatic, but it is quite true.

Your time is limited, so don't waste it living someone else's life. Don't be trapped by **dogma**²—which is living with the results of other people's thinking. Don't let the noise of others' opinions drown out your own inner voice. And most important, have the courage to follow your heart and intuition. They somehow already know what you truly want to become. Everything else is secondary.

When I was young, there was an amazing publication called *The Whole Earth Catalog*, which was one of the bibles of my generation. It was created by a fellow named Stewart Brand not far from here in Menlo Park, and he brought it to life with his poetic touch. This was in the late 1960's, before personal computers and desktop publishing, so it was all made with typewriters, scissors, and **polaroid camera**³. It was sort of like Google in **paperback**⁴ form, 35 years before Google came along: it was idealistic, and overflowing with neat tools and great notions.

Stewart and his team put out several issues of *The Whole Earth Catalog*, and then when it had run its course, they put out a final issue. It was the mid-1970s, and I was your age. On the back cover of their final issue was a photograph of an early morning country road, the kind you might find yourself **hitchhiking**⁵ on if you were so adventurous. Beneath it were the words: "Stay Hungry. Stay Foolish." It was their farewell message as they signed off. Stay Hungry. Stay Foolish. And I have always wished that for myself. And now, as you graduate to begin anew, I wish that for you.

Stay Hungry. Stay Foolish.

Thank you very much.

---

1 sedated 安静的
2 dogma 教条
3 polaroid camera 一次成影照相机
4 paperback 平装本
5 hitchhike 搭便车

英语演讲名篇赏析
Appreciation of Masterpiece English Speeches

▶ 文化快递

1. Serif and San Serif typefaces（Serif 或 San Serif 字体）

在西方国家罗马字母阵营中，字体分为两大种类：Sans Serif 和 Serif；有衬线字体英文名为 serif，无衬线字体英文名为 sans-serif。Serif 是在字的笔画开始及结束的地方有额外的装饰，而且笔画的粗细会因直横的不同而有不同。San Serif 是一种字母末端没有短线装饰线的字体。典型的非饰线字样没有开始或者结束的笔画，所有起承转合的笔画，看起来也都是一样粗细的。Serif 是一个字笔画的结尾，例如 M 的起点与终点。Serif 是由罗马刻印字母所发展出来的，用以改良字体的典雅程度与易读性。它们是先用毛笔书写，然后再刻出来的。Serif 活存到现在，是因为它们十分美丽及古典，而且它们阅读起来十分容易。对于细小的文本字体，非常适合用 Serif 字体。

2. Windows just copied the Mac（"微软"抄袭"苹果"）

多年来，苹果首席执行官乔布斯一直以来表示，微软 windows 操作系统窃取了苹果的许多创新方法，抄袭苹果的功能、界面。多年来双方一直存在着如此多的巧合。而如今苹果 Mac OS X 10.6 雪豹和微软的 windows 7 又存在着许多相似。他们已经成为计算领域的一部分，很难判断出谁最早出现功能。

▶ 参考译文

我今天很荣幸能和你们一起参加毕业典礼，斯坦福大学是世界上最好的大学之一。我从来没有从大学中毕业。说实话，今天也许是在我的生命中离大学毕业最近的一天了。今天我想向你们讲述我生活中的三个故事。不是什么大不了的事情，只是三个故事而已。

第一个故事是关于如何把生命中的点点滴滴串联起来。

我在 Reed 大学读了六个月之后就退学了，但之后作为旁听生又混了十八个月以后才真正离开。我为什么要退学呢？

故事从我出生的时候讲起。我的亲生母亲是一个年轻的，没有结婚的大学毕业生。她决定让别人收养我，她十分想让我被大学毕业生收养。所以在我出生的时候，她已经做好了一切的准备工作，能使得我被一个律师和他的妻子所收养。但是她没有料到，当我出生之后，律师夫妇突然决定他们想要一个女孩。所以我的生养父母（他们在待选名单上）突然在半夜接到了一个电话："我们现在这儿有一个不小心生出来的男婴，你们想要他吗？"他们回答道："当然！"但是我亲生母亲随后发现，我的养母从来没有上过大学，我的养父甚至从没有读过高中。她拒绝签这个收养合同。只是在几个月以后，我的父母答应她一定要让我上大学，那个时候她才软化同意。

在十七岁那年，我真的上了大学。但是我很愚蠢地选择了一个几乎和你们斯坦福大学一样贵的学校，我父母还处于蓝领阶层，他们几乎把所有积蓄都花在了我的学费上面。在六个月后，我已经看不到其中的价值所在。我不知道我真正想要做什么，我也不知道大学能怎样帮助我找到答案。但是在这里，我几乎花光了我父母这一辈子的全部积蓄。所以我决定要退学，我觉得这是个正确的决定。不能否认，我当时确实非常的害怕，但是现在回头看看，那的确是我这一生中最棒的一个决定。在我做出退学决定的那一刻，我终于可以不必去读那些令我提不起丝毫兴趣的课程了。然后我可以开始去修那些看起来有点意思的课程。

但是这并不是那么浪漫。我失去了我的宿舍，所以我只能在朋友房间的地板上面睡觉，我去捡可以换5美分的可乐罐，仅仅为了填饱肚子，在星期天的晚上，我需要走七英里的路程，穿过这个城市到海尔·克里什纳（注：位于纽约Brooklyn下城），只是为了能吃上好饭——这个星期唯一一顿好一点的饭，我喜欢那里的饭菜。我跟着我的直觉和好奇心走，遇到的很多东西，此后被证明是无价之宝。让我给你们举一个例子吧：

Reed大学在那时提供也许是全美最好的美术字课程。在这个大学里面的每个海报，每个抽屉的标签上面全都是漂亮的美术字。因为我退学了，不必去上正规的课程，所以我决定去参加这个课程，去学学怎样写出漂亮的美术字。我学到了serif和san serif字体，我学会了怎么样在不同的字母组合之中改变空白间距，还有怎么样才能作出最棒的印刷式样。那种美好、历史感和艺术精妙，是科学永远不能捕捉到的，我发现那实在是太迷人了。

当时看起来这些东西在我的生命中，好像都没有什么实际应用的可能。但是十年之后，当我们在设计第一台Macintosh电脑的时候，就不是那样了。我把当时我学的那些东西全都设计进了Mac。那是第一台使用了漂亮的印刷字体的电脑。如果我当时没有退学，就不会有机会去参加这个我感兴趣的美术字课程，Mac就不会有这么多丰富的字体以及赏心悦目的字体间距。而个人电脑就不会有现在这么美妙的字形了。当然我在大学的时候，还不可能把从前的点点滴滴串联起来，但是当我十年后回顾这一切的时候，真的豁然开朗了。

再次说明的是，你在向前展望的时候不可能将这些片断串联起来；你只能在回顾的时候将点点滴滴串联起来。所以你必须相信这些片断会在你未来的某一天串联起来。你必须要相信某些东西：你的勇气、目的、生命、因缘……这个过程从来没有令我失望，只是让我的生命更加地与众不同。

我的第二个故事是关于爱和失去。

我非常幸运，因为我在很早的时候就找到了我钟爱的东西。Woz和我在二十岁的时候就在父母的车库里面开创了苹果公司。我们工作得很努力，十年之后，这个公司从那两个车库中的穷小子发展到了超过四千名的雇员、价值超过二十亿的大公司。在公司成立的第九年，我们刚刚发布了最好的产品，那就是Macintosh。我也快要到三十岁了。在那一年，我被炒了鱿鱼。你怎么可能被你自己创立的公司炒了鱿鱼呢？嗯，在苹果快速成长的时候，我们雇用了一个很有天分的家伙和我一起管理这个公司，在最初的几年，公司运转得很好。但是

后来我们对未来的看法发生了分歧，最终我们吵了起来。当争吵不可开交的时候，董事会站在了他的那一边。所以在三十岁的时候，我被炒了。在这么多人目光下我被炒了。在而立之年，我生命的全部支柱离自己远去，这真是毁灭性的打击。

在最初的几个月里，我真是不知道该做些什么。我觉得我很令上一代的创业家们失望，我把他们交给我的接力棒弄丢了。我和创办惠普的David Pack、创办Intel的Bob Noyce见面，并试图向他们道歉。我把事情弄得糟糕透顶了。但是我渐渐发现了曙光，我仍然喜爱我从事的这些东西。苹果公司发生的这些事情丝毫的没有改变这些，一点也没有。我被驱逐了，但是我仍然钟爱我所做的事情。所以我决定从头再来。

我当时没有觉察，但是事后证明，从苹果公司被炒是我这辈子发生的最棒的事情。因为，作为一个成功者的负重感被作为一个创业者的轻松感觉所重新代替，没有比这更确定的事情了。这让我觉得如此自由，进入了我生命中最有创造力的一个阶段。

在接下来的五年里，我创立了一个名叫NeXT的公司，还有一个叫Pixar的公司，然后和一个后来成为我妻子的优雅女人相识。Pixar制作了世界上第一个用电脑制作的动画电影——"玩具总动员"，Pixar现在也是世界上最成功的电脑制作工作室。在后来的一系列运转中，Apple收购了NeXT，然后我又回到了Apple公司。我们在NeXT发展的技术在Apple的今天的复兴之中发挥了关键的作用。而且，我还和Laurence一起建立了一个幸福完美的家庭。

我可以非常肯定，如果我不被Apple开除的话，这其中一件事情也不会发生的。这个良药的味道实在是太苦了，但是我想病人需要这个药。有些时候，生活会拿起一块砖头向你的脑袋上猛拍一下。不要失去信仰。我很清楚唯一使我一直走下去的，就是我做的事情令我无比钟爱。你需要去找到你所爱的东西。对于工作是如此，对于你的爱人也是如此。你的工作将会占据生活中很大的一部分。你只有相信自己所做的是伟大的工作，你才能怡然自得。如果你现在还没有找到，那么继续找、不要停下来，只要全心全意地去找，在你找到的时候，你的心会告诉你的。就像任何真诚的关系，随着岁月的流逝只会越来越紧密。所以继续找，直到你找到它，不要停下来！

我的第三个故事是关于死亡的。

当我十七岁的时候，我读到了一句话："如果你把每一天都当作生命中最后一天去生活的话，那么有一天你会发现你是正确的。"这句话给我留下了一个印象。从那时开始，过了33年，我在每天早晨都会对着镜子问自己："如果今天是我生命中的最后一天，你会不会完成你今天想做的事情呢？"当答案连续多天是"No"的时候，我知道自己需要改变某些事情了。

"记住你即将死去"是我一生中遇到的最重要箴言。它帮我指明了生命中重要的选择。因为几乎所有的事情，包括所有的荣誉、所有的骄傲、所有对难堪和失败的恐惧，这些在死亡面前都会消失。我看到的是留下的真正重要的东西。你有时候会思考你将会失去某些东西,"记住你即将死去"是我知道的避免这些想法的最好办法。你已经赤身裸体了,你没有理由不去跟随自己内心的声音。

大概一年以前,我被诊断出癌症。我在早晨七点半做了一个检查,检查清楚地显示在我的胰腺有一个肿瘤。我当时都不知道胰腺是什么东西。医生告诉我那很可能是一种无法治愈的癌症,我还有三到六个月的时间活在这个世界上。我的医生叫我回家,然后整理好我的一切,那是医生对临终病人的标准程序。那意味着你将要把未来十年对你小孩说的话在几个月里面说完;那意味着把每件事情都安排好,让你的家人会尽可能轻松的生活;那意味着你要说"再见了"。

我拿着那个诊断书过了一整天,那天晚上我作了一个活切片检查,医生将一个内窥镜从我的喉咙伸进去,通过我的胃,然后进入我的肠子,用一根针在我的胰腺上的肿瘤上取了几个细胞。我当时是被麻醉的,但是我的妻子在那里,后来告诉我,当医生在显微镜下观察这些细胞的时候他们开始尖叫,因为这些细胞最后竟然是一种非常罕见的可以用手术治愈的胰腺癌症细胞。我做了这个手术,谢天谢地,现在我痊愈了。

那是我最接近死亡的时候,我希望这也是以后的几十年最接近的一次。从死亡线上又活了过来,我可以比以前把死亡只当成一种想象中的概念的时候,更肯定一点地对你们说:

没有人愿意死,即使人们想上天堂,也不会为了去那里而死。但是死亡是我们每个人共同的终点。从来没有人能够逃脱它。也应该如此。因为死亡就是生命中最好的一个发明。它将旧的清除以便给新的让路。你们现在是新的,但是从现在开始不久以后,你们将会逐渐变成旧的然后被送离人生舞台。我很抱歉这很戏剧性,但这是十分的真实。

你们的时间很有限,所以不要将他们浪费在重复其他人的生活上。不要被教条束缚,那意味着你和其他人思考的结果一起生活。不要被其他人喧嚣的观点掩盖你真正的内心的声音。还有最重要的是,你要有勇气去听从你直觉和心灵的指示——它们在某种程度上知道你想要成为什么样子,所有其他的事情都是次要的。

当我年轻的时候,有一本叫做"整个地球的目录"振聋发聩的杂志,它是我们那一代人的圣经之一。它是一个叫Stewart Brand的家伙在离这里不远的Menlo Park编辑的,他像诗一般神奇地将这本书带到了这个世界。那是六十年代后期,在个人电脑出现之前,所以这本书全部是用打字机,剪刀还有偏光镜制造的。有点像用软皮包装的google,在google出现三十五年之前:这是理想主义的,其中有许多灵巧的工具和伟大的想法。

Stewart和他的伙伴出版了几期的"整个地球的目录",当它完成了自己使命的时候,他们做出了最后一期的目录。那是在七十年代的中期,我正是你们的年纪。在最后一期的封底上是清晨乡村公路的照片(如果你有冒险精神的话,你可以自己找到这条路的),在照片之下有这样一段话:"求知若饥,虚心若愚。"这是他们停止了发刊的告别语。"求知若饥，虚心若愚。"我总是希望自己能够那样，现在，在你们即将毕业，开始新的旅程的时候，我也希望你们能这样：

求知若饥，虚心若愚。

非常感谢你们。

Lesson 2

The Way Ahead: Innovating Together in China

Task 1 Questions and Answers

Directions: Work in pairs. Read the following speech then take turns to ask and answer the following questions.
1. When was the speech delivered? Where?
2. Who delivered the speech? Who are involved in the speech?
3. What is the theme of the speech?
4. Why is there a need for the request?
5. How can the request be achieved?

Task 2 Dictation

Directions: Watch the authentic video of the speech. Then fill in the missing words in their appropriate forms. You may watch the video for three times.

China will start to play a very _____ role, and part of that is the _____ that has been made in having _____ universities, of which Tsinghua is really the _____ example. For Microsoft, we have a _____ to work with our partners here and make them successful, to make sure that there are _____ hundreds of software start-ups that not only sell in the market here but sell to the _____ world.

Task 3 Imitation and Play

Directions: Watch the authentic video of the speech. Then try to imitate one or two paragraphs you like with appropriate delivery techniques. First practice by yourself. Then work in groups of four to take turns to deliver the speech.

Task 4 **Discussion**

Directions: *Work in groups of four and discuss the following questions. You may locate some useful information from the script.*
1. What do you know about Bill Gates?
2. What does Bill Gates think of Tsinghua University and its graduates?
3. What is "Microsoft Distinguished Visiting Professorship" for? Who sponsored it? Who was the first recipient of it?
4. Is Bill Gates optimistic about what software can do for us in the future? How can it change our life?

Task 5 **Speaking Practice**

Directions: *Give a speech for about 300 words on a given topic which you are interested in. You may choose from the following:*
1. The Greatest Invention In My Eyes
2. Information is a Key to Success
3. If I Were the Richest Man in the World

The Way Ahead: Innovating Together in China
未来之路：与中国共同创新
Speech at Tsinghua University by Bill Gates
April 19, 2007

人物简介

比尔·盖茨（Bill Gates，1955年10月28日— ），美国企业家、软件工程师、慈善家以及微软公司的董事长，连续13年蝉联世界首富。2008年6月27日正式退出微软公司，并把580亿美元个人财产尽数捐到比尔与美琳达·盖茨基金会。2009年3月12日《福布斯》杂志公布全球富豪排名，比尔·盖茨以400亿美元资产重登榜首。他与保罗·艾伦一起创建了微软公司，曾任微软CEO和首席软件设计师。比尔·盖茨远见卓识以及他对个人计算机的先见之明使他在事业上取得了非凡的成绩。此外，盖茨和妻子Melinda捐赠了34.6亿美元建立了一个基金，用于支持在全球医疗健康和教育领域的慈善事业。

名篇导读

2007年4月19日上午，微软公司主席比尔·盖茨从北京清华大学校长顾秉林手中接过名誉博士学位证书，成为清华大学第13位名誉博士。学位授予仪式结束后，比尔·盖茨在清华大学主楼大厅发表了题为"未来之路：与中国共同创新"的演讲。在演讲中，盖茨阐释了自己对数字时代的创新见解，表达了对于推动创新、缩小数字鸿沟和扩大信息技术受益人群的愿望。盖茨认为，中国是世界上发展最快的国家之一，微软希望能为中国人民带来技术方面的最大便利。比尔·盖茨曾在1997年访问过清华大学。十年后故地重游，他表示："中国学生对科学技术研究的激情给我留下了非常深刻的印象，并成为我在北京开设微软亚洲研究院的重要原因之一。"

英文原文

Honourable President GU, faculty and students of Tsinghua University;

I'm very honored to be here receiving this degree from Tsinghua, which is one of the top universities in the world.

Throughout its 96 years, it not only produced outstanding scientists but also industry and government leaders. When I visited here in 1997—10 years ago—I was very impressed by the talent, the enthusiasm and the creativity of the students that I met at Tsinghua. And it inspired me to support Microsoft in creating a research lab here in Beijing.

That research lab has gone on to incredible success, led by Harry Shum and joined by top university graduates from this school and others. It's made huge contributions to Microsoft. And if you look at various conferences getting together to discuss the **state-of-the-art**[1] issues, the researchers from this lab are making huge contributions. Or if you look at the products, even the recent Windows Vista or Office 2007, we have substantial innovations in those products.

This is an incredible time to be a student at this University. The frontiers of science, including computer science, have never been nearer. The opportunity to improve people's lives in

---

1 state-of-art 最先进的，已经发展的

every way has never been stronger.

We've really just scratched the surface of the digital revolution. Yes, we have about a billion personal computers that are connected up to the Internet. And we've already started to transform the way people think studying information and sharing information. But there are so much more that we can do. The advances predicted by the **exponential**[1] improvement in not only the processor transistors but also what we have in storage or **optic**[2] **fiber**[3] **bandwidth**[4] give us an opportunity to apply software that can work in a far more powerful way.

For example, when we think about TV. Today it's just a passive, non-interactive situation, but that's in the process of changing: changing so that you can get any show that you want on the Internet, changing so that it can be interactive so that you can learn as you go home, changing so that the flexibility even to talk and collaborate with others will be part of that experience.

If you think about product design—and products are going to be designed digitally. I spent several hours yesterday at the Agricultural Rice Institute talking with the experts there about how they are using software technology to **sequence**[5] different rice varieties. And they're optimistic that they can come up with new varieties that will require less **fertilizer**[6], less water and yet increase the yield. And its advances like that ,that really reach out and change the lives not just of those of us who work in technology but people everywhere.

The advances in medicine are dependent on software, software that can manage the databases and understand the complex systems. I'm very optimistic that we can make big breakthroughs based on what software will provide.

And if you think about your mobile phone going from being just a voice device to being something that can be a "digital wallet", that can show you maps and you'll be able to talk to it and ask for information and it will go out to the Internet and find the things that you're interested in.

In terms of learning, by creating what we call the "student tablet" that will be very inexpensive and the size of a tablet but wirelessly connected to the Internet and able to record your voice or recognize your ink handwriting and yet provide learning experiences that are far more effective—and in fact bringing together all of the world's knowledge on the Internet in a very attractive form.

Teachers will be able to see the world's best lectures, and they'll be able to see the best materials and for the first time start to share with each other. And so for anyone who wants to learn or wants to teach, it will be a very, very different world.

We certainly have some very tough and interesting problems that I know the students here will be making breakthroughs in. Writing software that's reliable, that's totally secure, software

---

1 exponential 指数的
2 optic 眼视觉的；光学的
3 fiber 光纤；纤维，纤维物质
4 bandwidth 带宽
5 sequence 排序
6 fertilizer 肥料

that can handle **parallel execution**[1], software that's very easy to use and software that can solve some very tough problems, for example problems of ***artificial intelligence*** that we've already spent many decades working on. And so this is an amazing time to be working in the sciences and particularly in computer science.

It's also an amazing time to this country. What's going on in China and the growth of its economy with incredible contributions not just within the country but to the global economy as well—you know, starting to be a very major contributor in all the sciences, advances in the medical drugs, advances in computer science.

China will start to play a very substantial role, and part of that is the investment that has been made in having world-class universities, of which Tsinghua is really the shining example. For Microsoft, we have a commitment to work with our partners here and make them successful, to make sure that there are literally hundreds of software **start-ups**[2] that not only sell in the market here but sell to the entire world.

We also want to make sure that the digital advances are available to all the citizens. And so whether it's **displaced**[3] workers or **migrants**[4] or people who have disabilities–for example blind people–trying to use the computer, there are these special programs that we can put together to make sure that software really isn't just for the few but really is about **empowering**[5] everyone. A good example of that is the 170 Hope Cyber Schools where we provided lots of training.

This commitment to think long-term and this commitment to the future is something that the Chinese Government, this University and Microsoft all share. And so the opportunity of working together on new **curriculum**[6], faculty exchange: these have strengthened all three of our institutions.

In the last several years, over 2,000 students from 100 Asian universities have worked at our research center here and we've awarded over 200 fellowships, so it's really become a mixing ground for the most talented people in the region. And of course, the university that has the largest representation has been Tsinghua.

Many more researchers are teaching courses, including the course here called "Hot Topics in Computing Research" that I think is a very **novel**[7] type of course and I think will be a model for many other universities as well.

Today I get a chance to announce some new program between Microsoft and Tsinghua, which is the "Microsoft Distinguished Visiting Professorship" at Tsinghua. And under this program, our research group will support a world-renowned computer scientist every year to visit the University at Professor Yao's Institute for Theoretical Computer Science. And the first

---

1　parallel execution 并行执行
2　start-up 启动阶段
3　displace 取代，替换
4　migrant 移民
5　empowering 授权；准许
6　curriculum 全部课程，课程
7　novel 新奇的

recipient[1] of this—a very impressive recipient—is Professor Frans Kaashoek from MIT.

And so I hope you get a sense of my optimism—optimism about what software can do and the interesting breakthroughs we can all make, opportunities to use that—use it for making businesses more effective, making jobs more interesting, designing far better products than ever before but also using it for the handicapped, for education, for **outreach**[2] so that any student who has an opportunity to connect up to the Internet will have the same type of opportunities as most privileged students.

I know many of the tough problems you're working on today. It's fantastic for me to be here. You may realize that I'm actually getting an honorary degree from Tsinghua before I get an honorary from Harvard—actually just less than two months I'll be at Harvard to get my first degree from the school that I spent several years at.

So these are amazing times and, you know, I think the **intersection**[3] of what's going on in China, what's going on with companies like Microsoft to take this long-term approach and the great academic tradition that is **exemplified**[4] by the excellence of this University, I think, we can all have a very high expectation. And certainly we're committed to working with all of you to realize that potential.

Thank you!

▶ 文化快递

1. artificial intelligence（人工智能）

英文缩写为AI。它是研究、开发用于模拟、延伸和扩展人的智能的理论、方法、技术及应用系统的一门新的技术科学。人工智能是计算机科学的一个分支，它企图了解智能的实质，并生产出一种新的能以与人类智能相似的方式做出反应的智能机器。例如繁重的科学和工程计算本来是要人脑来承担的，现在计算机不但能完成这种计算，而且能够比人脑做得更快、更准确。

2. "an honorary degree from Tsinghua before I get an honorary from Harvard"

微软公司总裁比尔·盖茨获得清华大学名誉博士学位，成为清华大学第13位名誉博士。此次授予比尔·盖茨名誉博士学位的原因是"他关心支持教育事业的发展，对教育事业的支持和帮助赢得了国际教育界的广泛赞誉，而且他个人的奋斗成长经历更是激发了成千上万人以新的方式来思考创新的问题"。同年6月，盖茨获得他的母校——哈佛大学的荣誉学位。

---

1 recipient 接受者
2 outreach 延伸，拓广
3 intersection 十字路口，交叉路
4 exemplify 举例说明

▶ 参考译文

尊敬的顾校长，清华大学的老师、同学们：

获得清华大学这所世界一流大学的名誉博士学位，让我深感荣幸。

拥有着96年悠久历史的清华诞生了很多杰出的科学家、商业和政治领袖。1997年，也就是10年以前，我访问过清华。当时，中国学生的才华、热情和创新给我留下了深刻的印象。之后，我决定在中国设立微软亚洲研究院。

在沈向洋博士的领导和在清华等大学优秀毕业生的协助下，微软亚洲研究院取得了成功，为微软公司作出了巨大贡献。在讨论先进技术的各种国际会议上，你总可以见到他们的身影。他们也为微软新产品的诞生，Windows Vista或者是Office 2007，付出了辛勤的努力。

这对于身为这所大学的学生来说是难以置信的时刻。因为包括网络在内的科学的尖端从未如此触手可及，推动人类各方面发展的时机也从未如此强烈。

我们才刚刚开始接触到数字变革时代带来的奇妙体验。的确，全世界有十亿计算机用户连接互联网。与此同时，我们也刚刚开始改变着人们学习并且分享信息的方式。半导体、光纤技术的飞速发展赋予我们应用软件的机会，从而使我们的工作方式变得强大，更多的事物充斥我们的生活。

比如就拿电视来说，现在我们观看电视还处于被动接受孤立的处境。但是这是一个转型的过程。在未来，你可以从因特网下载节目，甚至可以在家进行互动和学习，在其中体验与他人交流合作的灵活性。

想想如果产品能够利用数字化进行设计将会怎样。昨天我花了几个小时的时间参观了中国农科院稻米研究所，看到那里的技术人员开始用软件来区分不同的稻米，为其排序。他们对今后用较少的农药和水培育出高产量的优良品种的前景表示乐观。而这不仅仅能够使我们这些从事科技研究人员的生活得到改善，而且还惠及到所有的人。

医学界已经开始用软件来管理数据库，推断复杂的系统。对基于这项软件所带来的巨大突破，我十分乐观。

想想移动电话从声控装置发展成为我们的"数字钱包"，可以显示地图，上网查找信息，与之进行信息交流，甚至还可以上网寻找你所感兴趣的东西。

就拿学习来说，通过制造出一种叫做"学生卡片"的廉价卡片，它能与互联网无线相连，记录你的声音，辨认出你的笔记并且提供有效的学习经历。事实上它以诱人的形式把互联网上全世界的知识都聚集起来。

这样，老师也可以看到世界各地的优秀教案和最好的学习材料，他们通过互联网首次进行分享。而对于每一个想要学习或者想要教书的人来说，这将会是一个非常不同的世界。

当然，我知道，还有一些艰巨并且有趣的问题等待在场的学生们来解决。书写软件虽然值得信赖，但是其未来还面临着很多挑战。软件能够执行一些并行执行的程序，方便使用并且能够解决一些棘手的问题。比如说：我们几十年来一直致力于的人工智能的研究。所以，在科学尤其是在计算机科学方面的研究是令人惊讶的。比如：如何使得用户更容易掌握？如何实现人工智能？但不管怎样，就计算机科学而言，我们所处的都是最激动人心的时代。

对这个国家来说，同样令人激动。中国的发展和其经济增长不仅对国家，对整个世界也是一个惊人的贡献。她开始在科学的领域里扮演主角，在医药和计算机科学领域渐渐处于领先地位。

中国将会扮演着一个很重要角色，其中就是要投资打造出世界级的大学。而清华就是一个闪光点。微软公司承诺与这儿的伙伴合作，愿意帮助中国公司的成长，保证数以百计的软件能够在本土乃至全世界上市。

我们也保证对所有的公民都能够享受到数码产品带来的优势。

无论是无家可归的工人，移民或是残疾人，比如说盲人，他们设法使用电脑，而我们把这些特殊的程序放在一块，确保软件不仅适用于少数人，而且还适用于每一个人。我们在170所网络希望学校所提供的培训就是一个很好的例子。

中国政府，清华大学和微软公司都应该对之给予未来长期的承诺。而我们之间的关系也将随着新课程的合作研发与人员的交流得到加强。

在过去的几年中，有来自100所亚太地区大学的超过2000名学生曾在微软亚洲研究院实习，并有200多人获得了研究资助，其中云集了这个领域内各路高手。当然，清华所占学生人数最多。

本学年将会有越来越多的微软亚洲研究院的研究人员在清华开设课程：包括"计算机研究的热门领域的研究"。我认为这是一门非常新奇的课程，对其他学校来说，这也是一门精品课程。今天，我还想借此机会宣布，微软公司将在清华设立"杰出访问学者"项目。在该项目下，微软亚洲研究院每年将资助一位世界知名的计算机专家到姚期智教授领导的理论计算机科学研究所讲学。第一位获邀来访的是美国麻省理工大学的弗朗斯·凯斯霍德教授。

所以我希望你们能够体味到我的乐观，一种怀着对未来软件领域可能出现的一些突破的乐观。它们能使商业变得更加有效，工作变得更加有趣，并且设计出比之前更好的产品，能够为残疾人所使用，为教育服务，甚至更广乃至每一位能够上网的学生能够和大多数优越的学生一样拥有平等的受教育机会。

我知道现在你们有许多困难需要克服。总之，我今天非常高兴来到贵校，并在接受我的母校哈佛大学2个月内颁给我名誉博士学位之前就成为清华的名誉博士。

所以这是一个惊人的年代。微软公司对于中国市场的专注是长期的，中国未来将怎样，微软未来将怎样的问题将由这所大学的优异成绩来证明。我们对于以学术严谨闻名的清华大学有着很高的期望。让我们携手努力，共创信息技术未来的辉煌！

谢谢大家。

Lesson 3

My Story and the Chinese Dream Behind It

Task 1 Questions and Answers

Directions: *Work in pairs. Read the following speech then take turns to ask and answer the following questions.*

1. When was the speech delivered? Where?
2. Who delivered the speech? Who are involved in the speech?
3. What is the theme of the speech?
4. Why is there a need for the request?
5. How can the request be achieved?

Task 2 Dictation

Directions: *Watch the authentic video of the speech. Then fill in the missing words in their appropriate forms. You may watch the video for three times.*

China will start to play a very _____ role, and part of that is the _____ that has been made in having _____ universities, of which Tsinghua is really the _____ example. For Microsoft, we have a _____ to work with our partners here and make them successful, to make sure that there are _____ hundreds of software start-ups that not only sell in the market here but sell to the _____ world.

Task 3 Imitation and Play

Directions: *Watch the authentic video of the speech. Then try to imitate one or two paragraphs you like with appropriate delivery techniques. First practice by yourself. Then work in groups of four to take turns to deliver the speech.*

Task 4 Discussion

Directions: *Work in groups of four and discuss the following questions. You may locate some useful information from the script.*

1. Do you know the speaker? What do you know about him?
2. How do Chinese people's life change in 1968, 1978, 1988, 1998 and 2008?
3. How do you like the structure of speech?

4. What are the differences between an American dream and a Chinese dream?

Task 5　Speaking Practice

Directions: *Give a speech to the class for 2-3 minutes on a topic which you are interested in. You may choose from the following:*

1. Differences Enrich the World
2. Mistakes and Progress
3. Language is Power
4. One World. One Dream

My Story and the Chinese Dream Behind It
我的故事与其背后的中国梦
Address at Yale University on December 20, 2010
By Bai Yansong

▶ 人物简介

　　白岩松（1968年8月20日— ），中央电视台著名主持人，出生于内蒙古自治区呼伦贝尔市海拉尔区，1985年考入北京广播学院新闻系。他于1989年分配至中央人民广播电台《中国广播报》工作，1993年3月进入中央电视台《东方时空》，后正式任中央电视台新闻评论部主持。自担任主持以来，他曾获"中国播音与主持"大奖特等奖、"中国金话筒奖"、2009年华语主持群星会获年度终身成就等奖项。 1997年开始，白岩松主持了香

港回归、三峡大坝截流、国庆五十周年庆典、澳门回归、第29届奥运会等大型现场直播节目，参与策划并主持《焦点访谈》、《中国之路》等节目。参加了"北京申办2008年奥运会"和"中国加入WTO"等的报道。他主持节目的风格深刻而不呆板，活泼而不媚俗，告别了简单播报与表演形式，成为新一代电视人的代表之一。

名篇导读

在每一个人的心中都有一个梦想，有的人想要当总统，有的人想要当艺术家，有的人要创造发明，有的人要改造社会。而白岩松以他个人成长为线索，浓缩了40年来中美关系的深刻变化，从家运到国运，用真情讲述了一个国家的梦想。他说，"40年前，当马丁·路德·金先生倒下的时候，他的那句话'我有一个梦想'传遍了全世界。但是，一定要知道，不仅仅有一个英文版的'我有一个梦想'。在遥远的东方，在一个几千年延续下来的中国，也有一个梦想。它不是宏大的口号，并不仅仅在政府那里存在，是属于每一个非常普通的中国人的'我有一个梦想！'"

白岩松向耶鲁学子展现了他激情幽默但不乏深刻含义的演讲。演讲中，他谈到自己从"文革"时代的小孩成长到北广的学生，到中央电视台主持和一个一岁儿童的父亲；从美国的9·11到次贷危机，从中国的神七飞天到汶川大地震爆发；从美国总统访华到中国城市的加州拉面。在成长的这四十年间，他向我们传达出，在两国共同经历悲喜和交流的过程中，在这日趋变平的世界里，中美两国应该带着正常的眼镜来平等看待对方，相互交流，相互进步。

英文原文

In the past twenty years, China has faced **three American presidents**, but till coming to Yale today, I never realized that China really just faced one university. Although, through these three presidents, I understand that the quality of Yale graduates is not so **even**[1].

Let me begin my main subject and let me give it a title, called "My Story and the Chinese Dream behind It".

I want to talk about five particular years. The first is 1968. That year I was born. But it was also a **chaotic**[2] year for the world. In France, there was this huge street disturbance, and in America, too. Then President Kennedy was **assassinated**[3]. However, I really did not cause all of these!

But that year what we remember more was *the assassination of Mr. Martin Luther King*. Although he fell that year, his words "I have a dream" stood up, not only stood up in America,

---

1   even 相等的；平均的
2   chaotic 混乱的
3   assassinate 刺杀

but across the whole world.

But sadly, not only for me, but for almost all Chinese, we did not know such a dream. It was hard to describe each Chinese as having his or her own dream. Because at that time, it was very hard for our Chinese to say that we had our own dreams, to turn our dreams to be a nation's dream, or even a leader's dream.

China and America were so far apart, no less far apart than the Moon and the Earth. But I didn't care about any of that. All I cared about was whether I could have a full meal. Because during the culture revolution, I had been sent into prison since two months I was born, therefore, in order to bring me some milk, my grandpa put up a fierce fight (had a fierce conflict with) with the guards. Clearly, I was born at a very inconvenient time, not only for China, but even for the world, there were problems.

In 1978, ten years later, I was 10. I still lived in the very little city that had only 200 thousand people at the time I was born. It was 2000 km from Beijing, if you wanted to read the newspaper from Beijing, you waited three days. So for us, there was no such thing as news.

That year my grandfather passed away. Two years before that my father passed away. So there was just my mother left to take care of me and my brother. Her monthly salary was not even ten dollars. As a result, even though I was 10, the word "dream" was still not in my vocabulary, and I would never think of it.

Until now, my mother, who brought my brother and me up alone, has not been establishing the new family; I could not see hope in this family, but only felt bitter cold every winter. Where we lived was close to the Soviet Union.

Yet the 1978 in which I could not see hope was also the year that a huge change took place, whether for China or for the relationship between China and America. That is a date that everybody here today should remember December 16, 1978, China and America officially established diplomatic relations. That was a big event. And two days after that, December 18 was when China opened **the 3rd Plenary Session of the Eleventh CPC Central Committee**[1]. You know that it was the beginning of thirty-one years of Reform and Opening. History, two great nations, and a very pitiful family all became **intertwined**[2] in a **theatrical**[3] way. Truthfully, from the small personal family, to the big family of the country, nobody then had any idea what the future would be like.

The next year was 1988, in this year I was 20. At this time I had already come out of the little border town to Beijing as a university student.

Although we have many people in China today criticizing China's university entrance exams and see many many **deficiencies**[4] in it, it must be said that it is such a system that allowed very ordinary people like me to have the opportunity to change our lives. Of course, at that time,

---

1　the 3rd Plenary Session of the Eleventh CPC Central Committee 中国共产党十一届三中全会
2　intertwine 缠结在一起；使缠结
3　theatrical 戏剧性的；夸张的；做作的
4　deficiency 缺乏

America was no longer a very distant country. It became very specific. It was no longer the "Imperialist America" of the past slogans, but it became the many details in our lives.

This was the first time that I tasted Coca-Cola. When I finished drinking it I believed China and America were truly so close, because it tasted just like Chinese medicine. That was a time when I took a crazy liking to rock'n'roll. That was a time when Michael Jackson still looked relatively handsome. More importantly, that was a time when China experienced very big **transformations**[1], as Reform and Opening had already gone on for ten years.

That year, China began experimenting with market pricing for many goods. It may feel like something totally **incomprehensible**[2] to you, but it was a big deal in China, a huge step, because before that the prices were decided by the government. But in that year, because price controls were relaxed, the whole country went on a crazy shopping **spree**[3]. Everybody all thought, how long could this last, so they had to get a whole life's worth of food and goods to bring home.

That year symbolized that China marched closer and closer to a market economy. Of course back then nobody knew that market economy could also have a **subprime**[4] crisis. Anyway, I know that 1988 was an extra important year for Yale, because a Yale **alumnus**[5] once again became an American President.

There comes another year—1998, that year, I was 30. I had already become a news **anchor**[6] at CCTV. More importantly, I had become the father of a one-year-old child. I started to realize that most things I concerned were not only about myself, but about my children and their next generations.

That year a very important thing happened between China and America, and the **protagonist**[7] was Clinton. Perhaps you remember his sexual scandal in America, but in China what we remember is his visit to China that year.

In June, when he visited China, he and President Jiang Zemin held an open press conference in the Great Hall of the People. Then he gave an open lecture at Peking University. The live anchor for both events was me. When President Clinton was about to leave China from Shanghai, a journalist asked him, "What left you the most profound impression during this visiting in China?" He said "I can't believe that both lectures are live broadcast." However, the live broadcast gave China the compliment, but American received the criticism, a very little criticism.

During Clinton's lecture at Peking University, because he used his own translator the whole time, therefore, today's **interpretation**[8] was much better than his interpretation.

I guessed that many Chinese viewers only knew that Clinton was definitely saying something, but what he said wasn't all that clear. So near the end of my live broadcast, I remarked

---

1　transformation 变化；核转换
2　incomprehensible 不可思议的
3　spree 狂欢
4　subprime 准一流的，近乎头等的；准最低贷款利率的
5　alumnus 校友
6　anchor 节目主持人
7　protagonist 主角
8　interpretation 口译

that it looked like for America to learn more about China, sometimes it needed to start with language, America, **inclusive**[1] of associated press and many other media, had all reported the sentence I have just mentioned. However, I wonder if they had reported my another word. I said "For both China and US, face-to-face was always better than back-to-back."

That was also the first year that I drove the first car in my life. For me this was unimaginable before, that Chinese people one day would also drive their own cars. A personal delight can also make a lasting impression, because sometimes the first time is the most unforgettable.

Then what I'd like to talk is the year 2008. In 2008, I was 40.

The words "I have a dream" that haven't been discussed for many years now were heard among so many Americans. It seemed like Obama really did not want to accept Yale's 20-year occupation of America. Using words like "change" and "dream", he even convinced Yale teachers and students to parade and celebrate his election to the Presidency, according to what I've heard.

From the detail, I found Yale teachers and students had exceeded themselves. But this was also a year in which the Chinese Dream showed clearly. After encountering many setbacks as any grand dream in the world is **destined**[2] to, it came through. Whether it was the long-awaited Beijing Olympics, or the first spacewalk by a Chinese aboard the Shenzhou 7, these were all dreams which we have waited for a long time since a long time ago. But the sudden Sichuan Earthquake made all this not as magnificent as we had expected.

This time, I believe that the way we treat life is **equivalent**[3] to American and any other nation in the world which treats life well. Eighty-thousand lives departed, and made every day of 2008 seem like a year.

I'm guessing that on Yale's campus, on every web site, in front of television and newspapers were also many people from China, and people in all parts of the world, who shed tears for these lost lives. However, just like forty years ago when Mr. Martin Luther King fell but allowed the words "I have a dream" to stand higher, more enduring, and seem ever more valuable, more Chinese people also came to understand that dreams are important, but lives are even more so.

During the Olympics, I passed my own fortieth birthday. That day I was full of emotional thoughts, because when the day of my birthday approached, I was broadcasting an exciting competition. Twenty-four hours later, when my birthday was passing, I was still broadcasting.

But that day I felt very fortunate. Because it was such a special fortieth birthday at the Beijng Olympics that made me realize the Chinese Dream behind my personal story. It was in this kind of forty years that I went from a far-away border-town kid who had no possibility of having a dream, to a newsman who could be at a big festival celebrated with all of humanity and who could communicate and share the happiness with them. This was a life story that took place in China. And in this year, China and America were not far apart. There was a bit of me in you and a bit of you in me, we needed each other.

1　inclusive 包括的，包罗广泛的
2　destine 命中注定，预定
3　equivalent 相等的，相当的，等效的

It was said that President Bush spent the longest time in any country abroad as President, and that was during the Beijing Olympics. Phelps took eight medals there, and his family was there by his side. All Chinese wished that **extraordinary**[1] family well. Of course, every dream will pass. In such a year, China and America almost **simultaneously**[2] found their new "I have a dream" moment, and it was so **coincidental**[3], and so deserving.

America is facing a very very difficult financial crisis, and it isn't only America, but it affects the whole world seriously.

Yesterday I got to New York. As soon as I **deplaned**[4], I went to Wall Street. There I saw the statue of President Washington. His gaze was permanently fixed on the huge American flag on the stock exchange. Interestingly, the hall behind the statue was holding an exhibition on "President Lincoln in New York", so President Lincoln's huge portrait was also on it, and he also gazed at the flag. I felt the very solemn weight of history.

When I left there, I told my colleague this. I said, many many years ago, if something like this **befell**[5] America, perhaps Chinese people would have taken pleasure, because see, America is miserable again. But today, Chinese people would especially wish that America get better soon, because we have hundreds of billions worth of money with America. We also have a huge quantity of products waiting to be put on **freighters**[6] and sent to America. If America's economy takes a step for the better, it means behind these products, another Chinese gets a raise, it means he **regains**[7] his employment and happiness in the family. So you had better understand that this is not a slogan.

What in particular I'd like to say is that, in the past 30 years, I don't know if you've noticed the Chinese Dream that is relevant to more and more ordinary Chinese people. I don't know what other country in this world, in the past 30 years, has changed the individual fates at this **magnitude**[8]. A kid from a remote small city on the **periphery**[9], a kid in despair, today has the chance to have an exchange with these Yale students, inclusive of many teachers and professors.

There are endless families like that during the 30 years China has experienced. Their grandparents are still on the farmland and working hard, with **scanty**[10] income. Their parents left the countryside and found jobs after graduation from universities, however, perhaps, the children and their generations are on abroad in the US at this moment, three generations, just like experiencing three eras. But in China, you can find families like this anytime. If I was not wrong, many students abroad who are at present here are living in these families, are you?

1　extraordinary 特别的，非凡的
2　simultaneously 同时地
3　coincidental 符合的，巧合的
4　deplane （使）下飞机
5　befall 降临，发生
6　freighter 货船
7　regain 重新获得
8　magnitude 巨大，广大，重大；（地震）级数
9　periphery 边缘；圆周；外围；边缘地带
10　scanty （大小或数量）不足的，勉强够的

So when we take a look into China, maybe what you are often concerned about are these political words like doctrine, socialism or other big words. Maybe we can change the viewpoint, and look at 1.3 billion very ordinary Chinese, their down-to-earth dreams, their **impulsive**[1] drive to change their fates, their still kindhearted **temperament**[2], and their diligent character. China today is made up of these words I just spoke.

In the past many years, Chinese seemed to be looking at America through a telescope. So everything good that is in America was **magnified**[3] by this telescope. Frequently people mentioned America was like this and like that, then look at us, when can we be like that.

In the past many years, Americans also seemed to be looking at China through a telescope, but I am guessing they held it backward, because what they saw was a **diminished**[4], always-doing-wrong, full-of-problems China. They overlooked 1.3 very ordinary Chinese people and this impulsive drive and urge of theirs to change their fate, which caused such huge transformations in our country. But I also always had this dream why do we need to use telescopes to look at each other?

I believe many students abroad at present will see the most real America, through their eyes and ears, to know American people's real thinking deeply rooted in their hearts. It was very difficult for them to change their **perception**[5] toward America no matter what kind of language being used, because, it is the feeling deriving from their hearts.

Of course I hope very many Americans have a chance to go see China, and not to look at China through the media. You know I don't really trust all of my colleagues. I'm just kidding. Actually I respect my American colleagues very much. I only hope that more and more American friends go to see a real China.

Because, at least, I dare to say that, even if in America you ate what was deemed to be the best Chinese food, it won't fetch a good price in China. Just like many many years ago, in every city of China there was this popular "California Beef Noodle" shop. Many Chinese all thought, anything from America was definitely very very tasty. So they all went to eat. Although it was not very tasty, they didn't complain because they knew it was from America. This fast-food chain existed in China for many years, until more and more Chinese people came to America, and searched every corner of California for a California Beef Noodle shop, and could not find a single one. Only then did more and more Chinese know that California doesn't have such beef noodle, so this chain store in China is in the process of disappearing. This is the kind of **discrepancy**[6] I am talking about. As we come and go, such misunderstandings will be fewer and fewer.

So lastly I just want to say one thing again. Forty years ago, when Mr. Martin Luther King fell down, his words "I have a dream" spread across the world. But, you must know that there

---

1 impulsive 冲动的
2 temperament 性格；气质
3 magnified 放大的
4 diminished 减退的
5 perception 知觉；觉察（力）；观念
6 discrepancy 矛盾；不符合（之处）

is not just an English version of "I have a dream". In the distant East, in China that has held on for thousands of years, there is also a dream. It isn't a **grandiose**[1] slogan, it doesn't lie with the government. It belongs to every ordinary Chinese. It is "I have a dream" written in Chinese.

Ok, thank you everyone!

▶ 文化快递

1. Three American Presidents in Yale（耶鲁大学的三位美国总统）

自1988年起，三位统领美国的总统都是耶鲁的毕业生，即老布什、克林顿与小布什。美国从来没有连续三位总统都毕业自同一所大学的，这在美国是史无前例的。三人的任期加起来，刚好20年。他们执政的20年，常常被戏谑得称为"Yale's 20-year occupation of America（耶鲁占领美国的20年）"。

2. The Assassination of President Kennedy（肯尼迪总统遇害）

约翰·肯尼迪是第35任美国总统，也是美国历史上最年轻的总统。他的执政时间从1961年1月20日开始到1963年11月22日在达拉斯遇刺身亡为止。美国总统历来是垄断资本集团的代言人。正是凭借得克萨斯州一批亿万富翁的大力资助，约翰·肯尼迪才得以在官场上步步高升，并聚集了三四千万美元的私人资产。1963年10月，肯尼迪宣布准备改革美国的税收政策，这直接触犯了美国众多石油垄断集团老板的经济利益，不少人当时就极不满意地表示"肯尼迪的政策欲置美国经济于死地"，而这也就是他们决心干掉肯尼迪的真正原因。肯尼迪遇刺事件实际上反映了美国国内不同利益集团之间不可调和的激烈斗争，肯尼迪则是这种斗争的直接牺牲品。

3. Subprime Crisis（次贷危机）

2007年2月13日爆发的次贷危机是指一场发生在美国，因次级抵押贷款机构破产、投资基金被迫关闭、股市剧烈震荡引起的金融风暴。它致使全球主要金融市场出现流动性不足。次贷危机席卷了美国、欧盟和日本等世界主要金融市场。目前已经成为国际上的一个热点问题。

4. California Beef Noodle（加州牛肉面大王）

在美国加州牛肉面并不常见，两家"美国加州牛肉面"的原料，包括面条、牛肉、香料以及制作工艺，均来自中国。"美国加州"的名称只是市场营销策略。

▶ 中文原文

过去的20年，中国一直在跟美国的三任总统打交道。但是，今天到了耶鲁大学我才知道，其实它只跟一所学校打交道。透过这三位总统我也明白了，耶鲁大学毕业生的水准也

---

1 grandiose 宏伟的

并不是很平均。

接下来，就进入我们今天的主题，如果要起个题目的话，应该叫《我的故事以及背后的中国梦》。

我要讲五个年份，第一要讲的年份是1968年。那一年我出生了。但是，那一年世界非常乱，在法国有巨大的街头的骚乱。在美国也有，然后美国总统候选人罗伯特·肯尼迪遇刺了。但是，的确这一切的原因都与我无关。

但是那一年，我们更应该记住的是马丁·路德·金先生遇刺。虽然，那一年他倒下了，但是"我有一个梦想"的这句话却真正地站了起来，不仅在美国站了起来，也在全世界站了起来。

但是，当时很遗憾，不仅仅是我，几乎很多的中国人并不知道这个梦想。因为当时中国人，每一个人很难说拥有自己的梦想，将自己的梦想变成了一个国家的梦想，甚至是领袖的一个梦想。

中国与美国的距离非常遥远，不亚于月亮与地球之间的距离。但是我并不关心这一切，我只关心我是否可以吃饱。因为我刚出生两个月就被关进了"文化大革命"的牛棚，因此我的爷爷为了给我送去牛奶和看守进行了非常激烈的搏斗。很显然，我的出生非常不是时候，不仅对于当时的中国来说，对于世界来说，似乎都有些问题。

接下来要讲的故事是1978年，十年之后，我十岁了。我依然生活在我出生的地方，那个只有20万人的非常非常小的城市。它离北京的距离有2000公里，它要想了解北京出的报纸的话，要在三天之后才能看见。所以，对于我们来说，是不存在新闻这个说法的。

那一年，我的爷爷去世了。而在两年前的时候，我的父亲去世了。所以，只剩下我母亲一个人抚养我们哥儿俩，她一个月的工资不到10美元。因此，即使10岁了，梦想这个词对我来说，依然是一个非常陌生的词汇，我从来不会去想它。

我母亲一直到现在也没有建立新的婚姻，是她一个人把我们哥俩抚养大。我看不到这个家庭的希望，只是会感觉，那个时候的每一个冬天都很寒冷。因为，我所生活的那个城市离苏联更近。

但是就在我看不到希望的1978年的时候，不管是中国这个国家，还有中国与美国这两个国家之间，都发生了非常巨大的变化。那是一个我们在座的所有人都该记住的年份1978年的12月16日，中国与美国正式建交，那是一个大事件。而在中美建交两天之后，12月18日，中国共产党十一届三中全会召开了，今天你们知道，那是中国改革开放31年的开始。历史将两个伟大的国家、一个非常可怜的家庭就如此戏剧性地交织在一起，不管是小的家庭，还是大的国家，其实当时谁都没有把握知道未来是什么样的。

接下来的年份，该讲1988年了，那一年我20岁。这个时候我已经从边疆的小城市来到了北京，成为一个大学生。

虽然，今天在中国依然还有很多的人在抨击中国的高考制度，认为它有很多很多的缺陷。但是，必须承认正是高考的存在，让我们这样一个又一个非常普通的孩子，拥有了改变命运的机会。当然，这个时候美国已经不再是一个很遥远的国家，它变得很具体，它也不再是那个过去口号当中的"美帝国主义"，而是变成了生活中很多的细节。

这个时候，我已经第一次尝试过可口可乐，而且喝完可口可乐之后会觉得中美两个国家真的是如此接近。因为，它几乎就跟中国的中药是一样的。那个时候，我已经开始非常狂热地去喜欢上摇滚乐。那个时候，正是迈克尔·杰克逊长得比较漂亮的时候。更重要的是，这个时候的中国，已经开始发生了非常大的变化。因为，改革已经进行了10年。

那一年，中国开始尝试放开很多商品的价格。这在你们看来是非常不可思议的事情。但是，在中国当时是一个很大的迈进，因为过去的价格都是由政府来决定的。但是就在那一年，因为放开了价格，引起了全国疯狂地抢购，大家都觉得这个时候会有多久呢？于是，要把一辈子用的食品和用品，都买回到家里头。

这一年也就标志着中国离市场经济越来越近了。当然，那个时候没有人知道市场经济也会有次贷危机。当然，我知道那一年1988年对于耶鲁大学来说是格外的重要，因为你们耶鲁的校友又有一个成为了美国的总统。

接下来又是一个新的年份1998年，那一年我30岁。我已经成为中央电视台的一个新闻节目主持人。更重要的是，我已经成为一个1岁孩子的父亲。我开始明白我所做的许多事情不仅要考虑我自己，还要考虑孩子及他们的未来。

那一年，在中美之间发生了一个非常重要的事件，主角就是克林顿。也许在美国你记住的是性丑闻。但是，在中国记住的是，他那一年访问了中国。

在6月份他访问中国的时候，在人民大会堂和江泽民主席进行了一个开放的记者招待会，然后又在北京大学进行了一个开放的演讲，这两场活动的直播主持人都是我。当克林顿总统在上海即将离开中国的时候，记者问道："这次访问中国，您印象最深的是什么？"他说："我最想不到的是这两场讲座居然都直播了。不过，直播让中国受到了表扬，而美国却受到了批评。"当然只是一个很小的批评。

在北大的演讲当中，由于整个克林顿总统的演讲，用的全是美方所提供的翻译。因此，他翻译的那个水准远远达不到今天我们翻译的水准。

我猜想有很多的中国观众，是知道克林顿一直在说话，但是说的是什么，不太清楚。所以，我在直播结束的时候，说了这样的一番话 "看样子美国需要对中国有更多的了解，有的时候要从语言开始"，美国包括美联社在内的很多媒体都报道了我的这句话。但是，我说的另外一句话不知道他们有没有报道？我说，"对于中美这两个国家来说，面对面永远要好过背对背。"

当然也是在这一年年初，我开上了人生的第一辆车。这是我在过去从来不会想到的，中国人有一天也可以开自己的车。个人的喜悦，也会让你印象很久，因为往往第一次才是最难忘的。

接下来，我要讲述的是2008这一年，这一年我40岁。

很多年大家不再谈论的"我有一个梦想"这句话了，但是在这一年我听到太多的美国人在讲。

看样子奥巴马的确不想再接受耶鲁占领美国20年这样的事实了（耶鲁大学一直盛产总统，而出身哈佛大学的奥巴马终结了这一事实）。他用"改变"以及"梦想"这样的词汇，让耶鲁大学的师生在他当选总统之后举行游行，甚至庆祝。

在这个细节中，让我看到了耶鲁师生的超越。但是这一年，也是中国梦非常明显的一年。它就像全世界所有的伟大梦想，注定都要遭受很多的挫折才能显现出来一样。无论是期待了很久的北京奥运会，还是神舟七号中国人第一次在太空行走，那都是很多年前，我们期待了很久的梦想。但是，突如其来的四川汶川特大地震，让这一切都变得没有我们期待中的那么美好。

这个时候中国人对于生命的看待，我相信跟美国人和世界上一切善待生命的民族都是一样的。8万个生命的离开，让整个2008年中国人度日如年。

我猜得到在耶鲁校园里头，在每一个网页、电视以及报纸的前面，也有很多的来自中国的人，以及世界各地的人们，为这些生命流下眼泪。但是，就像40年前，马丁·路德·金先生倒下，却让"我有一个梦想"这句话站得更高，站得更久，站得更加让人觉得极其有价值一样，更多的中国人也明白了，梦想很重要，但是生命更重要。

在北京奥运会期间，我度过了自己的40岁的生日。那一天，我感慨万千。虽然，周围的人不会知道。因为时间进入到我的生日那一天的时候，我在直播精彩的比赛。24小时之后，当这个时间要走出我生日这一天的时候，我也依然在直播。

但是，这一天我觉得非常的幸运。因为，正是这样一个特殊的，在北京奥运会期间的40岁，让我意识到了我的故事背后的中国梦。正是在这样的40年的时间里头，我从一个根本不可能有梦想的，一个遥远边疆的小城市里的孩子，变成了一个可以在全人类欢聚的一个大的节日里头，分享以及传播这种快乐的新闻人，这是一个在中国发生的故事。而在这一年，中国和美国相距并不遥远，你中有我，我中有你，彼此需要。

布什总统据说度过了他作为总统以来在国外、一个国家待得最长的一段时间，就是在北京奥运会期间。菲尔普斯在那儿拿到了8块金牌，而他的家人都陪伴在他的身边，所有的中国人都为这样一个特殊的家庭祝福。当然，任何一个这样的梦想都会转眼过去。在这样的一个年份里头，中美两国历史上几乎是第一次同时发出了"我有一个新的梦想"的时候，如此的巧合，如此的应该。

美国面临了一次非常非常艰难的金融危机，当然不仅仅是美国的事情，也对全世界有重大的影响。

昨天我到达纽约，刚下了飞机，我去的第一站就是华尔街，我看到了华盛顿总统的雕像，他的视线是那么永久不变地在盯着证券交易所上那面巨大的美国国旗。而非常奇妙的是，在这个雕像后面的展览馆里正在举行"林肯总统在纽约"这样的一个展览。因此，林肯总统的大幅的画像也挂在那上面，他也在看那面国旗。我读出了非常悲壮的一种历史感。

在离开那个地方的时候，我对我的同事说了这样一句话：："很多很多年前如果美国发生了这样状况的时候，也许中国人会感到很开心。"因为，大家会说："你看，美国又糟糕了！"但是，今天中国人会格外地希望美国尽早地好起来，因为我们有几千亿的钱在美国，我们还有大量的产品等待着装上货船，送到美国来，如果美国的经济进一步好起来的话，在这些货品的背后，就是一个又一个中国人增长的工资，是他重新拥有的就业岗位以及家庭的幸福。因此，你明白，这不是一个口号的宣传。

今天我特别要讲的是，在过去的30年里头，你们是否注意到了，与一个又一个普通的中国人紧密相关的中国梦。我不知道世界上还有哪个国家，在过去这30年的时间里头，让个人的命运发生了这么大的变化。一个边远小城市的孩子，一个绝望中的孩子，今天有机会在耶鲁跟各位同学交流，当然也包括很多老师和教授。

中国经历了这30年，有无数个这样的家庭。他们的爷爷奶奶依然守候在土地上，仅有微薄的收入，千辛万苦。他们的父亲母亲，已经离开了农村，通过考大学，在城市里已经有了很好的工作，而这个家庭的孙子孙女也许此刻就在美国留学，三代人，就像经历了三个时代。但是在中国，你随时可以看到这样的家庭。如果我没有说错的话，现场的很多个中国留学生，他们的家庭也许就是这样。对么？

那么，在我们去观察中国的时候，也许你经常关注的是"主义"，"社会主义"或其他庞大的政治词汇，或许该换一个视角去看13亿个非常普通的中国人。他们并没有宏大的梦想、改变命运的那种冲动，依然善良的性格和勤奋的那种品质。今天的中国是由刚才的这些词汇构成。

在过去的很多年里头，中国人看美国，似乎在用望远镜看。美国所有的美好的东西，都被这个望远镜给放大了。经常有人说美国怎么怎么样，美国怎么怎么样，你看我们这儿什么时候能这样。

在过去的好多年里头，美国人似乎也在用望远镜在看中国。但是，我猜测可能拿反了。因为，他们看到的是一个缩小了的、错误不断的、有众多问题的一个中国。他们忽视了13亿非常普通的中国人，改变命运的这种冲动和欲望，使这个国家发生了如此巨大的变化。但是，我也一直有一个梦想：为什么要用望远镜来看彼此？

我相信现场在座的很多个来自中国的留学生，他们会用自己的眼睛看到了最真实的美国，用自己的耳朵去了解最真实的来自美国人内心的想法。无论再用什么样的文字也很难改变他们对美国的看法。因为，这来自他们内心的感受。

当然我也希望非常多的美国人，有机会去看看中国，而不是在媒体当中去看中国。你知道，我并不太信任我所有的同行。开一个玩笑。其实美国的同行是我非常尊敬的同行。我只是希望越来越多的美国的朋友去看一个真实的中国。

因为，我起码敢确定一件事情，即使在美国你吃到的被公认为最好的中国菜，在中国却很难卖出好价钱。就像很多很多年之前，在中国所有的城市里流行着一种叫加州牛肉面，加利福尼亚牛肉面。相当多的中国人都认为，美国来的东西一定非常非常好吃。所以，他们都去吃了。即使没那么好吃的话，由于觉得这是美国的也就不批评了。这个连锁的快餐店在中国存在了很多年，直到有越来越多的中国人来到美国，在加州四处寻找加州牛肉面。但是，一家都没有找到的时候，越来越多的中国人知道，加州是没有这种牛肉面的。于是，这个连锁店在中国，现在处于消失的过程当中。你看，这就是一种差异。但是，当人来人往之后，这样的一种误会就会越来越少。

所以，最后我只想再说一句。40年前，当马丁·路德·金先生倒下的时候，他的那句话"我有一个梦想"传遍了全世界。但是，一定要知道，不仅仅有一个英文版的"我有一个梦想"。在遥远的东方，在一个几千年延续下来的中国，也有一个梦想。它不是宏大的口号，并不仅仅在政府那里存在，它是属于每一个非常普通的中国人，而它用中文写成："我有一个梦想！"

好，谢谢各位！

Lesson 4

Feelings, Failure and Finding Happiness

Task 1　Questions and Answers

Directions: *Work in pairs. Read the following speech then take turns to ask and answer the following questions.*

1. When was the speech delivered? Where?
2. Who delivered the speech? Who are involved in the speech?
3. What is the theme of the speech?
4. Why is there a need for the request?
5. How can the request be achieved?

Task 2 Dictation

Directions: *Watch the authentic video of the speech. Then fill in the missing words in their appropriate forms. You may watch the video for three times.*

And, meanwhile, I was trying to sit _____ like Barbara and make myself talk like Barbara. And I thought, well, I could make a pretty _____ Barbara. And if I could _____ out how to be myself, I could be a pretty good Oprah. I was trying to sound _____ like Barbara. And sometimes I didn't read my _____, because something inside me said, this should be _____. So, I wanted to get the news as I was giving it to the people.

Task 3 Imitation and Play

Directions: *Watch the authentic video of the speech. Then try to imitate one or two paragraphs you like with appropriate delivery techniques. First practice by yourself. Then work in groups of four to take turns to deliver the speech.*

Task 4 Paraphrasing

Directions: *Work in groups of four and paraphrase the following sentences into simple English. Use specific details and examples to support yourself. You may locate some useful information from the script.*

1. If you really want to fly, just harness your power to your passion.
2. Nobody's journey is seamless or smooth. We all stumble.
3. Don't react against a bad situation; merge with that situation instead.
4. What matters most is what's inside.
5. Live not for battles won. / Live not for the-end-of-the-song. / Live in the along.
6. Life is a reciprocal exchange. To move forward you have to give back.
7. Not everybody can be famous. But everybody can be great, because greatness is determined by service.

Task 5 Speaking Practice

Directions: *Give a speech to the class for 2-3 minutes on the topic "Should Pop Stars Enjoy Their Privacy".*

Feelings, Failure and Finding Happiness
感觉、失败及寻找幸福

Commencement Speech of Stanford Class of 2008
By Oprah Winfrey

人物简介

奥普拉·温弗瑞（1954年1月29日— ）美国著名的脱口秀主持人，拥有美国"传媒女皇"之称。出生于美国密西西比。奥普拉19岁开始其广播生涯，于1984年来到芝加哥，主持早间脱口秀节目"芝加哥早晨"。节目在不到一年的时间里就取得了很大的成功。1986年，奥普拉成立了自己的制作公司——哈泼公司，并以她的名字命名脱口秀节目《奥普拉脱口秀》。她幽默机智的风格便迅速捕获了美国无数观众的心，成为美国的文化现象。奥普拉作为娱乐界的慈善家也是享有盛名。她将收入的10%投入慈善事业。她特别关注教育领域，建立了私人的慈善组织"奥普拉·温弗瑞基金会"，支持全世界妇女、儿童的教育。美国《名利场》杂志评价她说："在大众文化中，她的影响力，可能除了教皇以外，比任何大学教授、政治家或者宗教领袖都大。"

名篇导读

"这整个世界，我们所居住的宇宙，就像个大教室，等着我们一个学分、一个学分去学习，有时必须重修、补考，甚至被'当掉'。我的秘诀是，毫不迟疑地打开试卷，用真正的我去面对，从中学到自我改进，追求更深层次的理解、被理解与成长。"

经历过不堪回首的童年、叛逆堕落的少女时代的奥普拉靠着"一个人可以非常清贫、困顿、低微，但是不可以没有梦想"的简单信念，实现了丑小鸭到黑天鹅的美丽蜕变。而她也将那份艰难岁月所带来的宝贵经验带到了斯坦福大学的校园里，与千万学子们共勉。

在斯坦福大学08届毕业典礼上，奥普拉与学生们分享了三个主题：感觉、失败与快乐。她认为"感觉"就像生命中的GPS，对于每个决定，要问问内心的感觉，勇敢地相信它；在重新定义"成功"的时候，奥普拉认为，成功并不代表拥有多少金钱，真正的财富是能带给你真正的富足的有意义的工作；在面对"失败"的时候，奥普拉认为，没有任何人一生风平浪静，面对生活中的危机、困境、失意，只要你从摔跤中学到教训，就站起来，拍拍灰尘，就能继续下去。否则，失败会以另外一种样式，继续出现在你面前，促使你继续克服它。演讲充分展现出幽默，亲密，自白的"脱口秀"式风格，整篇讲稿也较为口语化。

对全世界数以百万计的人们来说，奥普拉是美国精神与创业成功的象征，她的故事是从身无分文到坐拥亿万的活生生的写照。她不仅是著名的电视节目主持人、娱乐界明星慈善活动家，而且还是"美国最便捷、最诚实的精神病医生"。

英文原文

Thank you, President Hennessy, and to the **trustees**[1] and the faculty, to all of the parents and grandparents, to you, the Stanford graduates. Thank you for letting me share this amazing day.

I need to begin by letting everyone in on a little secret. The secret is that Kirby Bumpus, Stanford Class of '08, is my **goddaughter**[2]. So, I was thrilled when President Hennessy asked me to be your Commencement speaker, because this is the first time I've been allowed on campus since Kirby's been here.

You see, Kirby's a very smart girl. She wants people to get to know her on her own terms, she says. Not in terms of who she knows. So, she never wants anyone who's first meeting her to know that I know her and she knows me. So, when she first came to Stanford for new student orientation with her mom, I hear that they arrived and everybody was so welcoming, and somebody came up to Kirby and they said, "Oh my god, that's Gayle King!" Because a lot of people know Gayle King as my BFF (best friend forever) and so somebody comes up to Kirby, and they say, " Oh my god, is that Gayle King?" And Kirby's like, "Uh-huh. She's my mom." And so the person says, "Oh my god, does it mean, like, you know Oprah Winfrey?" And Kirby says, "Sort of."

I said, "Sort of? You sort of know me?" Well, I have photographic proof. I have pictures which I can e-mail to you all of Kirby riding horsey with me on all fours. So, I more than sort-of know Kirby Bumpus. And I'm so happy to be here, just happy that I finally, after four years, get to see her room. There's really nowhere else I'd rather be, because I'm so proud of Kirby,

---

1 trustee 受托人
2 goddaughter 教女

who graduates today with two degrees, one in human bio and the other in psychology. Love you, Kirby Cakes! That's how well I know her. I can call her Cakes.

And so proud of her mother and father, who helped her get through this time, and her brother, Will. I really had nothing to do with her graduating from Stanford, but every time anybody's asked me in the past couple of weeks what I was doing, I would say, "I'm getting ready to go to Stanford."

I just love saying "Stanford". Because the truth is, I know I would have never gotten my degree at all, 'cause I didn't go to Stanford. I went to Tennessee State University. But I never would have gotten my diploma at all, because I was supposed to graduate back in 1975, but I was short one credit. And I figured, I'm just going to forget it, 'cause, you know, I'm not going to march with my class. Because by that point, I was already on television. I'd been in television since I was 19 and a sophomore. Granted, I was the only television anchor person that had an 11 o'clock **curfew**[1] doing the 10 o'clock news.

Seriously, my dad was like, "Well, that news is over at 10:30. Be home by 11."But that didn't matter to me, because I was earning a living. I was on my way. So, I thought, I'm going to let this college thing go and I only had one credit short. But, my father, from that time on and for years after, was always on my case, because I did not graduate. He'd say, "Oprah Gail"—that's my middle name—"I don't know what you're gonna do without that degree." And I'd say, "But, Dad, I have my own television show." And he'd say, "Well, I still don't know what you're going to do without that degree." And I'd say, "But, Dad, now I'm a talk show host." He'd say, "I don't know how you're going to get another job without that degree."

So, in 1987, Tennessee State University invited me back to speak at their commencement. By then, I had my own show, was nationally **syndicated**[2]. I'd made a movie, had been nominated for an Oscar and founded my company, Harpo. But I told them, I cannot come and give a speech unless I can earn one more credit, because my dad's still saying I'm not going to get anywhere without that degree.

So, I finished my coursework, I turned in my final paper and I got the degree. And my dad was very proud. And I know that, if anything happens, that one credit will be my **salvation**[3].

But I also know why my dad was insisting on that diploma, because, as B. B. King put it, "The beautiful thing about learning is that nobody can take that away from you." And learning is really in the broadest sense what I want to talk about today, because your education, of course, isn't ending here. In many ways, it's only just begun.

The world has so many lessons to teach you. I consider the world, this Earth, to be like a school and our life the classrooms. And sometimes here in this Planet Earth School the lessons often come dressed up as **detours**[4] or **roadblocks**[5]. And sometimes as full-blown crises. And

1 curfew 宵禁
2 syndicate 成为组合
3 salvation 救助
4 detours 岔路
5 roadblock 路障

the secret I've learned to getting ahead is being open to the lessons, lessons from the grandest university of all, that is, the universe itself.

It's being able to walk through life eager and open to self-improvement and that which is going to best help you evolve, 'cause that's really why we're here, to evolve as human beings. To grow into being more of ourselves, always moving to the next level of understanding, the next level of compassion and growth.

I think about one of the greatest compliments I've ever received: I interviewed with a reporter when I was first starting out in Chicago. And then many years later, I saw the same reporter. And she said to me, "You know what? You really haven't changed. You've just become more of yourself."

And that is really what we're all trying to do, become more of ourselves. And I believe that there's a lesson in almost everything that you do and every experience, and getting the lesson is how you move forward. It's how you enrich your spirit. And, trust me, I know that inner wisdom is more precious than wealth. The more you spend it, the more you gain.

So, today, I just want to share a few lessons—meaning three—that I've learned in my journey so far. And aren't you glad? Don't you hate it when somebody says, "I'm going to share a few," and it's 10 lessons later? And, you're like, "Listen, this is my graduation. This is not about you." So, it's only going to be three.

The three lessons that have had the greatest impact on my life have to do with feelings, with failure and with finding happiness.

A year after I left college, I was given the opportunity to co-anchor the 6 o'clock news in Baltimore, because the whole goal in the media at the time I was coming up was you try to move to larger markets. And Baltimore was a much larger market than Nashville. So, getting the 6 o'clock news co-anchor job at 22 was such a big deal. It felt like the biggest deal in the world at the time.

And I was so proud, because I was finally going to have my chance to be like Barbara Walters, which is who I had been trying to **emulate**[1] since the start of my TV career. So, I was 22 years old, making $22,000 a year. And it's where I met my best friend, Gayle, who was an **intern**[2] at the same TV station. And once we became friends, we'd say, "Oh my god, I can't believe it! You're making $22,000 and you're only 22. Imagine when you're 40 and you're making $40,000!"

When I turned 40, I was so glad that didn't happen.

So, here I am, 22, making $22,000 a year and, yet, it didn't feel right. It didn't feel right. The first sign, as President Hennessy was saying, was when they tried to change my name. The news director said to me at the time, "Nobody's going to remember Oprah. So, we want to change your name. We've come up with a name we think that people will remember and people will like. It's a friendly name: Suzie."

Hi, Suzie. Very friendly. You can't be angry with Suzie. Remember Suzie. But my name

---

1 emulate 模仿
2 intern 实习生

wasn't Suzie. And, you know, I'd grown up not really loving my name, because when you're looking for your little name on the lunch boxes and the license plate tags, you're never going to find Oprah.

So, I grew up not loving the name, but once I was asked to change it, I thought, well, it is my name and do I look like a Suzie to you? So, I thought, no, it doesn't feel right. I'm not going to change my name. And if people remember it or not, that's OK.

And then they said they didn't like the way I looked. This was in 1976, when your boss could call you in and say, "I don't like the way you look." Now that would be called a **lawsuit**[1], but back then they could just say, "I don't like the way you look." Which, in case some of you in the back, if you can't tell, is nothing like Barbara Walters? So, they sent me to a **salon**[2] where they gave me a **perm**[3], and after a few days all my hair fell out and I had to shave my head. And then they really didn't like the way I looked, because now I am black and bald and sitting on TV. Not a pretty picture.

But even worse than being bald, I really hated, hated, hated being sent to report on other people's tragedies as a part of my daily duty, knowing that I was just expected to observe, when everything in my instinct told me that I should be doing something, I should be lending a hand. So, as President Hennessy said, I'd cover a fire and then I'd go back and I'd try to give the victims blankets. And I wouldn't be able to sleep at night because of all the things I was covering during the day.

And, meanwhile, I was trying to sit gracefully like Barbara and make myself talk like Barbara. And I thought, well, I could make a pretty **goofy**[4] Barbara. And if I could figure out how to be myself, I could be a pretty good Oprah. I was trying to sound elegant like Barbara. And sometimes I didn't read my copy, because something inside me said, this should be spontaneous. So, I wanted to get the news as I was giving it to the people. So, sometimes, I wouldn't read my copy and it would be, like, six people on a **pileup**[5] on I-40. Oh, my goodness.

And sometimes I wouldn't read the copy—because I wanted to be spontaneous—and I'd come across a list of words I didn't know and I'd mispronounce. And one day I was reading copy and I called Canada "ca nada". And I decided, this Barbara thing's not going too well. I should try being myself.

But at the same time, my dad was saying, "Oprah Gail, this is an opportunity of a lifetime. You better keep that job." And my boss was saying, "This is the nightly news. You're an anchor, not a social worker. Just do your job."

So, I was **juggling**[6] these messages of expectation and obligation and feeling really miserable with myself. I'd go home at night and fill up my journals, 'cause I've kept a journal

---

1 lawsuit 诉讼
2 salon 沙龙
3 perm 烫发
4 goofy 傻瓜
5 pileup 连环撞车
6 juggling 欺诈

since I was 15—so I now have volumes of journals. So, I'd go home at night and fill up my journals about how miserable I was and frustrated. Then I'd eat my anxiety. That's where I learned that habit.

And after eight months, I lost that job. They said I was too emotional. I was too much. But since they didn't want to pay out the contract, they put me on a talk show in Baltimore. And the moment I sat down on that show, the moment I did, I felt like I'd come home. I realized that TV could be more than just a playground, but a platform for service, for helping other people lift their lives. And the moment I sat down, doing that talk show, it felt like breathing. It felt right. And that's where everything that followed for me began.

And I got that lesson. When you're doing the work you're meant to do, it feels right and every day is a bonus, regardless of what you're getting paid.

It's true. And how do you know when you're doing something right? How do you know that? It feels so. What I know now is that feelings are really your GPS system for life. When you're supposed to do something or not supposed to do something, your emotional guidance system lets you know. The trick is to learn to check your ego at the door and start checking your gut instead. Every right decision I've made—every right decision I've ever made—has come from my gut. And every wrong decision I've ever made was a result of me not listening to the greater voice of myself.

If it doesn't feel right, don't do it. That's the lesson. And that lesson alone will save you, my friends, a lot of grief. Even doubt means don't. This is what I've learned. There are many times when you don't know what to do. When you don't know what to do, get still, get very still, until you do know what to do.

And when you do get still and let your internal motivation be the driver, not only will your personal life improve, but you will gain a competitive edge in the working world as well. Because, as Daniel Pink writes in his best-seller, *A Whole New Mind*, we're entering a whole new age. And he calls it the Conceptual Age, where traits that set people apart today are going to come from our hearts—right brain—as well as our heads. It's no longer just the logical, linear, rules-based thinking that matters, he says. It's also empathy and joyfulness and purpose, inner traits that have **transcendent**[1] worth.

These qualities bloom when we're doing what we love, when we're involving the wholeness of ourselves in our work, both our **expertise**[2] and our emotion.

So, I say to you, forget about the fast lane. <u>If you really want to fly, just harness your power to your passion</u>. Honor your calling. Everybody has one. Trust your heart and success will come to you. So, how do I define success? Let me tell you, money's pretty nice. I'm not going to stand up here and tell you that it's not about money, 'cause money is very nice. I like money. It's good for buying things.

But having a lot of money does not automatically make you a successful person. What you

---

1 transcendent 卓越的
2 expertise 专门技术

want is money and meaning. You want your work to be meaningful, because meaning is what brings the real richness to your life. What you really want is to be surrounded by people you trust and treasure and by people who cherish you. That's when you're really rich. So, lesson one, follow your feelings. If it feels right, move forward. If it doesn't feel right, don't do it.

Now I want to talk a little bit about failings, because nobody's journey is **seamless**[1] or smooth. We all stumble. We all have setbacks. If things go wrong, you hit a dead end—as you will—it's just life's way of saying time to change course. So, ask every failure—this is what I do with every failure, every crisis, every difficult time—I say, what is this here to teach me? And as soon as you get the lesson, you get to move on. If you really get the lesson, you pass and you don't have to repeat the class. If you don't get the lesson, it shows up wearing another pair of pants—or skirt—to give you some remedial work.

And what I've found is that difficulties come when you don't pay attention to life's whisper, because life always whispers to you first. And if you ignore the whisper, sooner or later you'll get a scream. Whatever you resist persists. But, if you ask the right question—not why is this happening, but what is this here to teach me?—it puts you in the place and space to get the lesson you need.

My friend Eckhart Tolle, who's written this wonderful book called *A New Earth* that's all about letting the awareness of who you are stimulate everything that you do, he puts it like this: He says, don't react against a bad situation; merge with that situation instead. And the solution will arise from the challenge. Because surrendering yourself doesn't mean giving up; it means acting with responsibility.

Many of you know that, as President Hennessy said, I started this school in Africa. And I founded the school, where I'm trying to give South African girls a shot at a future like yours—Stanford. And I spent five years making sure that school would be as beautiful as the students. I wanted every girl to feel her worth reflected in her surroundings. So, I checked every **blueprint**[2], I picked every pillow. I was looking at the **grout**[3] in between the bricks. I knew every **thread**[4] count of the sheets. I chose every girl from the villages, from nine provinces. And yet, last fall, I was faced with a crisis I had never anticipated. I was told that one of the dorm **matrons**[5] was suspected of sexual abuse.

That was, as you can imagine, devastating news. First, I cried—actually, I **sobbed**[6]—for about half an hour. And then I said, let's get to it; that's all you get, a half an hour. You need to focus on the now, what you need to do now. So, I contacted a child **trauma**[7] specialist. I put together a team of investigators. I made sure the girls had counseling and support. And Gayle and

---

1 seamless 无缝的
2 blueprint 蓝图
3 grout 水泥
4 thread 线
5 matron （学校的）女舍监
6 sob 啜泣
7 trauma 外伤

I got on a plane and flew to South Africa.

And the whole time I kept asking that question: What is this here to teach me? And, as difficult as that experience has been, I got a lot of lessons. I understand now the mistakes I made, because I had been paying attention to all of the wrong things. I'd built that school from the outside in, when what really mattered was the inside out. So, it's a lesson that applies to all of our lives as a whole. What matters most is what's inside. What matters most is the sense of integrity, of quality and beauty. I got that lesson. And what I know is that the girls came away with something, too. They have emerged from this more **resilient**[1] and knowing that their voices have power.

And their resilience and spirit have given me more than I could ever give to them, which leads me to my final lesson—the one about finding happiness—which we could talk about all day, but I know you have other **wacky**[2] things to do.

Not a small topic this is, finding happiness. But in some ways I think it's the simplest of all. Gwendolyn Brooks wrote a poem for her children. It's called "Speech to the Young : Speech to the Progress-Toward." And she says at the end, "Live not for battles won. / Live not for the-end-of-the-song. / Live in the along." She's saying, like Eckhart Tolle, that you have to live for the present. You have to be in the moment. Whatever has happened to you in your past has no power over this present moment, because life is now.

But I think she's also saying, be a part of something. Don't live for yourself alone. This is what I know for sure: In order to be truly happy, you must live along with and you have to stand for something larger than yourself. Because life is a **reciprocal**[3] exchange. To move forward you have to give back. And to me, that is the greatest lesson of life. To be happy, you have to give something back.

I know you know that, because that's a lesson that's woven into the very fabric of this university. It's a lesson that Jane and Leland Stanford got and one they've **bequeathed**[4] to you. Because all of you know the story of how this great school came to be, how the Stanfords lost their only child to **typhoid**[5] at the age of 15. They had every right and they had every reason to turn their backs against the world at that time, but instead, they **channeled**[6] their grief and their pain into an act of grace. Within a year of their son's death, they had made the founding grant for this great school, pledging to do for other people's children what they were not able to do for their own boy.

The lesson here is clear, and that is, if you're hurting, you need to help somebody ease their hurt. If you're in pain, help somebody else's pain. And when you're in a mess, you get yourself out of the mess helping somebody out of theirs. And in the process, you get to become a member

---

1 resilient 恢复
2 wacky 古怪的
3 reciprocal 相互的；互惠的；倒数的
4 bequeath 把……遗赠
5 typhoid 伤寒
6 channel 引导

of what I call the greatest fellowship of all, the **sorority**[1] of compassion and the **fraternity**[2] of service.

The Stanfords had suffered the worst thing any mom and dad can ever endure, yet they understood that helping others is the way we help ourselves. And this wisdom is increasingly supported by scientific and sociological research. It's no longer just woo-woo soft-skills talk. There's actually a helper's high, a spiritual surge you gain from serving others. So, if you want to feel good, you have to go out and do some good.

But when you do good, I hope you strive for more than just the good feeling that service provides, because I know this for sure, that doing good actually makes you better. So, whatever field you choose, if you operate from the **paradigm**[3] of service, I know your life will have more value and you will be happy.

I was always happy doing my talk show, but that happiness reached a depth of fulfillment, of joy, that I really can't describe to you or measure when I stopped just being on TV and looking at TV as a job and decided to use television, to use it and not have it use me, to use it as a platform to serve my viewers. That alone changed the **trajectory**[4] of my success.

So, I know this—that whether you're an actor, you offer your talent in the way that most inspires art. If you're an **anatomist**[5], you look at your gift as knowledge and service to healing. Whether you've been called, as so many of you here today getting doctorates and other degrees, to the professions of business, law, engineering, humanities, science, medicine, if you choose to offer your skills and talent in service, when you choose the paradigm of service, looking at life through that paradigm, it turns everything you do from a job into a gift. And I know you haven't spent all this time at Stanford just to go out and get a job.

You've been enriched in countless ways. There's no better way to make your mark on the world and to share that abundance with others. My constant prayer for myself is to be used in service for the greater good.

So, let me end with one of my favorite quotes from Martin Luther King. Dr. King said, "Not everybody can be famous." And I don't know, but everybody today seems to want to be famous.

But fame is a **trip**[6]. People follow you to the bathroom, listen to you **pee**[7]. It's just—try to pee quietly. It doesn't matter, they come out and say, "Oh my god, it's you. You peed."

That's the fame trip, so I don't know if you want that.

So, Dr. King said, "Not everybody can be famous. But everybody can be great, because greatness is determined by service." Those of you who are history scholars may know the rest of that passage. He said, "You don't have to have a college degree to serve. You don't have to

---

1 sorority 妇女联合会
2 fraternity 友爱
3 paradigm 榜样
4 trajectory 轨道
5 anatomist 分析家
6 trip 代价
7 pee 小便

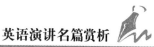

make your subject and verb agree to serve. You don't have to know about Plato or Aristotle to serve. You don't have to know Einstein's theory of relativity to serve. You don't have to know the second theory of thermodynamics in physics to serve. You only need a heart full of grace and a soul generated by love."

In a few moments, you'll all be officially Stanford's '08.

You have the heart and the smarts to go with it. And it's up to you to decide, really, where will you now use those gifts? You've got the diploma, so go out and get the lessons, 'cause I know great things are sure to come.

You know, I've always believed that everything is better when you share it, so before I go, I wanted to share a graduation gift with you. Underneath your seats you'll find two of my favorite books. Eckhart Tolle's *A New Earth* is my current book club selection. Our New Earth webcast has been downloaded 30 million times with that book. And Daniel Pink's *A Whole New Mind: Why Right-Brainers Will Rule the Future* has reassured me I'm in the right direction.

I really wanted to give you cars but I just couldn't pull that off! Congratulations, '08!

文化快递

1. B. B. King（B·B·金）

Blues Boy King是美国歌手，吉他演奏家，作曲家，号称"蓝调音乐之王"。他的作品既有纯布鲁斯的，也有乡村音乐风格的，还有流行和摇滚的，每一种形式中都夹杂着布鲁斯的成分。独特的小颤音足使他的唱风与众不同。作为BLUES王国的主宰，他一直有着无上的自信，能够从任何抒情诗中表达出微妙的语感。同时，他的表现力丰富，善于使用不同的曲调演唱同一句歌词。奥普拉引用B·B·King的"关于学习的美好在于别人不会把知识从你身上拿走"是告诉大家在人的一生中都要怀有坦然学习的心态。

2. Barbara Walters（芭芭拉·沃尔斯特）

芭芭拉·沃尔斯特，是世界知名女主持人，以深度采访知名人士而见长，主持美国著名新闻杂志性节目《20/20》，曾因在已七十高龄时采访邓小平，而在中国有着较高的知名度。该节目由美国ABC播出，它的报道题材涉及范围广，对国内国际时政、社会问题、儿童问题等都曾有报道。

3. Speech to the Young: Speech to the Progress-toward（致青年和终将到来的进步）

格温多林·布鲁克斯在她的一生中创作了大量的诗歌，她出版了二十多部诗集，她是全世界著名的用诗歌的语言来增强人们对美国黑人文化的了解的人。她在二十世纪四五十年代创作了许多反映黑人生活的诗歌，她的诗歌描写了黑人社会中的贫穷、种族不平等和吸毒的现象，她还创作了反映黑人妇女抗争的事迹。她的这首Speech to the Young: Speech to the progress-toward中的 "Live not for battles won. Live not for the-end-of-the-song. Live in the along." 传达了活在当下的意思。

4. Eckhart Tolle's *A New Earth*（艾克哈特·托尔的《新世界》）

艾克哈特·托尔（Eckhart Tolle），生于德国，伦敦大学毕业后，在剑桥大学担任研究员和导师。29岁那年，一次意外的经历彻底改变了他的生活。在接下来的几年里，他致力于解释、整合和深化这种变化。他用一种简单明了的语言，传达了古代心灵导师简单而深刻的信息：我们可以摆脱痛苦并进入内心的平和世界。在这本书中，作者经由自己的亲身经历，描绘了痛苦之身如何控制人类，而我们又如何能够借助于临在之光，也就是意识的觉醒，从痛苦之身中破茧而出。那份对痛苦之身的知晓，就足以开始转化的过程。接下来要做的，就是接纳——允许自己在痛苦之身爆发的时刻完全地去感受当下的感觉。而随着全人类觉醒的到来，在我们现有的基础上，将会出现一个新世界——人类不再认同于思想，也就是小我的心智，因而能够获得真正的内在自由。

5. Daniel Pink's *A Whole New Mind*（丹尼尔·平克的《全新思维》）

《全新思维》的作者是美国前副总统戈尔御用文人、著名趋势分析家、知名预言家丹尼尔·平克。他提出"知识不再是力量，感性才是力量。"书中阐述了这个原本属于一群高喊知识就是力量、重视理性分析的世界正在转化为一个重视创新、同理心，与整合力的感性时代。今后全世界渴望的人才，需要六种感性能力，而这六种关键能力又来自两种感知：高感性与高体会。

参考译文

汉尼斯校长，全体教员，家长，还有斯坦福的毕业生们，非常感谢你们。感谢你们让我和你们分享这美好的一天。

我很乐意和大家分享个小秘密来作为这次演讲的开始。这个秘密就是科比·巴姆珀斯，斯坦福2008年的毕业生，是我的教女。所以当汉尼斯校长让我来做演讲时，我受宠若惊，因为自从科比来这上学以来，这是我第一次被允许到斯坦福来。

正如你们知道的那样科比是一个非常聪明的女孩。她说，她希望大家通过她自己的努力了解她，而不是她认识谁。因此她从来不希望每一个第一次见到她的人知道她认识我。当她和她妈妈第一次来到斯坦福参加开学典礼时，我听说每个人都十分热情。他们说："我的天啊，那是盖尔·金"。因为很多人都知道盖尔·金是我最好的朋友，所以有些人走到科比面前，对科比说："我的天啊，那是盖尔·金吗？"科比说："嗯，她是我妈妈。"然后人们说："我的天啊，难道说，你认识奥普拉·温弗瑞？"科比说："有点吧。"

我说："有一点。你有一点认识我。"我还有照片为证。我可以把科比和我骑马时的照片用邮件发给你们。因此我不仅仅只是有点认识科比·巴姆珀斯。我非常高兴来到这里，因为四年来我第一次来到她的寝室。我为科比感到自豪，因为她获得了人类生物学和心理学的双学位。这就是我多么的了解她。我可以叫她"蛋糕"。

我为她的父母感到骄傲,她的父母给了她很大帮助,还有她的哥哥威尔。我对科比大学四年真的没有什么帮助。但是在过去的几周里,每当人们问我在做什么时,我都会说:"我正准备去斯坦福。"

我就是喜欢这样说斯坦福(用一种奇怪的语调)。因为这是真的,我知道根本不会拿到我的学位,因为我没有去斯坦福念书。我去了田纳西州立大学。但是我本来不会拿到我的毕业证,因为我本应该在1975年毕业,但是我少了一个学分。我认为我还是会忘了这件事。你们知道,我不会比得上我的同班同学。因为我已经上了电视。我在19岁还是大学二年级的时候就已经上了电视。我是唯一一个电视节目主持人,虽然有11点的宵禁,却做着10,点钟的新闻。

严肃地说,我爸爸告诉我,"好吧,新闻10:30结束。11点之前到家。"但是这对我并不重要,因为我已经自食其力了。我在走我自己的路。所以我想,我不能让关于我大学的那件事就这么过去,我还少一个学分。但是我的父亲从那时起却成了问题。由于我没有毕业,他总是说:"奥普拉·吉尔(我的中间名字),我不知道没有学位你能做些什么。"然后我说:"但是,爸爸,我已经有我自己的电视节目啦。"他说:"好吧,但是我还是不知道没有那个学位你能干什么。"我说:"但是,爸爸,现在我已经是脱口秀的主持人了。"他还是说:"我不知道没有那个学位你怎么去找其他的工作。"

在1987年,田纳西州立大学邀请我回去做他们的毕业典礼演讲。在那时,我已经有了自己的电视节目,并加入了国家联合会。我制作了一部电影,并被奥斯卡提名,而且成立了我自己的公司哈伯特。可我告诉他们,我不能去演讲除非我得到那一个学分,因为我爸爸总是说没了那学位我将一事无成。

因此,我完成了我的课程,上交了我的毕业论文,然后拿到了学位。我的爸爸非常的骄傲。从此我知道,无论什么事发生,那一个学分是我的救世主

但是我知道为什么我爸爸总是坚持让我获得文凭,因为,正如B·B·金所说:"关于学习的美好在于别人不会把知识从你身上拿走。"学习正是我今天想说的,因为你们的教育并没有在这里结束。在很多情况下,这才是刚刚开使。

这个世界将会教会你们很多。我认为这个世界,这个地球,就像一个学校,我们人生就是教室。有时这些课程会是弯路和障碍。有时会充满危机。我所学的应付这一切的秘密就是去勇于面对,正如我们面对大学课程一样。

我们能够充满激情的去生活和自我提高,这就是我们存在的意义。不断自我提高,去追求人生的更高境界,去追求更高级别的理解和自我提高。

我记得我所受到的最大的赞扬就是当我刚刚在芝加哥开始工作时,我采访了一个记者。很多年以后我们又见面了。她对我说:"你知道吗?你一点也没有变。你变得更为自我了。"

这就是我们一直努力在做的,去做我们自己。我坚信你们会从每一件做过的事上学到

经验，这样你们就会取得进步。这样你们丰富了心灵。相信我，内在的智慧比外在的财富更加珍贵。你越是使用它，你就得到更多。

今天我想和大家分享我人生的三个经验。你们难道不觉得高兴吗？你们是否会反感，当有人对你说："我想分享一些"但事实上却是10个经验。你们肯定在想："听着，这是我的毕业典礼，不是你的"。因此这里只有三个经验我想和大家分享。

这三个经验对我的人生产生了很大影响，它们是关于感情，失败和追求幸福。

当我离开大学一年后，在巴尔的摩我得到了一个共同主持6点新闻的机会。在那时媒体界的最大目标就是获得更大的市场，而巴尔的摩是一个比纳什维尔大得多的市场，因此在22岁时得到这个机会对我来说非常重要。它那时对我来说仿佛是世界上最重要的事。

我非常自豪，因为我终于有机会去效法芭芭拉·沃特斯。而她正是我从业以来一直效法的对象。那时我22岁，每年挣22,000美元。我遇到了在电视台做实习生的盖尔，我们立刻成了好朋友。我们说："我的天啊，真难以置信。你在22岁时每年能挣22,000美元。想象一下吧，当你40岁时你每年就会挣40,000美元"。

当我真的40岁时，我很高兴这并没有成真。

这就是我，22岁时每年挣22,000美元，然而，这种感觉并不好。首先，正如汉尼斯校长所说，当他们试图让我改名字。那时导演对我说："没人会记住奥普拉这个名字。因此我们想让你改名字。我们已经为你想了一个大家都会记住和喜欢的名字——苏茜。"

苏茜，一个很友善的名字。你不会厌恶苏茜。记住苏茜吧。但是我的名字不是苏茜。你们可以看到，自小我就不怎么喜欢我的名字。因为当你在午餐箱和牌号寻找你的名字时，你永远也不会找奥普拉。

我从小就不怎么喜欢我的名字，但是当我被告知去改名字时，我想，好吧，那是我的名字，但是苏茜真的适合我吗？因此我想，它并不适合我。我不会改我的名字。我也不介意人们是否记得住我的名字，这没什么大不了的。

然后他们还对我说他们不喜欢我的长相。那是在1976年，你的老板可以那么说。但是如果是现在的话，那就是一件很严重的事了。可是那时他们还是说："我不喜欢你的造型。"我根本不像芭芭拉·沃特斯。于是他们把我送到沙龙，给我烫了发。可是几天后我的头发一团糟。我不得不剃光我的头发。此时他们更不喜欢我的造型了。因为作为一个光头黑人坐在摄影机前，我肯定不漂亮的。

比光头更令我讨厌的是我不得不把播报别人遭受的痛苦作为我的日常工作。我深知我期待去观察，我的内心告诉我，我应该做些什么了。我需要为他人提供帮助。正如汉尼斯校长所说的那样，我播报了一起火灾，然后应当去给受害者拿毯子。由于白天播报的那些新闻导致我晚上难以入睡。

与此同时我尽量表现的优雅一些，使我更像芭芭拉。我认为我可能会成为一个傻傻

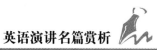

的芭芭拉。如果我做回我自己,我就会成为一个很棒的奥普拉。我努力像芭芭拉那样优雅。有时我并不读我的稿件,因为我的内心告诉我这是不自主的。所以我想为大家播报一些我想要的新闻。有时,我不会播报像6个人在连环车祸中受伤这类的新闻。哦,我的天啊。

有时出于内心的本能,我不会去播报一些新闻。我还会遇到一些不认识的和念错的词。一天当我播新闻时,我把加拿大读错了。我想这样下去学芭芭拉可不大好。我应该做回我自己。

但那时我爸爸却对我说:"这是你一生的机会。你最好继续那份工作。"我的老板也说:"这是晚间新闻。你是播报员,不是福利工作者。还是做你的本职工作吧。"

我歪曲了这些期待和义务,并感觉很糟。晚上回到家后我会记日记。自从15岁时我就开始记日记了,于是现在我已经有了好几卷日记。我晚上回到家后,我会记录下我是多么的不幸和沮丧。然后我消除了焦虑。这就是我如何养成了那个习惯。

8个月后我失去了那份工作。他们说我太情绪化了。但因为他们不想违背合约,他们就让我去巴尔的摩主持一档脱口秀节目。从我开始主持那档节目的一刻起,我感觉好像回到了家一样。我意识到电视不应该仅仅是一个娱乐场,更应该是一个以服务为目的的平台,以帮助他人更好的生活。当我开始主持节目的时候,就像呼吸一样。感觉好极啦。这就是我工作的真正开始。

这就是我学到的经验。当你做的是一份你喜欢的工作时,那感觉棒极了。无论你能挣到多少钱,你都会有很大收获。

这是真的。但是你怎么知道你所做的是对的呢?你怎么知道呢?我所知道的就是你的内心是你人生的导航系统。当你应该或者不应该做某事时,你的内心会告诉你怎样去做。关键是去面对你自己,面对你自己的内心。我所做过的所有正确选择都是源自我内心的。我所做过的所有错误选择都是因为没有听取来自我内心的声音。

如果感觉不好,就不要去做。这就是我的经验。我的朋友,这个经验会帮你避免很多痛苦。甚至怀疑都意味着不要去做。这就是我所学到的。有很多次当你不知道如何去做时,什么也不要做,直到你知道怎么做为止。

当你什么也不要做时,让你的内心作为驱动力。不仅仅你的个人生活会提高,你在工作中也会获得竞争力。正如丹尼尔·平克在他的畅销书《全新思维》中所说的那样,我们进入了一个新时代,一个他称之为概念时代的时代。人们的内心使人与人之间产生隔阂。他说,重要的不仅仅是逻辑上的,线性的,直尺式的思维方式。移情,快乐,目标和内部特质同样也有卓越的价值。

当我们做自己喜欢的事时,当我们全身心地投入到工作中时,这些特质就会焕发生机。

因此我对你说,忘掉那些快车道吧。如果你真的想飞翔,就把你的力量投入到你的激情当中。尊重你内心的召唤。每一个人都会有的。相信你的心灵，你会成功的。那么我是如何定义成功的呢？让我告诉你，钱很美好。我不会告诉你们成功与钱无关，因为钱是好东西。我喜欢钱。它能买东西。

但是拥有很多钱并不能使你自然而然的成为一个成功者。你想要的是钱和意义。你想你的工作更有意义。因为有意义使你的生活更加充实。你所希望得到的是被信任你珍视你的人包围。这才是你真正富有的时候。因此，第一个经验，跟随你的心灵。如果感觉对了，就继续前进。如果感觉不对，就不要做了。

现在我想谈谈失败。没有人的一生是一帆风顺的。我们都会遇到困难，受到挫折。如果事情出错了，你进入了死胡同，这正是生活在告诉你是时候改变了。所以，每当遇到困难和危机时，我都会问它教会了我什么？只要你吸取了教训，你就会继续前进。如果你真正吸取了教训，你就会顺利通过考验，不用再去经受失败了。如果你没有吸取教训，它会以另外一种形式出现在你面前并给你一些补救。

我注意到当你没有仔细对待生活的细节时，困难就会出现。因为生活总是提前低声的告诫你。如果你忽视了这个低声的告诫，过不了多久你就会得到一个惊声尖叫，无论你怎样反抗。但是如果你不去想为什么困难会发生，而是去反思困难会教给我什么时，你就会学到你需要的东西。

我的朋友艾克哈特·托尔。他写了一本非常棒的书，名叫的《新世界》。这本书就是关于让你的意识激励你去做事。他说，不要去反抗困境，相反，要融入到其中。事情会变的越来越好的。因为暂时的屈服并不意味着放弃，它意味着一种责任感。

你们当中很多人都知道，正如汉尼斯校长所说，我在非洲创办了一个学校。我希望给南非的女孩们一个像你们一样的未来。我花了5年时间来确保学校会像学生们一样好。我想让每一个女孩感觉到自己的价值受到重视。所以我检查了每一个设计图，亲自挑选每个枕头，甚至检查砖块间的水泥。我知道每一个细节。每一学生都是我从9个省的村落里亲自选出来的。然而，去年的秋天我却遇到了一个我从未预料的危机。我被告知有一名宿舍管理员涉嫌性虐待。

你们可以想象得到这是多么令人沮丧的消息啊。首先，我哭了，啜泣了大约半个小时。然后我说，我们得面对它。一个半小时，这就是你全部所能得到的。你需要把注意力集中到现在，现在你应该做些什么。所以我联系了一位儿科创伤专家。我派了一队调查人员。我确定女孩们得到了安慰和支持。盖尔和我坐上飞机飞向南非。

整个过程中我都在问自己："这件事教会了我什么？"虽然这个经历十分困难，但是我学到了很多。我意识到自己所犯的错误，因为我一直以来都把注意力集中在错事上。我从外向内建造了那所学校，然而真正对我有意义的是从内向外的去建造它。最重要的是我对正直，品质和美好的理解。我学到了那个教训。我也明白女孩们也学到了一些事。她们从中恢复了过来并意识到她们的声音是有影响力的。

她们的恢复力和精神给了我很多东西，以至于比我给她们的还多。接下来是我最后的经验——关于寻找幸福，我可以谈论一整天，但是我知道你们有其他古怪的事要做。

　　追求幸福并不是一个小话题。但在某种程度上来说它又是最简单的话题。格温多林·布鲁克斯为她的孩子写了一首诗，诗名是《对年轻人和未来进步的演讲》。在诗的最后她说道，不要为了战胜而生活，不要为了歌曲的结尾而生活，要享受生活。她说，你应当为了现在而生活，无论过去发生了什么都不应该影响到现在，因为生活就是过好现在。

　　我想她还说过，去参与一些事。不要仅仅为了自己而生活。我可以非常肯定的是为了追求真正的快乐，你必须为了一些更有意义的事而生活。生活是互动的。为了前进，你必须后退。对于我而言，这是人生中最重要的经验。想要获得快乐你必须付出。

　　我知道你们已经很了解了，因为这个经验已经深深的融入了斯坦福。这个经验是简和勒兰德传承给你们的。因为你们所有的人都知道这座伟大的大学是如何建成的。斯坦福夫妇的独子在15岁时得了伤寒离开了他们。他们有权利和理由去恨这个世界，但是他们却用优雅的行动疏导了心中的悲伤。在他们儿子死后不到一年内，他们已经为这所伟大的大学筹集了建设经费，并发誓要为别人的孩子做一些他们自己的孩子不能得到的事。

　　这个经验非常明显，那就是，如果你受了伤，你需要帮助他人减轻伤痛。如果你感到痛苦，帮助他人减轻痛苦。如果你的生活一团糟，去帮助其他处在困难中的人摆脱困境。这样一来，你就变成了妇女联谊会或是互助会中最伟大的一员。

　　斯坦福夫妇遭受了世上父母所能遭受的最大痛苦，然而他们懂得通过帮助他人来帮助自己。这种智慧渐渐地被科学和社会学研究所证实。这不仅仅是某种软技能的谈话。这事实上是在帮助者的高度，一种从帮助别人而获得的精神大爆发。所以如果你想快乐，去帮助别人吧。

　　但是当你做好事时，我希望你不仅仅是为了获得的快乐，因为我深知做好事可以让你变得更棒。所以无论你怎样选择，若你能以服务他人为榜样，我相信你的生活会更有价值，你也会更快乐。

　　我也很高兴做我的脱口秀节目，那种快乐是一种更深层次的成就感，我很难去表达和衡量。我决定以电视作为我的职业，我要用电视这个平台来为我的观众服务，而不是让电视利用我。这改变了我成功的轨迹。

　　我知道无论你是否是一名演员，你都应该把你的才智贡献给能够鼓舞他人的事业。如果你是一名剖析家，你应当把你们的智慧投入到医治他人当中。无论你是否被召唤，你们中的很多人在经济、法律、人权、科学、医药方面都获得了诸如博士一类的学位，如果你们决定把你们的技能和智慧奉献给服务他人，选择把服务他人作为榜样，你们的工作就会变成一种天赋。我知道你们在斯坦福所在的一切就是为了出去找一份工作。

你们在很多方面都得到了提高。没有其他更好的方式能够让你给这个世界留下印记并且分享你的丰富的才智。我永恒的祈祷就是让自己能够为他人提供更好的服务。

就让我引用马丁·路德·金的话来作为结束语吧。他说:"不是所有人都会出名。"我不知道,但似乎今天所有人都想出名。

但是成名也是一种代价。有些人会尾随你到卫生间,听你尿尿。你会尽量尿的轻一些。这没什么大不了的。他们会对你说:"我的天啊,是你!你尿尿啦。"

这就是成名的代价,我不知道你们是否喜欢。

所以,正如马丁·路德金所说,"不是所有人都会成名。但每个人都可以变的伟大,因为伟大是通过为他人服务而界定的。"你们当中学历史的人可能会知道他接下来的话,"为别人提供服务,并不一定要有大学学历,并不一定要主谓一致,并不一定要认识柏拉图和亚里士多德,并不一定要会爱因斯坦的相对论,并不一定要了解热力学第二定律。你所需要的是一颗优雅的心灵和充满爱的灵魂。"

不久你们就会正式成为斯坦福大学2008年的毕业生了。

你们有聪明才智。你们将会决定如何利用它。说真的,你们将会如何利用它呢?你们拿到了学位。走向社会吧,我坚信伟大的事将会发生的。

你们知道,我一直坚信,如果你和他人分享,那么事情就会变得更好。所以在我离开之前,我想和大家分享一下毕业礼物。在你们的座位底下,你们会发现两本我最喜欢的书。艾克哈特·托尔的《新世界》流行书俱乐部的精选品。我们的《新世界》广播已经被下载3亿次。丹尼尔·平克的《全新思维:为什么会正确思维的人将统治未来:》使我确定我在人生的正轨上。

我真的想送大家轿车,只是开不过来!祝贺大家!08年的毕业生们!

Lesson 5

The Fringe Benefits of Failure and the Importance of Imagination

Task 1 Questions and Answers

Directions: *Work in pairs. Read the following speech then take turns to ask and answer the following questions.*

1. When was the speech delivered? Where?
2. Who delivered the speech? Who are involved in the speech?

3. What is the theme of the speech?
4. Why is there a need for the request?
5. How can the request be achieved?

Task 2 Dictation

Directions: *Watch the authentic video of the speech. Then fill in the missing words in their appropriate forms. You may watch the video for three times.*

If you choose to use your status and influence to raise your voice on _____ of those who have no voice; if you choose to _____ not only with the powerful, but with the powerless; if you_____ the ability to _____ yourself into the lives of those who do not have your advantages, then it will not only be your proud families who celebrate your _____, but thousands and millions of people whose reality you have helped _____ for the better. We do not need _____ to transform the world, we carry all the power we need inside ourselves already: we have the power to imagine better.

Task 3 Imitation and Play

Directions: *Watch the authentic video of the speech. Then try to imitate one or two paragraphs you like with appropriate delivery techniques. First practice by yourself. Then work in groups of four to take turns to deliver the speech.*

Task 4 Discussion

Directions: *Work in groups of four and discuss the following questions. You may locate some useful information from the script.*

1. What do you know about J. K. Rowling? What contribute to the success of Harry Porter?
2. Do you agree to the statement that "You might be driven by a fear of failure quite as much as a desire for success. (Line 2, Paragraph 17)"? Why or why not?
3. What are the benefits of failure, according to J. K. Rowling?
4. Is imagination a necessity for a writer?
5. Can you use specific details or examples to share your understanding of the statement that "As is a tale, so is life: not how long it is, but how good it is, is what matters"?

Task 5 Writing

Directions: *Write a speech for about 300 words on the topic of **If I Were Harry Porter**.*

The Fringe Benefits of Failure and the Importance of Imagination
失败的附带益处与想象的重要性

Harvard University Commencement Address
By J.K. Rowling

🔴 人物简介

乔安妮·凯瑟琳·罗琳（Joanne Kathleen Rowling，笔名J.K. Rowling：1966年7月31日— ），生于英国的格温特郡的普通医院，毕业于英国埃克塞特大学（University Of Exeter），学习法语和古典文学，获文理学士学位，其著有作品集《哈利·波特》系列。生为单身母亲，罗琳早期的创作生活极其艰辛。她的第一本书《哈利·波特与魔法石》前后共写了5年，她时常到住家附近的一家咖啡馆里，伴着咖啡馆的氛围和女儿吵闹声中创作她的哈利波特，而作品出版之后，哈利·波特迅速成为风靡全球的童话人物，《哈利·波特》系列创作系列小说一共有七部，被译成70多种语言，在200多个国家销售。而罗琳的生活也随这作品的成名发生了翻天覆地的变化。罗琳的座右铭是："你必须要自己做得更好。人通常是和自己的以前比较，而我则是和未来比较。"

🔴 名篇导读

42岁的罗琳回首自己的大学时光，那时的她在内心的追求与亲人的要求之间进行抗争。父母希望她能摆脱贫穷带来的恐惧、压力和沮丧以及随之带来的心胸狭窄，卑微低下和艰难困苦。而罗琳在毕业之后的7年经历了一次巨大的失败，婚姻和工作双双失利带给她沉重的压力和恐惧，从中她学到了比宝石还要珍贵的东西——沉着、从容的人生态度，并在失败堆积成的硬石般的基础上，开始重铸她的人生。

罗琳在她的演说中提到了两个主题的选择，第一个主题是关于失败的。她谈到："失败给了我内心的安宁，这种安宁是不会从一帆风顺的经历中得到的。失败让我认识自己，这些无法从其他地方学到。我发现自己有坚强的意志，而且，自我控制能力比自己想象的还要强，我也发现自己拥有比红宝石更珍贵的朋友。"第二个主题是想象力，她强调，想象力不仅仅是人类设想还不存在的事物这种独特的能力，为所有发明和创新提供源泉，它还是人类改造和揭露现实的能力，使我们同情自己不曾经受的他人苦难。

本篇演讲稿中，罗琳对她所走过的人生有着深刻的理解，从经历失败到重铸自己，她向哈佛学子传达对生活的诠释：生活就像故事，不在乎长短，而在于质量，这才是最重要的。

英文原文

President Faust, members of the Harvard Corporation and the Board of Overseers, members of the faculty, proud parents, and, above all, graduates,

The first thing I would like to say is "thank you". Not only has Harvard given me an extraordinary honour, but the weeks of fear and **nausea**[1] I have endured at the thought of giving this commencement address have made me lose weight. A win-win situation! Now all I have to do is take deep breaths, **squint**[2] at the red banners and convince myself that I am at the world's largest *Gryffindor reunion*.

Delivering a commencement address is a great responsibility; or so I thought until I cast my mind back to my own graduation. The commencement speaker that day was the distinguished British philosopher *Baroness Mary Warnock*. Reflecting on her speech has helped me enormously in writing this one, because it turns out that I can't remember a single word she said. This liberating discovery enables me to proceed without any fear that I might **inadvertently**[3] influence you to abandon promising careers in business, the law or politics for the **giddy**[4] delights of becoming a gay wizard.

You see? If all you remember in years to come is the gay "wizard" joke, I've come out ahead of Baroness Mary Warnock. Achievable goals: the first step to self-improvement.

Actually, I have **wracked**[5] my mind and heart for what I ought to say to you today. I have asked myself what I wish I had known at my own graduation, and what important lessons I have learned in the 21 years that have expired between that day and this.

I have come up with two answers. On this wonderful day when we are gathered together to celebrate your academic success, I have decided to talk to you about the benefits of failure. And

---

1 nausea 恶心，反胃
2 squint 眯眼
3 inadvertently 不注意，疏忽地
4 giddy 头晕的
5 wrack 破坏

as you stand on the threshold of what is sometimes called "real life", I want to **extol**[1] the crucial importance of imagination.

These may seem **quixotic**[2] or paradoxical choices, but please bear with me.

Looking back at the 21-year-old that I was at graduation is a slightly uncomfortable experience for the 42-year-old that she has become. Half my lifetime ago, I was striking an uneasy balance between the ambition I had for myself, and what those closest to me expected of me.

I was convinced that the only thing I wanted to do, ever, was to write novels. However, my parents, both of whom came from **impoverished**[3] backgrounds and neither of whom had been to college, took the view that my overactive imagination was an amusing personal **quirk**[4] that would never pay a mortgage, or secure a pension.

I know that the irony strikes with the force of a cartoon **anvil**[5] now, but…

So they hoped that I would take a vocational degree; I wanted to study English Literature. A compromise was reached that in **retrospect**[6] satisfied nobody, and I went up to study Modern Languages. Hardly had my parents' car rounded the corner at the end of the road than I **ditched**[7] German and **scuttled**[8] off down the Classics corridor.

I cannot remember telling my parents that I was studying Classics; they might well have found out for the first time on graduation day. Of all the subjects on this planet, I think they would have been hard put to name one less useful than Greek **mythology**[9] when it came to securing the keys to an executive bathroom.

I would like to make it clear, in **parenthesis**[10], that I do not blame my parents for their point of view. There is an expiry date on blaming your parents for **steering**[11] you in the wrong direction; the moment you are old enough to take the wheel, responsibility lies with you. What is more, I cannot criticise my parents for hoping that I would never experience poverty. They had been poor themselves, and I have since been poor, and I quite agree with them that it is not an **ennobling**[12] experience. Poverty **entails**[13] fear, and stress, and sometimes depression; it means a thousand petty **humiliations**[14] and hardships. Climbing out of poverty by your own efforts, that is indeed something on which to pride yourself, but poverty itself is **romanticized**[15] only by fools.

---

1 extol 称赞
2 quixotic 狂想家的
3 impoverished 贫乏，枯燥
4 quirk 怪癖
5 anvil 铁钻
6 retrospect 回顾
7 ditch 丢弃
8 scuttle 奔跑
9 mythology 神话
10 parenthesis 附带
11 steering 掌舵，指导
12 ennoble 授予爵位
13 entail 牵涉；需要；使必要
14 humiliation 耻辱；丢脸
15 romanticize 使浪漫化

What I feared most for myself at your age was not poverty, but failure.

At your age, in spite of a distinct lack of motivation at university, where I had spent far too long in the coffee bar writing stories, and far too little time at lectures, I had a **knack**[1] for passing examinations, and that, for years, had been the measure of success in my life and that of my peers.

I am not dull enough to suppose that because you are young, gifted and well-educated; you have never known hardship or heartbreak. Talent and intelligence never yet **inoculated**[2] anyone against the **caprice**[3] of the Fates, and I do not for a moment suppose that everyone here has enjoyed an existence of **unruffled**[4] privilege and contentment.

However, the fact that you are graduating from Harvard suggests that you are not very well-acquainted with failure. <u>You might be driven by a fear of failure quite as much as a desire for success</u>. Indeed, your conception of failure might not be too far from the average person's idea of success, so high have you already flown academically.

Ultimately, we all have to decide for ourselves what constitutes failure, but the world is quite eager to give you a set of criteria if you let it. So I think it fair to say that by any conventional measure, a mere seven years after my graduation day, I had failed on an **epic**[5] scale. An exceptionally short-lived marriage had **imploded**[6], and I was jobless, a lone parent, and as poor as it is possible to be in modern Britain, without being homeless. The fears that my parents had had for me, and that I had had for myself, had both come to pass, and by every usual standard, I was the biggest failure I knew.

Now, I am not going to stand here and tell you that failure is fun. That period of my life was a dark one, and I had no idea that there was going to be what the press has since represented as a kind of fairy tale **resolution**[7]. I had no idea then how far the tunnel extended, and for a long time, any light at the end of it was a hope rather than a reality.

So why do I talk about the benefits of failure? Simply because failure meant a stripping away of the **inessential**[8]. I stopped pretending to myself that I was anything other than what I was, and began to direct all my energy into finishing the only work that mattered to me. Had I really succeeded at anything else, I might never have found the determination to succeed in the one **arena**[9] I believed I truly belonged. I was set free, because my greatest fear had been realized, and I was still alive, and I still had a daughter whom I adored, and I had an old typewriter and a big idea. And so bottom became the solid foundation on which I rebuilt my life.

You might never fail on the scale I did, but some failure in life is inevitable. It is impossible

---

1 knack 技巧
2 inoculate 灌输
3 caprice 反复无常
4 unruffled 平静的
5 epic 史诗的
6 implode 内爆
7 resolution 决心
8 inessential 无关紧要的
9 arena 表演场地，舞台；竞技场

to live without failing at something, unless you live so cautiously that you might as well not have lived at all—in which case, you fail by default.

Failure gave me an inner security that I had never attained by passing examinations. Failure taught me things about myself that I could have learned no other way. I discovered that I had a strong will, and more discipline than I had suspected; I also found out that I had friends whose value was truly above the price of **rubies**[1].

The knowledge that you have emerged wiser and stronger from setbacks means that you are, ever after, secure in your ability to survive. You will never truly know yourself, or the strength of your relationships, until both have been tested by adversity. Such knowledge is a true gift, for all that it is painfully won, and it has been worth more to me than any qualification I ever earned.

So given a Time Turner, I would tell my 21-year-old self that personal happiness lies in knowing that life is not a check-list of acquisition or achievement. Your qualifications, your **CV**[2], are not your life, though you will meet many people of my age and older who confuse the two. Life is difficult, and complicated, and beyond anyone's total control, and the humility to know that will enable you to survive its **vicissitudes**[3].

Now you might think that I chose my second theme, the importance of imagination, because of the part it played in rebuilding my life, but that is not wholly so. Though I personally will defend the value of bedtime stories to my last **gasp**[4], I have learned to value imagination in a much broader sense. Imagination is not only the uniquely human capacity to envision that which is not, and therefore the **fount**[5] of all invention and innovation. In its arguably most **transformative**[6] and **revelatory**[7] capacity, it is the power that enables us to **empathise**[8] with humans whose experiences we have never shared.

One of the greatest formative experiences of my life preceded Harry Potter, though it informed much of what I subsequently wrote in those books. This revelation came in the form of one of my earliest day jobs. Though I was **sloping off**[9] to write stories during my lunch hours, I paid the rent in my early 20s by working at the African research department at Amnesty International's headquarters in London.

There in my little office I read hastily **scribbled**[10] letters smuggled out of **totalitarian**[11] regimes by men and women who were risking imprisonment to inform the outside world of what was happening to them. I saw photographs of those who had disappeared without trace, sent to

---

1 rubies 红宝石
2 CV 个人简历
3 vicissitudes 盛衰变迁
4 gasp 喘气
5 fount 源泉
6 transformative 有改革能力的
7 revelatory 启示性的
8 empathise 移情，共鸣
9 slope off 溜走
10 scribble 潦草地书写
11 totalitarian 极权主义者

Amnesty by their desperate families and friends. I read the testimony of **torture**[1] victims and saw pictures of their injuries. I opened handwritten, **eye-witness**[2] accounts of summary trials and executions, of kidnappings and rapes.

Many of my co-workers were ex-political prisoners, people who had been displaced from their homes, or fled into exile, because they had the **temerity**[3] to speak against their governments. Visitors to our offices included those who had come to give information, or to try and find out what had happened to those they had left behind.

I shall never forget the African torture victim, a young man no older than I was at the time, who had become mentally ill after all he had endured in his homeland. He trembled uncontrollably as he spoke into a video camera about the brutality inflicted upon him. He was a foot taller than I was, and seemed as fragile as a child. I was given the job of **escorting**[4] him back to the Underground Station afterwards, and this man whose life had been shattered by cruelty took my hand with **exquisite**[5] courtesy, and wished me future happiness.

And as long as I live I shall remember walking along an empty corridor and suddenly hearing, from behind a closed door, a scream of pain and horror such as I have never heard since. The door opened, and the researcher poked out her head and told me to run and make a hot drink for the young man sitting with her. She had just had to give him the news that in **retaliation**[6] for his own **outspokenness**[7] against his country's regime, his mother had been seized and executed.

Every day of my working week in my early 20s I was reminded how incredibly fortunate I was, to live in a country with a democratically elected government, where legal representation and a public trial were the rights of everyone.

Every day, I saw more evidence about the evils humankind will inflict on their fellow humans, to gain or maintain power. I began to have nightmares, literal nightmares, about some of the things I saw, heard and read.

And yet I also learned more about human goodness at Amnesty International than I had ever known before.

Amnesty mobilizes thousands of people who have never been tortured or imprisoned for their beliefs to act on behalf of those who have. The power of human empathy, leading to collective action, saves lives, and frees prisoners. Ordinary people, whose personal well-being and security are assured, join together in huge numbers to save people they do not know, and will never meet. My small participation in that process was one of the most humbling and inspiring experiences of my life.

Unlike any other creature on this planet, humans can learn and understand, without having

---

1 torture 拷问
2 eye-witness 目击证人
3 temerity 鲁莽
4 escort 护送
5 exquisite 精挑细选
6 retaliation 报复，反击
7 outspokenness 直言无讳

experienced. They can think themselves into other people's minds, imagine themselves into other people's places.

Of course, this is a power, like my brand of fictional magic, that is morally neutral. One might use such an ability to **manipulate**[1], or control, just as much as to understand or sympathise.

And many prefer not to exercise their imaginations at all. They choose to remain comfortably within the bounds of their own experience, never troubling to wonder how it would feel to have been born other than they are. They can refuse to hear screams or to peer inside cages; they can close their minds and hearts to any suffering that does not touch them personally; they can refuse to know.

I might be tempted to envy people who can live that way, except that I do not think they have any fewer nightmares than I do. Choosing to live in narrow spaces leads to a form of mental **agoraphobia**[2], and that brings its own terrors. I think the **willfully**[3] unimaginative see more monsters. They are often more afraid.

What is more, those who choose not to empathise enable real monsters. For without ever committing an act of **outright**[4] evil ourselves, we **collude**[5] with it, through our own **apathy**[6].

One of the many things I learned at the end of that Classics corridor down which I **ventured**[7] at the age of 18, in search of something I could not then define, was this, written by the Greek author Plutarch: What we achieve **inwardly**[8] will change outer reality.

That is an astonishing statement and yet proven a thousand times every day of our lives. It expresses, in part, our inescapable connection with the outside world, the fact that we touch other people's lives simply by existing.

But how much more are you, Harvard graduates of 2008, likely to touch other people's lives? Your intelligence, your capacity for hard work, the education you have earned and received, give you unique status, and unique responsibilities. Even your nationality sets you apart. The great majority of you belong to the world's only remaining superpower. The way you vote, the way you live, the way you protest, the pressure you bring to bear on your government, has an impact way beyond your borders. That is your privilege, and your burden.

If you choose to use your status and influence to raise your voice on behalf of those who have no voice; if you choose to identify not only with the powerful, but with the powerless; if you retain the ability to imagine yourself into the lives of those who do not have your advantages, then it will not only be your proud families who celebrate your existence, but thousands and millions of people whose reality you have helped transform for the better. We do not need magic

---

1 manipulate 操控
2 agoraphobia 陌生环境恐怖症
3 willfully 任性固执地
4 outright 率直地
5 collude 共谋
6 apathy 冷漠
7 venture 敢于去做
8 inwardly 内心的

英语演讲名篇赏析
Appreciation of Masterpiece English Speeches

to transform the world, we carry all the power we need inside ourselves already: we have the power to imagine better.

I am nearly finished. I have one last hope for you, which is something that I already had at 21. The friends with whom I sat on graduation day have been my friends for life. They are my children's **godparents**[1], the people to whom I've been able to turn in times of few trouble, people who have been kind enough not to sue me when I took their names for Death Eaters. At our graduation we were bound by enormous affection, by our shared experience of a time that could never come again, and, of course, by the knowledge that we held certain photographic evidence that would be exceptionally valuable if any of us ran for Prime Minister.

So today, I wish you nothing better than similar friendships. And tomorrow, I hope that even if you remember not a single word of mine, you remember those of Seneca, another of those old Romans I met when I fled down the Classics corridor, in retreat from career ladders, in search of ancient wisdom:

<u>As is a tale, so is life: not how long it is, but how good it is, is what matters.</u>
Thank you very much.
I wish you all very good lives.

文化快递

1. Gryffindor（格莱芬多）
《哈利·波特》魔法学校霍格沃茨的一个学院，是哈利、罗恩、赫敏所在的学院。

2. Seneca（塞内加）
古罗马悲剧家（约公元前4—公元65年）生于罗马帝国行省西班牙，早年到罗马受过很好的修辞学训练，擅长演说，对哲学、宗教、伦理道德和自然科学都有研究和著作，是古罗马斯多葛派的代表人物之一。他提倡简朴的生活和内心的宁静，鄙弃财富，却从尼禄那里获得大量钱财，使他成为罗马帝国一大富豪。

3. Amnesty International（大赦国际）
大赦国际，于1961年5月28日在伦敦成立。其宗旨是"动员公众舆论，促使国际机构保障人权宣言中提出的言论和宗教自由"；"致力于为释放由于信仰而被监禁的人以及给他们的家庭发放救济"等方面的工作。其活动是"为良心犯寻求释放，即那些在各地因个人的信仰、肤色、性别、种族、语言和宗教在没有使用或鼓吹暴力的情况下而被拘禁的人；为所有政治犯争取公平迅速的审判，并为那些被指控有罪或审判而被拘禁的人代言；反对对任何囚犯实施死刑和酷刑，或其他残忍、不人道或侮辱性的待遇或惩罚。"每年召开一次理事会会议。其资金来源于个人捐款、会费和当地筹款。大赦国际组织在全球150个国家和地区拥有110万名以上的会员，有80多个国家的4349个地区性

---
1 godparents 教父母

组织会员及54个国家会员。该组织在纪念《世界人权宣言》30周年时获联合国人权奖，1977年获诺贝尔和平奖。

4. Baroness Mary Warnock（玛丽·沃洛克）

男爵夫人玛丽·沃洛克（Mary Warnock）出生于1924年4月14日，是英国著名的哲学家、教育家、心理学家和存在主义者，玛丽·沃洛克的实现目标为：启迪你们迈出了个人改善的第一步。其著作为《20世纪之伦理》。

5. Death Eaters（食死徒）

《哈里·波特》中的人物角色，伏地魔的追随者。

▶ 参考译文

福斯特主席，哈佛公司和监察委员会的各位成员，各位老师、家长、全体毕业生们：

首先请允许我说一声谢谢。哈佛不仅给了我无上的荣誉，连日来为这个演讲经受的恐惧和紧张，更令我减肥成功。这真是一个双赢的局面。现在我要做的就是深呼吸几下，眯着眼睛看看前面的大红横幅，安慰自己正在世界上最大的魔法学院聚会上。

发表毕业演说是一个巨大的责任，至少在我回忆自己当年的毕业典礼前是这么认为的。那天做演讲的是英国著名的哲学家巴瑞尼斯·玛丽·沃纳克，对她演讲的回忆，对我写今天的演讲稿，产生了极大的帮助，因为我不记得她说过的任何一句话了。这个发现让我释然，让我不再担心我可能会无意中影响你放弃在商业，法律或政治上的大好前途，转而醉心于成为一个快乐的魔法师。

你们看，如果在若干年后你们还记得"快乐的魔法师"这个笑话，那就证明我已经超越了巴瑞尼斯·玛丽·沃纳克。建立可实现的目标——这是提高自我的第一步。

实际上，我为今天应该和大家谈些什么绞尽了脑汁。我问自己什么是我希望早在毕业典礼上就该了解的，而从那时起到现在的21年间，我又得到了什么重要的启示。

我想到了两个答案。在这美好的一天，当我们一起庆祝你们取得学业成就的时刻，我希望告诉你们失败有什么样的益处；在你们即将迈向"现实生活"的道路之际，我还要褒扬想象力的重要性。

这些似乎是不切实际或自相矛盾的选择，但请先容我讲完。

回顾21岁刚刚毕业时的自己，对于今天42岁的我来说，是一个稍微不太舒服的经历。可以说，我人生的前一部分，一直挣扎在自己的雄心和身边的人对我的期望之间。

我一直深信，自己唯一想做的事情，就是写小说。不过，我的父母，他们都来自贫穷的背景，没有任何一人上过大学，坚持认为我过度的想象力是一个令人惊讶的个人怪癖，根本不足以让我支付按揭，或者取得足够的养老金。

我现在明白反讽就像用卡通铁砧去打击你，但……

他们希望我去拿个职业学位，而我想去攻读英国文学。最后，达成了一个双方都不甚

满意的妥协：我改学现代语言。可是等到父母一走开，我立刻放弃了德语而报名学习古典文学。

我不记得将这事告诉了父母，他们可能是在我毕业典礼那一天才发现的。我想，在全世界的所有专业中，他们也许认为，不会有比研究希腊神话更没用的专业了，根本无法换来一间独立宽敞的卫生间。

我想澄清一下：我不会因为父母的观点，而责怪他们。埋怨父母给你指错方向是有一个时间段的。当你成长到可以控制自我方向的时候，你就要自己承担责任了。尤其是，我不会因为父母希望我不要过穷日子，而责怪他们。他们一直很贫穷，我后来也一度很穷，所以我很理解他们。贫穷并不是一种高贵的经历，它带来恐惧、压力、有时还有绝望，它意味着许许多多的羞辱和艰辛。靠自己的努力摆脱贫穷，确实可以引以为豪，但贫穷本身只有对傻瓜而言才是浪漫的。

我在你们这个年龄，最害怕的不是贫穷，而是失败。

我在你们这么大时，明显缺乏在大学学习的动力，我花了太久时间在咖啡吧写故事，而在课堂的时间却很少。我有一个通过考试的诀窍，并且数年间一直让我在大学生活和同龄人中不落人后。

我不想愚蠢地假设，因为你们年轻、有天分，并且受过良好的教育，就从来没有遇到困难或心碎的时刻。拥有才华和智慧，从来不会使人对命运的反复无常有所准备；我也不会假设大家坐在这里冷静地满足于自身的优越感。

相反，你们是哈佛毕业生的这个事实，意味着你们并不很了解失败。你们也许极其渴望成功，所以非常害怕失败。说实话，你们眼中的失败，很可能就是普通人眼中的成功，毕竟你们在学业上已经达到很高的高度了。

最终，我们所有人都必须自己决定什么算作失败，但如果你愿意，世界是相当渴望给你一套标准的。所以我承认命运的公平，从任何传统的标准看，在我毕业仅仅七年后的日子里，我的失败达到了史诗般空前的规模：短命的婚姻闪电般地破裂，我又失业成了一个艰难的单身母亲。除了流浪汉，我是当代英国最穷的人之一，真的一无所有。当年父母和我自己对未来的担忧，现在都变成了现实。按照惯常的标准来看，我也是我所知道的最失败的人。

现在，我不打算站在这里告诉你们，失败是有趣的。那段日子是我生命中的黑暗岁月，我不知道它是否代表童话故事里需要历经的磨难，更不知道自己还要在黑暗中走多久。很长一段时间里，前面留给我的只是希望，而不是现实。

那么为什么我要谈论失败的好处呢？因为失败意味着剥离掉那些不必要的东西。我因此不再伪装自己、远离自我，而重新开始把所有精力放在对我最重要的事情上。如果不是没有在其他领域成功过，我可能就不会找到，在一个我确信真正属于我的舞台上取得成功的决心。我获得了自由，因为最害怕的虽然已经发生了，但我还活着，我仍然有一个我深爱的女儿，我还有一个旧打字机和一个很大的想法。所以困境的谷底，成为我重建生活的坚实基础。

　　你们可能永远没有达到我经历的那种失败程度，但有些失败，在生活中是不可避免的。生活不可能没有一点失败，除非你生活的万般小心，而那也意味着你没有真正在生活了。无论怎样，有些失败还是注定地要发生。

　　失败使我的内心产生一种安全感，这是我从考试中没有得到过的。失败让我看清自己，这也是我通过其他方式无法学会的。我发现，我比自己认为的要有更强的意志和决心。我还发现，我拥有比宝石更加珍贵的朋友。

　　从挫折中获得智慧、变得坚强，意味着你比以往任何时候都更有能力生存。只有在逆境来临的时候，你才会真正认识你自己，了解身边的人。这种了解是真正的财富，虽然是用痛苦换来的，但比我以前得到的任何资格证书都有用。

　　如果给我一部时间机器，我会告诉21岁的自己，人的幸福在于知道生活不是一份漂亮的成绩单，你的资历、简历，都不是你的生活，虽然你会碰到很多与我同龄或更老一点的人今天依然还在混淆两者。生活是艰辛的，复杂的，超出任何人的控制能力，而谦恭地了解这一点，将使你历经沧桑后能够更好的生存。

　　对于第二个主题的选择——想象力的重要性——你们可能会认为是因为它对我重建生活起到了帮助，但事实并非完全如此。虽然我愿誓死捍卫睡前要给孩子讲故事的价值观，我对想象力的理解已经有了更广泛的含义。想象力不仅仅是人类设想还不存在的事物这种独特的能力，为所有发明和创新提供源泉，它还是人类改造和揭露现实的能力，使我们同情自己不曾经受的他人苦难。

　　其中一个影响最大的经历发生在我写哈利波特之前，为我随后写书提供了很多想法。这些想法成形于我早期的工作经历，在20多岁时，尽管我可以在午餐时间里悄悄写故事，可为了付房租，我做的主要工作是在伦敦总部的大赦国际研究部门。

　　在我的小办公室，我看到了人们匆匆写的信件，它们是从极权主义政权被偷送出来的。那些人冒着被监禁的危险，告知外面的世界他们那里正在发生的事情。我看到了那些无迹可寻的人的照片，它们是被那些绝望的家人和朋友送来的。我看过拷问受害者的证词和被害的照片。我打开过手写的目击证词，描述绑架和强奸犯的审判和处决。

　　我有很多的同事是前政治犯，他们已离开家园流离失所，或逃亡流放，因为他们敢于怀疑政府、独立思考。来我们办公室的访客，包括那些前来提供信息，或想设法知道那些被迫留下的同志发生了什么事的人。

　　我将永远不会忘记一个非洲酷刑的受害者，一名当时还没有我大的年轻男子，他因在故乡的经历而精神错乱。在摄像机前讲述被残暴地摧残的时候，他颤抖失控。他比我高一英尺，却看上去像一个脆弱的儿童。我被安排随后护送他到地铁站，这名生活已被残酷地打乱的男子，小心翼翼地握着我的手，祝我未来生活幸福。

只要我活着,我还会记得,在一个空荡荡的的走廊,突然从背后的门里,传来我从未听过的痛苦和恐惧的尖叫。门打开了,调查员探出头请求我,为坐在她旁边的青年男子,调一杯热饮料。她刚刚给他的消息是,为了报复他对国家政权的批评,他的母亲已经被捕并执行了枪决。

在我20多岁的那段日子,每一天的工作,都在提醒我自己是多么幸运。生活在一个民选政府的国家,依法申述与公开审理,是所有人的权利。

每一天,我都能看到更多有关恶人的证据,他们为了获得或维持权力,对自己的同胞犯下暴行。我开始做噩梦,真正意义上的噩梦,全都和我所见所闻有关。

同时在这里我也了解到更多关于人类的善良,比我以前想象的要多很多。

大赦动员成千上万没有因为个人信仰而受到折磨或监禁的人,去为那些遭受这种不幸的人奔走。人类同理心的力量,引发集体行动,拯救生命,解放囚犯。个人的福祉和安全有保证的普通百姓,携手合作,大量挽救那些他们素不相识,也许永远不会见面的人。我用自己微薄的力量参与了这一过程,也获得了更大的启发。

不同于在这个星球上任何其他的动物,人类可以学习和理解未曾经历过的东西。他们可以将心比心、设身处地的理解他人。

当然,这种能力,就像在我虚构的魔法世界里一样,在道德上是中立的。一个人可能会利用这种能力去操纵控制,也有人选择去了解同情。

而很多人选择不去使用他们的想象力。他们选择留在自己舒适的世界里,从来不愿花力气去想想如果生在别处会怎样。他们可以拒绝去听别人的尖叫,看一眼囚禁的笼子;他们可以封闭自己的内心,只要痛苦不触及个人,他们可以拒绝去了解。

我可能会受到诱惑,去嫉妒那样生活的人。但我不认为他们做的噩梦会比我更少。选择生活在狭窄的空间,可以导致不敢面对开阔的视野,给自己带来恐惧感。我认为不愿展开想象的人会看到更多的怪兽,他们往往更感到更害怕。

更甚的是,那些选择不去同情的人,可能会激活真正的怪兽。因为尽管自己没有犯下罪恶,我们却通过冷漠与之勾结。

我18岁开始从古典文学中汲取许多知识,其中之一当时并不完全理解,那就是希腊作家普鲁塔克所说:我们内心获得的,将改变外在的现实。

那是一个惊人的论断,在我们生活的每一天里被无数次证实。它指明我们与外部世界有无法脱离的联系,我们以自身的存在接触着他人的生命。

但是,哈佛大学的2008届毕业生们,你们多少人有可能去触及他人的生命?你们的智慧,你们努力工作的能力,以及你们所受到的教育,给予你们独特的地位和责任。甚至你们的国籍也让你们与众不同,你们绝大部分人属于这个世界上唯一的超级大国。你们表决的方式,你们生活的方式,你们抗议的方式,你们给政府带来的压力,具有超乎寻常的影响力。这是你们的特权,也是你们的责任。

如果你选择利用自己的地位和影响，去为那些没有发言权的人发出声音；如果你选择不仅与强者为伍，还会同情帮扶弱者；如果你会设身处地为不如你的人着想，那么你的存在，将不仅是你家人的骄傲，更是无数因为你的帮助而改变命运的成千上万人的骄傲。我们不需要改变世界的魔法，我们自己的内心就有这种力量：那就是我们一直在梦想，让这个世界变得更美好。

　　我的演讲要接近尾声了。对你们，我有最后一个希望，也是我21岁时就有的。毕业那天坐在我身边的朋友现在是我终身的挚交，他们是我孩子的教父母，是在我遇到麻烦时愿意伸出援手，在我用他们的名字给哈利波特中的"食死徒"起名而不会起诉我的朋友。我们在毕业典礼时坐在了一起，因为我们关系亲密，拥有共同的永远无法再来的经历，当然，也因为假想要是我们中的任何人竞选首相，那照片将是极为宝贵的关系证明。

　　所以今天我可以给你们的，没有比拥有知己更好的祝福了。明天，我希望即使你们不记得我说的任何一个字，你们还能记得哲学家塞内加的一句至理名言。我当年没有顺着事业的阶梯向上攀爬，转而与他在古典文学的殿堂相遇，他的古老智慧给了我人生的启迪：

　　生活就像故事一样：不在乎长短，而在于质量，这才是最重要的。

　　非常感谢大家。

　　我祝愿你们都有美好的生活。

Lesson 6

Heal the Kids

Task 1　**Questions and Answers**

Directions: *Work in pairs. Read the following speech then take turns to ask and answer the following questions.*

1. When was the speech delivered? Where?
2. Who delivered the speech? Who are involved in the speech?
3. What is the theme of the speech?
4. Why is there a need for the request?
5. How can the request be achieved?

Task 2　**Dictation**

Directions: *Watch the authentic video of the speech. Then fill in the missing words in their appropriate forms. You may watch the video for three times.*

Love, ladies and gentlemen, is the human family's most _____ legacy, its richest bequest, its golden inheritance. And it is a _____ that is handed down from one generation to another. Previous ages may not have had the _____ we enjoy. Their houses may have lacked electricity, and they _____ their many kids into small homes without central _____. But those homes had no darkness, nor were they cold. They were lit _____ with the glow of love and they were warmed snugly by the very heat of the human heart. Parents, undistracted by the lust for luxury and _____ accorded their children primacy in their lives.

Task 3 Group List

Directions: *Go through the script. Locate information on* **The tenets of Children's Universal Bill of Rights** *(Paragraph 14). First fill in the blank with missing words. Then work in groups of four, make a list according to the importance of these tenet and explain why you rank these tenets that way.*

The tenets of Children's Universal Bill of Rights are:

1. The right to _____.
2. The right to _____.
3. The right to _____.
4. The right to _____.
5. The right to _____.
6. The right to _____.
7. The right to _____.

Task 4 Discussion

Directions: *Work in groups of four and discuss the following questions. Do you agree or disagree to the following statement. Use specific details or examples to support yourself. You may also locate some useful information from the script.*

1. All of us are products of our childhood.
2. Today children are constantly encouraged to grow up faster, as if this period known as childhood is a burdensome stage, to be endured and ushered through, as swiftly as possible.
3. But it all begins with forgiveness, because to heal the world, we first have to heal ourselves.
4. In a world filled with hate, we must still dare to hope. Keep hop alive. In a world filled with anger, we must still dare to comfort. In a world filled with despair, we must still dare to dream. And in a world filled with distrust, we must still dare to believe.

Task 5 Speaking Practice

Directions: *Give a speech to the class for 2-3 minutes on the topic "The Best Gift (s) I've Got From My Parents".*

Heal the Kids
拯救儿童

Address at Oxford University in March 2001
By Michael Jackson

🔊 **人物简介**

迈克尔·约瑟夫·杰克逊（Michael Joseph Jackson，简称MJ，1958年8月29日—2009年6月25日），世界级流行音乐歌手、作曲家、作词家、舞蹈家、演员、导演、唱片制作人、慈善家、时尚引领者，被誉为"流行音乐之王（King of Pop）"。迈克尔·杰克逊出身在阿肯色州的一个路德教牧师家庭，从小就受到严厉的家庭管教，在父亲的引导和组织下成立了演唱蓝调音乐的The Jackson 5，并于1964年首次亮相，后来又于1971年成功开始独唱生涯。1979年成年后发行第一张专辑《Off The Wall》就被誉为迪斯科音乐经典之作，1982年发行第二张专辑《Thriller》，奠定了迈克尔歌王的地位，并对整个流行乐坛产生了巨大的影响。杰克逊的音乐曲风完美地融合了黑人节奏蓝调与白人摇滚并且形成独特的MJ乐风，他的魔幻般的太空舞步让无数的明星效仿。他一生都致力于慈善事业，他用音乐歌颂大爱、种族团结与世界和平。他设立了许多慈善机构，其捐款超过三亿美元，创立了规模最大的"治愈世界基金会（Heal the World Foundation）"（1992年成立），"拯救儿童基金会"（2001年成立）和"迈克尔·杰克逊烧伤中心"（1984年成立）等慈善机构约三十九个。

遗憾的是，因其私人医生莫里违规操作注射镇静剂过量，导致杰克逊心脏病突发逝世。迈克尔·杰克逊给予了这世界魔幻魅力般的歌舞、博爱善良的救助、高尚的品格和永恒的纯真，却因根深蒂固的种族主义而被世人长久地误解。他是这样描述人和艺术之间的特殊关系的："当我站在镜前时看着自己，我知道，我是个黑人！我将自己投入了我的艺术。我相信所有艺术的顶峰都是物质与精神，人与神的完美结合。我相信这是一切艺术存在的原因。"

▶ 名篇导读

《拯救儿童》（"Heal the Kids"）是迈克尔·杰克逊于2001年3月6日应朋友之邀，前往英国牛津大学学生俱乐部所作的演讲。本次演讲是他留给世人唯一一次公开演讲。演讲的目的是启动"拯救孩子"工程。在演讲中，杰克逊回忆了自己不快乐的童年，回忆了父亲的严厉管教，从父亲细微的动作体会到父亲并没有吝啬内心深处对自己的爱，父亲的爱尽管严酷，但还是一种爱。与此同时，他呼吁我们要宽恕父母并且教他们如何去爱，呼吁天下父母给孩子享受童年快乐的权利，用爱去拯救一个孤寂的世界。

杰克逊的个人经历贯穿了整篇演讲稿。能够感受出，整场演讲无不透露出他的真情。他在文章中大量引用的经典来自圣雄甘地、杰西·杰克逊的语录以及圣经中的《十诫》。而他以歌唱的形式呼吁大家共同拯救世界堪称经典。正如杰克逊在演讲结束后那首歌中所唱的那样："Heal the world, make it a better place, for you and for me and the entire human race..."要拯救这个世界，我们必须拯救自己内心的那颗童心。当父母的心通过孩子的心而恢复童真的时候，当我们学会宽容、相互补偿、共同进步时，一个新世界和一个新时代便诞生了。

▶ 英文原文

Thank you, thank you dear friends, from the bottom of my heart, for such a loving and spirited welcome, and thank you, Mr President, for your kind invitation to me which I am so honoured to accept. I also want to express a special thanks to you Shmuley, who for 11 years served as **rabbi**[1] here at Oxford. You and I have been working so hard to form Heal the Kids, as well as writing our book about childlike qualities, and in all of our efforts you have been such a supportive and loving friend. And I would also like to thank Toba Friedman, our director of operations at Heal the Kids, who is returning tonight to the **alma mater**[2] where she served as a Marshall scholar, as well as Marilyn Piels, another central member of our Heal the Kids team.

I am humbled to be lecturing in a place that has previously been filled by such notable figures as Mother Theresa, Albert Einstein, Ronald Reagan, Robert Kennedy and Malcolm X. I've even heard that Kermit the Frog has made an appearance here, and I've always felt a **kinship**[3] with Kermit's message that it's not easy being green. I'm sure he didn't find it any easier being up

---

1　rabbi 拉比，犹太教对有学问的犹太人（老师）的尊称。
2　alma mater 母校
3　kinship 亲属关系

here than I do!

As I looked around Oxford today, I couldn't help but be aware of the majesty and **grandeur**[1] of this great institution, not to mention the brilliance of the great and gifted minds that have **roamed**[2] these streets for centuries. The walls of Oxford have not only housed the greatest philosophical and scientific geniuses-they have also **ushered**[3] forth some of the most cherished creators of children's literature, from J.R.R. Tolkien to CS Lewis. Today I was allowed to **hobble**[4] into the dining hall in Christ Church to see Lewis Carroll's Alice in Wonderland **immortalised**[5] in the **stained glass**[6] windows. And even one of my own fellow Americans, the beloved Dr Seuss **graced**[7] these halls and then went on to leave his mark on the imaginations of millions of children throughout the world.

I suppose I should start by listing my qualifications to speak before you this evening.

Friends, I do not claim to have the academic expertise of other speakers who have addressed this hall, just as they could lay little claim at being adept at the **moonwalk**[8] —and you know, Einstein in particular was really TERRIBLE at that. But I do have a claim to having experienced more places and cultures than most people will ever see. Human knowledge consists not only of libraries of **parchment**[9] and ink-it is also comprised of the volumes of knowledge that are written on the human heart, **chiselled**[10] on the human soul, and **engraved**[11] on the human psyche. And friends, I have encountered so much in this relatively short life of mine that I still cannot believe I am only 42. I often tell Shmuley that in soul years I'm sure that I'm at least 80—and tonight I even walk like I'm 80! So please **harken**[12] to my message, because what I have to tell you tonight can bring healing to humanity and healing to our planet.

Through the grace of God, I have been fortunate to have achieved many of my artistic and professional aspirations realised early in my lifetime. But these friends are accomplishments, and accomplishments alone are not **synonymous**[13] with who I am. Indeed, the cheery five-year-old who belted out Rockin Robin and Ben to adoring crowds was not indicative of the boy behind the smile.

Tonight, I come before you less as an **icon**[14] of pop (whatever that means anyway), and more as an icon of a generation, a generation that no longer knows what it means to be children. <u>All of us are products of our childhood.</u> But I am the product of a lack of a

---

1 grandeur 宏伟
2 roam 漫步
3 usher 引导
4 hobble 蹒跚
5 immortalise 使不朽
6 stained glass 彩色玻璃
7 grace 使高雅
8 moonwalk 太空漫步
9 parchment 羊皮纸
10 chisel 刻
11 engrave 雕刻
12 harken 听
13 synonymous 同义的
14 icon 偶像

childhood, an absence of that precious and wondrous age when we **frolic**¹ playfully without a care in the world, basking in the adoration of parents and relatives, where our biggest concern is studying for that big spelling test come Monday morning. Those of you who are familiar with the Jackson Five know that I began performing at the tender age of five and that ever since then, I haven't stopped dancing or singing.

But while performing and making music undoubtedly remain as many of my greatest joys, when I was young I wanted more than anything else to be a typical little boy. I wanted to build tree houses, have water balloon fights, and play hide and seek with my friends. But fate had it otherwise and all I could do was envy the laughter and playtime that seemed to be going on all around me. There was no **respite**² from my professional life. But on Sundays I would go Pioneering, the term used for the missionary work that Jehovahs Witnesses do. And it was then that I was able to see the magic of other peoples childhood. Since I was already a celebrity, I would have to don a disguise of fat suit, wig, beard and glasses and we would spend the day in the suburbs of Southern California, going door-to-door or making the rounds of shopping malls, distributing our *Watchtower* magazine. I loved to set foot in all those regular suburban houses and catch sight of the shag rugs and La-Z-Boy armchairs with kids playing Monopoly and grandmas baby-sitting and all those wonderful, ordinary and **starry**³ scenes of everyday life. Many, I know, would argue that these things seem like no big deal. But to me they were **mesmerising**⁴. I used to think that I was unique in feeling that I was without a childhood. I believed that indeed there were only a handful people with whom I could share those feelings.

When I recently met with Shirley Temple, the great child star of the 1930s and 40s, we said nothing to each other at first, we simply cried together, for she could share a pain with me that only others like my close friends Elizabeth Taylor and McCauley Culkin know. I do not tell you this to gain your sympathy but to impress upon you my first important point: It is not just Hollywood child stars that have suffered from a non-existent childhood. Today, its a universal **calamity**⁵, a global catastrophe. Childhood has become the great casualty of modern-day living. All around us we are producing scores of kids who have not had the joy, who have not been accorded the right, who have not been allowed the freedom, or knowing what its like to be a kid. <u>Today children are constantly encouraged to grow up faster, as if this period known as childhood is a **burdensome**⁶ stage, to be endured and ushered through, as swiftly as possible.</u> And on that subject, I am certainly one of the worlds greatest experts.

Our's is a generation that has witnessed the **abrogation**⁷ of the parent-child **covenant**⁸. Psychologists are publishing libraries of books detailing the destructive effects of denying one's

---

1　frolic 嬉戏
2　respite 休息期间；缓解，暂缓
3　starry 闪闪发光
4　mesmerising 使人催眠的
5　calamity 灾难
6　burdensome 累赘
7　abrogation 废除
8　covenant 盟约；契约

children the unconditional love that is so necessary to the healthy development of their minds and character. And because of all the neglect, too many of our kids essentially, have to raise themselves. They are growing more distant from their parents, grandparents and other family members, as all around us the **indestructible**[1] bond that once glued together the generations, **unravels**[2]. This violation has bred a new generation, Generation O let us call it, that has now picked up the torch from Generation X. The O stands for a generation that has everything on the outside-wealth, success, fancy clothing and fancy cars, but an aching emptiness on the inside. That cavity in our chests, that **barrenness**[3] at our core, that void in our centre is the place where the heart once beat and which love once occupied. And it's not just the kids who are suffering. It's the parents as well. For the more we cultivate little-adults in kids-bodies, the more removed we ourselves become from our own child-like qualities, and there is so much about being a child that is worth retaining in adult life.

Love, ladies and gentlemen, is the human family's most precious legacy, its richest **bequest**[4], its golden inheritance. And it is a treasure that is handed down from one generation to another. Previous ages may not have had the wealth we enjoy. Their houses may have lacked electricity, and they squeezed their many kids into small homes without central heating. But those homes had no darkness, nor were they cold. They were lit bright with the glow of love and they were warmed **snugly**[5] by the very heat of the human heart. Parents, undistracted by the lust for luxury and status, accorded their children **primacy**[6] in their lives.

As you all know, our two countries broke from each other over what Thomas Jefferson referred to as "certain inalienable rights". And while we Americans and British might dispute the justice of his claims, what has never been in dispute is that children have certain obvious rights, and the gradual erosion of those rights has led to scores of children worldwide being denied the joys and security of childhood. I would therefore like to propose tonight that we install in every home a Children's Universal Bill of Rights, the **tenets**[7] of which are:

1. The right to be loved without having to earn it
2. The right to be protected, without having to deserve it
3. The right to feel valuable, even if you came into the world with nothing
4. The right to be listened to without having to be interesting
5. The right to be read a bedtime story, without having to compete with the evening news or Easter Day
6. The right to an education without having to dodge bullets at schools

---

1　indestructible 不可毁灭的
2　unravels 解开；拆散
3　barrenness 荒芜
4　bequest 遗产
5　snugly 紧密地
6　primacy 主要
7　tenets 主旨

7. The right to be thought of as adorable-(even if you have a face that only a mother could love).

Friends, the foundation of all human knowledge, the beginning of human consciousness, must be that each and every one of us is an object of love. Before you know if you have red hair or brown, before you know if you are black or white, before you know of what religion you are a part, you have to know that you are loved.

About twelve years ago, when I was just about to start my Bad tour, a little boy came with his parents to visit me at home in California. He was dying of cancer and he told me how much he loved my music and me. His parents told me that he wasn't going to live, that any day he could just go, and I said to him, "Look, I am going to be coming to your hometown in Kansas to start my tour in three months. I want you to come to the show. I am going to give you this jacket that I wore in one of my videos." His eyes lit up and he said, "You are gonna GIVE it to me?" I said, "Yeah, but you have to promise that you will wear it to the show." I was trying to make him hold on. I said, "When you come to the show I want to see you in this jacket and in this glove" and I gave him one of my **rhinestone**¹ gloves-and I never usually give the rhinestone gloves away. And he was just in heaven.But maybe he was too close to heaven, because when I came to his town, he had already died, and they had buried him in the glove and jacket. He was just 10 years old. God knows, I know, that he tried his best to hold on. But at least when he died, he knew that he was loved, not only by his parents, but even by me, as a near stranger, I also loved him. And with all of that love he knew that he didn't come into this world alone, and he certainly didnt leave it alone.

If you enter this world knowing you are loved and you leave this world knowing the same, then everything that happens in between can be dealt with. A professor may **degrade**² you, but you will not feel degraded, a boss may **crush**³ you, but you will not be crushed, a corporate **gladiator**⁴ might **vanquish**⁵ you, but you will still triumph. How could any of them truly prevail in pulling you down? For you know that you are an object worthy of love. The rest is just packaging.

But if you don't have that memory of being loved, you are condemned to search the world for something to fill you up. But no matter how much money you make or how famous you become, you will still fell empty. What you are really searching for is unconditional love, unqualified acceptance. And that was the one thing that was denied to you at birth.

Friends, let me paint a picture for you. Here is a typical day in America—six youths under the age of 20 will commit suicide, 12 children under the age of 20 will die from firearms—remember this is a DAY, not a year—399 kids will be arrested for drug abuse, 1,352 babies will be born to teen mothers. This is happening in one of the richest, most developed countries in the

---

1 rhinestone 莱茵石（人造钻石）
2 degrade 使降级
3 crush 压碎，挤碎
4 gladiator 争论者
5 vanquish 征服

history of the world.

Yes, in my country there is an epidemic of violence that parallels no other industrialised nation. These are the ways young people in America express their hurt and their anger. But don't think that there is not the same pain and **anguish**[1] among their counterparts in the United Kingdom. Studies in this country show that every single hour, three teenagers in the UK **inflict**[2] harm upon themselves, often by cutting or burning their bodies or taking an **overdose**[3]. This is how they have chosen to cope with the pain of neglect and emotional agony.

In Britain, as many as 20% of families will only sit down and have dinner together once a year. Once a year! And what about the **time-honoured**[4] tradition of reading your kid a bedtime story? Research from the 1980s showed that children who are read to, had far greater literacy and significantly **outperformed**[5] their peers at school. And yet, less than 33% of British children ages two to eight have a regular bedtime story read to them. You may not think much of that until you take into account that 75% of their parents DID have that bedtime story when they were that age.

Clearly, we do not have to ask ourselves where all of this pain, anger and violent behaviour comes from. It is self-evident that children are thundering against the neglect, quaking against the indifference and crying out just to be noticed. The various child protection agencies in the US say that millions of children are victims of **maltreatment**[6] in the form of neglect, in the average year. Yes, neglect. In rich homes, privileged homes, wired to the **hilt**[7] with every electronic **gadget**[8]. Homes where parents come home, but they're not really home, because their heads are still at the office.

And their kids? Well, their kids just make do with whatever emotional **crumbs**[9] they get. And you don't get much from endless TV, computer games and videos. These hard, cold numbers which for me, wrench the soul and shake the spirit, should indicate to you why I have devoted so much of my time and resources into making our new Heal the Kids initiative a **colossal**[10] success. Our goal is simple—to recreate the parent and child bond, renew its promise and light the way forward for all the beautiful children who are destined one day to walk this earth. But since this is my first public lecture, and you have so warmly welcomed me into your hearts, I feel that I want to tell you more. We each have our own story, and in that sense statistics can become personal.

They say that parenting is like dancing. You take one step, your child takes another. I have

---

1 anguish 痛苦
2 inflict 造成损伤
3 overdose 药量过多
4 time-honoured 由来已久的
5 outperform 比……出色
6 maltreatment 虐待
7 hilt 刀柄
8 gadget 小玩意
9 crumbs 面包屑
10 colossal 巨大的

discovered that getting parents to re-dedicate themselves to their children is only half the story. The other half is preparing the children to re-accept their parents.

When I was very young I remember that we had this crazy mutt of a dog named "Black Girl", a mix of wolf and **retriever**[1]. Not only wasn't she much of a guard dog, she was such a scared and nervous thing that it is a wonder she did not pass out every time a truck **rumbled by**[2], or a thunderstorm swept through Indiana. My sister Janet and I gave that dog so much love, but we never really won back the sense of trust that had been stolen from her by her previous owner. We knew he used to beat her. We didn't know with what. But whatever it was, it was enough to **suck**[3] the spirit right out of that dog.

A lot of kids today are hurt puppies who have **weaned**[4] themselves off the need for love. They couldn't care less about their parents. Left to their own devices, they cherish their independence. They have moved on and have left their parents behind. Then there are the far worse cases of children who harbour **animosity**[5] and resentment toward their parents, so that any **overture**[6] that their parents might undertake would be thrown forcefully back in their face.

Tonight, I don't want any of us to make this mistake. That's why I'm calling upon all the world's children—beginning with all of us here tonight—to forgive our parents, if we felt neglected. Forgive them and teach them how to love again. You probably weren't surprised to hear that I did not have an **idyllic**[7] childhood. The strain and tension that exists in my relationship with my own father is well documented.

My father is a tough man and he pushed my brothers and me hard, really hard, from the earliest age, to be the best performers we could be. He had great difficulty showing affection. He never really told me he loved me. And he never really complimented me either. If I did a great show, he would tell me it was a good show. And if I did an OK show...he would say nothing.

He seemed **intent**[8], above all else, on making us a commercial success. And at that he was more than **adept**[9]. My father was a managerial genius and my brothers and I owe our professional success, in no small measure, to the forceful way that he pushed us. He trained me as a showman and under his guidance I couldn't miss a step.

But what I really wanted was a Dad. I wanted a father who showed me love. And my father never did that. He never said I love you while looking me straight in the eye, he never played a game with me. He never gave me a **piggyback**[10] ride, he never threw a pillow at me, or a water balloon.

But I remember once when I was about four years old, there was a little **carnival**[11] and he

---

1 retriever 猎犬
2 rumble by 轰隆隆呼啸而过
3 suck 吸，吮
4 wean 断奶
5 animosity 憎恶
6 overture 提案；前奏曲
7 idyllic 田园般的
8 intent 意图
9 adept 熟练
10 piggyback 背在肩上的
11 carnival 嘉年华

picked me up and put me on a pony. It was a tiny gesture, probably something he forgot five minutes later. But because of that moment I have this special place in my heart for him. Because that's how kids are, the little things mean so much to them and for me, that one moment meant everything. I only experienced it that one time, but it made me feel really good, about him and about the world.

But now I am a father myself, and one day I was thinking about my own children, Prince and Paris and how I wanted them to think of me when they grow up. To be sure, I would like them to remember how I always wanted them with me wherever I went, how I always tried to put them before everything else. But there are also challenges in their lives. Because my kids are stalked by paparazzi, they can't always go to a park or a movie with me.

So what if they grow older and resent me, and how my choices impacted their youth? Why weren't we given an average childhood like all the other kids, they might ask? And at that moment I pray that my children will give me the benefit of the doubt. That they will say to themselves: "Our daddy did the best he could, given the unique circumstances that he faced. He may not have been perfect, but he was a warm and decent man, who tried to give us all the love in the world."

I hope that they will always focus on the positive things, on the sacrifices I willingly made for them, and not criticise the things they had to give up, or the errors I've made, and will certainly continue to make, in raising them. For we have all been someone's child, and we know that despite the very best of plans and efforts, mistakes will always occur. That's just being human.

And when I think about this, of how I hope that my children will not judge me unkindly, and will forgive my shortcomings, I am forced to think of my own father and despite my earlier denials, I am forced to admit that he must have loved me. He did love me, and I know that.

There were little things that showed it. When I was a kid I had a real sweet tooth—we all did. My father, he did try My favourite food, the satisfied sweetie, was **glazed doughnuts**[1] and my father knew that. So every few weeks I would come downstairs in the morning and there on the kitchen counter was a bag of glazed doughnuts - no note, no explanation - just the doughnuts. It was like Santa Claus.

Sometimes I would think about staying up late at night, so I could see him leave them there, but just like with Santa Claus, I didn't want to ruin the magic for fear that he would never do it again. My father had to leave them secretly at night, so as no one might catch him with his guard down. He was scared of human emotion, he didn't understand it or know how to deal with it. But he did know doughnuts.

And when I allow the **floodgates**[2] to open up, there are other memories that come rushing back, memories of other tiny gestures, however imperfect, that showed that he did what he could. So tonight, rather than focusing on what my father didn't do, I want to focus on all the things he

---

1 glazed doughnuts 炸面包圈
2 floodgates 闸门

did do and on his own personal challenges. I want to stop judging him.

I have started reflecting on the fact that my father grew up in the South, in a very poor family. He came of age during the Depression and his own father, who struggled to feed his children, showed little affection towards his family and raised my father and his **siblings**[1] with an iron fist. Who could have imagined what it was like to grow up a poor black man in the South, robbed of dignity, **bereft**[2] of hope, struggling to become a man in a world that saw my father as **subordinate**[3]. I was the first black artist to be played on MTV and I remember how big a deal it was even then. And that was in the 1980s!

My father moved to Indiana and had a large family of his own, working long hours in the steel mills, work that kills the lungs and humbles the spirit, all to support his family. Is it any wonder that he found it difficult to expose his feelings? Is it any mystery that he hardened his heart, that he raised the emotional **ramparts**[4]? And most of all, is it any wonder why he pushed his sons so hard to succeed as performers, so that they could be saved from what he knew to be a life of indignity and poverty?

I have begun to see that even my father's **harshness**[5] was a kind of love, an imperfect love, to be sure, but love nonetheless. He pushed me because he loved me. Because he wanted no man ever to look down at his offspring.

And now with time, rather than bitterness, I feel blessing. In the place of anger, I have found **absolution**[6]. And in the place of revenge, I have found **reconciliation**[7]. And my initial fury has slowly given way to forgiveness.

Almost a decade ago, I founded a charity called Heal the World. The title was something I felt inside me. Little did I know, as Shmuley later pointed out, that those two words form the **cornerstone**[8] of *Old Testament* prophecy. Do I really believe that we can heal this world, that is **riddled**[9] with war and **genocide**[10], even today?

And do I really think that we can heal our children, the same children who can enter their schools with guns and hatred and shot down two beautiful students just at the beginning of their lives. A horrified reminder of guns and hatred at Columbine almost two years ago? Or children who can beat a defenceless **toddler**[11] to death, like the tragic story of Jamie Bulger? Of course I do, or I wouldn't be here tonight.

But it all begins with forgiveness, because to heal the world, we first have to heal ourselves. And to heal the kids, we first have to heal the child within, each and every one of us. As an

---

1　siblings 兄弟姐妹
2　bereft 剥夺
3　subordinate 下级；次要的
4　rampart 堡垒；防御墙
5　harshness 严酷
6　absolution 赦免
7　reconciliation 斡旋，调解
8　cornerstone 基石
9　riddle 困扰
10　genocide 种族灭绝
11　toddler 蹒跚学步的孩子

adult, and as a parent, I realise that I cannot be a whole human being, nor a parent capable of unconditional love, until I put to rest the ghosts of my own childhood.

And that's what I'm asking all of us to do tonight. Live up to the fifth of the Ten Commandments. Honour your parents by not judging them. Give them the benefit of the doubt. That is why I want to forgive my father and to stop judging him. I want to forgive my father, because I want a father, and this is the only one that I've got.

I want the weight of my past lifted from my shoulders and I want to be free to step into a new relationship with my father, for the rest of my life, **unhindered**[1] by the **goblins**[2] of the past.

In a world filled with hate, we must still dare to hope. Keep **hop**[3] alive. In a world filled with anger, we must still dare to comfort. In a world filled with despair, we must still dare to dream. And in a world filled with distrust, we must still dare to believe.

To all of you tonight who feel let down by your parents, I ask you to let down your disappointment. To all of you tonight who feel cheated by your fathers or mothers, I ask you not to cheat yourself further. And to all of you who wish to push your parents away, I ask you to extend you hand to them instead.

I am asking you, I am asking myself, to give our parents the gift of unconditional love, so that they too may learn how to love from us, their children. So that love will finally be restored to a desolate and lonely world. Shmuley once mentioned to me an ancient Biblical **prophecy**[4] which says that a new world and a new time would come, when "the hearts of the parents would be restored through the hearts of their children".

My friends, we are that world, we are those children.

Mahatma Gandhi said, "The weak can never forgive. Forgiveness is the **attribute**[5] of the strong." Tonight, be strong. Beyond being strong, rise to the greatest challenge of all—to restore that broken **covenant**[6]. We must all overcome whatever **crippling**[7] effects our childhoods may have had on our lives and in the words of Jesse Jackson, forgive each other, **redeem**[8] each other and move on.

This call for forgiveness may not result in "Oprah moments" the world over, with thousands of children making up with their parents, but it will at least be a start, and we will all be so much happier as a result.

And so ladies and gentlemen, I conclude my remarks tonight with faith, with joy and excitement. From this day forward, may a new song be heard.

Let that new song be the sound of children laughing.

Let that new song be the sound of children playing.

---

1 unhindered 无法阻止的
2 goblins 小妖精
3 hop 跳跃
4 prophecy 预言
5 attribute 属性
6 covenant 契约
7 crippling 受挫的
8 redeem 赎回，补偿，恢复

Let that new song be the sound of children singing.

And let that new song be the sound of parents listening.

Together, let us create a symphony of hearts, marvelling at the miracle of our children and basking in the beauty of love.

Let us heal the world and blight its pain.

And may we all make beautiful music together.

God bless you, and I love you.

文化快递

1. Heal the World（"拯救世界"慈善组织）

"拯救世界"是由迈克尔·杰克逊于1992年创立的慈善组织，组织的名称与歌曲"Heal the World"同名。在建立组织之前，杰克逊就对人道主义、公平和世界和平表现出极大的热情。该慈善组织的建立是为孩子们提供医药，并且同世界人民的饥荒、人们的无家可归和对儿童的剥削和虐待进行抗争。杰克逊申明他想要改善全世界儿童的生存条件。2001年2月，杰克逊首先发起了拯救儿童的运动，发起这项运动的目的是为了提升儿童福利。在这项运动中，杰克逊表示："'拯救儿童'能够帮助成年人和家长们意识到：应该用我们的力量来改变孩子们的世界。"

2. Guns and Hatred at Columbine（哥伦拜恩校园枪击事件）

哥伦拜恩校园事件是指1999年4月20日于美国科罗拉多州杰佛逊郡哥伦拜恩高中（Columbine High School）发生的校园枪击事件。制造事件的是两名青少年学生——埃里克·哈里斯和迪伦·克莱伯德配备枪械和爆炸物进入校园，枪杀了12名学生和1名教师，造成其他24人受伤，两人随即自杀身亡。这起事件被视为美国历史上最血腥校园枪击事件之一。

3. Old Testament Prophecy（旧约全书）

旧约全书是基督宗教的启示性经典文献。是由犹太人所写，尔后被基督教所抢。其内容和希伯来圣经一致，但编排不同。主要包括摩西五经、历史书、诗歌智慧书、大先知书、小先知书，总共39卷（希伯来古本为24卷），分律法书、历史书、智慧书、先知书四类。从公元前12世纪至公元前2世纪，陆续用希伯来语写成。

4. Ten Commandments（《十诫》）

《十诫》语出《圣经》，《圣经·出埃及记》载，十诫是耶和华所授，并命摩西颁布施行。内容是：不许拜别神；不许制造和敬拜偶像；不许妄称耶和华名；须守安息日为圣日；须孝父母；不许杀人；不许奸淫；不许偷盗；不许作假见证；不许贪恋他人财物。

5. Mahatma Gandhi（圣雄甘地）

圣雄甘地是印度民族主义运动和国大党领袖。他既是印度国父，也是印度最伟大的政治领袖。他带领国家迈向独立，脱离英国的殖民统治。他的"非暴力"的哲学思想，即他所说的"satyagraha"，影响了全世界的民族主义者和那些争取和平变革的国际运动。

6. Jesse Jackson（杰西·杰克逊）

杰西·杰克逊是美国著名的黑人运动领袖，1941生于南卡罗来纳州格林维尔，在贫困中长大。他先后在伊利诺伊大学、北卡罗来纳农业和技术学院、芝加哥神学院学习。1968年，杰西·杰克逊被委任为浸礼会牧师。

7. Oprah moments（奥普拉时刻）

"奥普拉时刻"是指在奥普拉脱口秀节目上真情流露的时刻，因为在奥普拉的脱口秀节目中，她会用自己的真情实感与对方进行交流，真情的流露十分常见。

参考译文

谢谢，谢谢各位亲爱的朋友，对大家如此热烈的欢迎，我由衷的表示感谢，谢谢主席，对您的盛意邀请，我感到万分荣幸。同时，我特别地感谢犹太教律法家希墨利，感谢您11年来在牛津所做的工作。你我一直都在为"拯救儿童"组织努力地工作着，也写出了孩子般品质的书，并且在我们的共同努力下，你已经成为我的一个乐于伸出援助之手而又可爱的朋友。但自始至终你都给予极大的支持和爱心。我还要感谢"拯救儿童"的理事多巴·弗里德曼她将于今晚返回母校，在此，她曾经作为一个马歇尔学者在母校工作过。当然还感谢我们"拯救儿童"组织的另一位中心成员玛丽莲·皮尔斯。

能来到这样一个曾经汇集过德兰修女、爱因斯坦、罗纳德·里根、罗伯特·肯尼迪和马尔柯姆·埃克斯等著名人物的地方演讲我感到受宠若惊。听说"青蛙"可米特曾经来过这里，我也和他有同感就是，没有深厚阅历的人来这里可并不容易，但我相信他一定没有想到我竟会这么容易地做到。

今天我参观牛津大学，真得忍不住被这一伟大建筑的宏伟壮观所吸引，更不必说这世纪之城才俊云集的绚烂了。牛津不仅荟萃了最出色沉着的科学英才，还引导出了从托尔金到刘易斯等不少极富爱心的儿童文学家。今天，我被允许在教堂餐厅里参观了雕刻在彩色玻璃窗里的路易斯·卡罗尔的爱丽斯梦游仙境。同时发现还有我的一位美国同胞，亲爱的苏斯先生也为此增色，启发着全世界的千万儿童的想象力。

今晚，我想先从我为何能有幸在这里为你们讲话开始。

朋友们，正如其他一些来此的演讲者不善于月球漫步一样，我也并不具备他们所拥有的学术专业知识——而且，大家都知道，爱因斯坦在这方面尤其让人敬畏。但是我可以说，比起大多数人，在其他文化方面我拥有更丰富的经验。人类文明不仅仅包括图书馆中纸墨记载的，还包括那些记在人们内心的，刻进人们灵魂的，印入人类精神的。而且朋友们，在我相对短暂的生命里我经历了这么多，以至于我真的难以相信自己只有42岁。我经常对施穆雷说我的心理年龄肯定至少有80了，今晚我甚至像个80岁老人一样走路。那么就请大家听我说,因为今天我一定要对大家讲的或许会让大家一起来治愈人道,拯救地球!

多亏上帝的恩典,我很幸运地提前实现了自己一生的艺术和职业抱负。但这些成绩和我是谁,完全不同性质。事实上,在崇拜者面前活泼快乐地表演摇滚罗宾和本的五岁小男孩并不意味笑容背后的他也同样快乐。

今晚,我不想以一个流行偶像的身份出现在大家面前,我更愿意作一代人的见证,一代不再了解作为孩子有什么意义的人。大家都有过童年,可我却缺少它,缺少那些宝贵的美妙的无忧无虑嬉戏玩耍的时光,而那些日子我们本该惬意地沉浸在父母亲人的疼爱中,为星期一重要的拼写考试下工夫做准备。熟悉"杰克逊五岁"的朋友都知道我5岁时就开始表演,从那以后,就再也没有停止过跳舞唱歌。

虽然音乐表演的确是我最大的乐趣,可是小的时候我更想和其他的男孩子一样,搭树巢、打水仗、捉迷藏。但是命中注定我只能羡慕那些笑声和欢乐,我的职业生活不容停歇。 不过,作为耶和华见证人,每个礼拜天我都要去参加教会工作,那时,我就会设想自己的童年和别人的一样充满魔力。而自从我成名以后,我就不得不用肥大的衣服、假发、胡须和眼镜把自己伪装起来。我们在加州南部的郊区度过一整天,挨家挨户串门,或者在购物中心闲逛,发放我们的《了望台》杂志。我也喜欢到普通的家庭里去,看那些粗毛地毯,看那些小家伙们过家家,看所有的精彩普通闪亮的日常生活情景。我知道很多人会认为这没什么大不了,可对我却充满了诱惑。我常常想自己这种没有童年的感觉是独一无二的,我想能和我分享这种感觉的人更是少之又少。

前些时候,我有幸遇到了三四十年代的一位童星秀兰·邓波儿,一见面我们什么都不说,只是一起哭,因为她能分担我的痛苦,这种痛苦只有我的一些密友,伊丽莎白·泰勒和麦尔利·库尔全他们才能体会到。我说这些并不是要博得大家的同情,只是想让大家牢记一点——这种失去童年的痛苦不仅仅属于好莱坞的童星。现在,这已经成为全世界的灾难。童年成了当代生活的牺牲品。我们使很多孩子不曾拥有欢乐,不曾得到相应的权利,不曾获得自由,而且还认为一个孩子就该是这样的。 现在,孩子们经常被鼓励长大得快一些,好像这个叫做童年的时期是一个累赘的阶段,大人们很不耐烦地想着法儿让它尽可能地快些结束。在这个问题上,我无疑是世界上最专业的人士之一了。

我这一代正是废除亲子盟约必要性的见证。心理学家在书中详述了不给予孩子绝对的爱而导致的毁灭性影响,这种无条件的爱对他们精神和人格的健康发展是极其必要的。因为被忽视,很多孩子就封闭自己。他们渐渐疏远自己的父母亲,祖父母以及其他的家庭成员,我们身边那种曾经团结过一代人的不灭的凝集力就这样散开了。这种违背常理的行为造就了一代新人,他们拥有所有外在的东西——财富、成功、时装和跑车,但他们的内心却是痛苦和空虚。胸口的空洞,心灵的荒芜,那些空白的地方曾经搏动着我们的心脏,曾经被爱占据。其实,不仅孩子们痛苦,父母亲也同样受煎熬。我们越是让孩子们早熟,我们就越来越远离了天真,而这种天真就算成年人也值得拥有。

爱，女士们先生们，爱是人类家庭最珍贵的遗产，是最贵重的馈赠，是最无价的传统，是我们应该代代相传的财富。以前，我们或许没有现在所享受的富有，房子里可能没有电，很多孩子挤在没有取暖设施的狭小房间里。但这些家庭里没有黑暗，也没有寒冷。他们点燃爱之光，贴紧的心让他们感到温暖。父母不为各种享受和权利的欲望分心，孩子才是他们的生活中最重要的。

我们都知道，我们两国在托马斯·杰弗逊提出的所谓"几个不可妥协的权利"上决裂。当我们美国人和英国人在争执各自要求的公平时，又有什么关于孩子们不可妥协的权利之争呢，对这些权利的逐步剥夺已经导致了世界上的很多孩子失去欢快乐趣和童年的安全感。因此我建议今晚我们就为每个家庭建立一部全体儿童权利条约，这些条例是：

1. 不必付出就可享受的被爱的权利
2. 不必乞求就可享有的被保护的权利
3. 即使来到这个世界时一无所有，也要有被重视的权利
4. 即使不引人注意也会有被倾听的权利
5. 不须要与晚间新闻和复活节抗争，就能在睡觉前听一段故事的权利
6. 不须要躲避子弹，可以在学校受教育的权利
7. 哪怕你只有妈妈才会爱的脸蛋，也要有被人尊重的权利。

朋友们，人类所有知识的创立，人类意识的萌芽必然需要我们每一个人都成为被爱的对象。哪怕你不知道自己的头发是红色还是棕色，不知道自己是白人还是黑人，不知道自己信仰哪个宗教，你也应该知道自己是被爱着的。

大概12年前，我正好在准备我的"真棒"巡演，一个小男孩和他的父母亲来加州看我。癌症正在威胁着他的生命，他告诉我他非常爱我和我的音乐。他的父母告诉我他生命将尽，说不上哪一天就会离开，我就对他说："你瞧，三个月之后我就要到堪萨斯州你住的那个城市去开演唱会，我希望你来看我的演出，我还要送给你一件我在一部录影带里穿过的夹克。"他眼睛一亮，说："你要把它送给我?" 我说："当然，不过你必须答应我穿着它来看我的演出。"我只想尽力让他坚持住，就对他说："我希望在我的演唱会上看见你穿着这件夹克戴着这只手套。"于是，我又送了一只镶着莱茵石的手套给他。一般我决不送手套给别人。但他就要去天堂了。不过，也许他离那儿实在太近，我到他的城市时，他已经走了，他们埋葬他时给他穿上那件夹克戴上那只手套。他只有10岁。上帝知道，我知道，他曾经多么努力地支持过。但至少，在他离开时，他知道自己是被深爱着的，不仅被父母亲，甚至还有几乎是个陌生人的我也同样爱他。拥有了这些爱，他知道他不是孤独地来到这个世界，同样也不是孤独地离开。

如果你降临或离开这个世界时都感到被爱，那么这些时间里发生的所有意外你都能对付得了。教授可能降你的级，可你自己并没有降级，老板可能排挤你，可你不会被排挤掉，一个辩论对手可能会击败你，可你却仍能胜利。他们怎么能真正战胜你击倒你呢?因

为你知道你是值得被爱的，其余的只是一层包装罢了。

可是，如果你没有被爱的记忆，你就无法发现世界上有什么东西能够让你充实。无论你挣了多少钱，无论你有多出名，你仍然觉得空虚。你真正寻找的只是无条件的爱和完全的包容。而这些在你诞生时就被拒绝给予。

朋友们，让我给大家描述一下这样的情景，在美国每一天将有——6个不满20岁的青年自杀，12个20岁以下的孩子死于武器——记住这只是一天，不是一年。另外还有399个年轻人因为服用麻醉品而被逮捕，1352个婴儿被十几岁的妈妈生出来，这都发生在世界上最富有最发达的国家。

是的，我国所充斥的暴力，其他的工业化国家无法相提并论。这只是美国年轻人宣泄自己所受的伤害和愤怒的途径，但是，难道英国就没有同样烦恼痛苦的人么？调查表明英国每小时都会有三个十来岁的孩子自残，经常割烫自己的身体或者服用过量药剂。这是他们现在用来发泄痛苦烦恼的方法。

在大不列颠，有20%的家庭一年只能聚在一起吃一次晚饭，一年才一次！80年代研究发现，听故事长大的孩子都有较强的识读能力和动手能力，而且，远比看着学的有效果。然而，英国只有不到33%的二至八岁的孩子才能固定地在睡前听段故事。如果我们没有意识到75%的家长在他们的那个年龄都是听着故事过来的，那么大家可能就不会想到什么了。

很显然，我们没有问过自己这些痛苦愤怒和暴力从何而来。不言而喻，孩子们特别憎恨被忽略，害怕冷漠，他们哭泣只是为了引起注意。在美国，各种儿童保护机构表示，平均每年，有千万儿童成为了因忽略冷漠的受害者，这是一种虐待！富有的家庭，幸运的家庭，完全被电子器件束缚了。父母亲回到家里，可是他们没有真正回家，他们的灵魂还在办公室。

那么他们的孩子们又如何呢？孩子们只好以他们所能得到的点滴感情勉强过活。无休止地看电视、玩电脑游戏、看录像，孩子们又能从中得到多少呢！这些让我觉得扭曲灵魂震撼心灵的又冷又硬的东西正好可以让大家明白，我为什么要花费这么多时间精力来支援拯救孩子的活动让它能获得巨大的成功。我们的目的很简单——重建父母儿女之间的融洽关系，重许我们的承诺去点亮所有终究有一天会来到这个世界美丽孩子们的前行路途。这次公开演讲之后，你们能对我敞开心扉，我觉得我会和你们聊更多。不过如果对我们每个人各自的故事都作统计的话就可能侵犯个人隐私了。

有人说，抚养孩子就像跳舞。你走一步，你的孩子跟一步。而我发觉养育孩子时，你对孩子的付出只是故事的一半，而另一半就是孩子对父母的回报。

在我小时候，我记得我们有一只名叫"黑姑娘"的疯狂的狼狗，它不仅不能看家，而且很胆小并且神经质，甚至对卡车的声音和印第安纳的雷雨也恐惧不已，我的妹妹珍妮和我在她身上用了不少心，但是我们没能赢得她的信任，这份被他以前的主人偷走的爱。她以前的主人总是打她，我们不知道为了什么，但是无论因为什么，都足以使这条狗失魂落魄。

如今许多冷漠的年轻人都是受伤害的可怜人，在需要爱的时候却被切断了爱的乳汁。他们一点也不关心他们的父母。他们依赖于自己的聪明才智，捍卫他们的独立。他们不停地向前进，而把父母抛在了后面。还有更糟的孩子，他们怨恨父母，甚至父母任一可能的提议都会被强硬地驳回。

今晚，我不希望我们之中任何人犯这样的错误，这就是为什么我正号召全世界的孩子——和我们今晚在场的人一起，宽恕我们的父母，如果我们觉得曾被父母忽略，那么宽恕他们并且教他们如何再次去爱。当你听说我不曾拥有一个田园牧歌式的幸福童年时，您可能并不吃惊，因为我和我父亲的紧张关系就是一例。

我父亲是个严厉的人，从记事起，他努力地让我们尽量做好的演员，他不善于表达爱，他从不说他爱我，也从未夸奖我，如果我表现得很棒，他会说不错，如果我表现得还行，他就什么也不说。

我的父亲一心想要让我们在商业上取得成功。他是个天才管理者，而且他把这一目标看得高于一切，他精于此道胜过其他。我和我的哥哥们在事业上不成功，他就以强迫的方式训练我们成为演员，在他的指导下，我没有错过任何一个机遇。

但我真正想要的是一个让我感觉到爱的父亲，我的父亲却不是这样，在他直视着我时从不说爱我，从未和我玩过一个游戏，没有玩过骑马，没有扔过枕头，没有玩过水球，

但我记得我四岁那年，有一个小的狂欢节，他把我放在小马上。这样小的一个动作，或许他五分钟后就忘记了，但因为那一刻，在我心里，他有了一个特别的位置，这就是孩子，很小的事情对他们意味着很多，对我亦如此，那一刻意味着一切。我仅仅经历过一次，但那感觉真好，父亲真好，这个世界真好。

但是现在我自己也当爸爸了，有一天我正在想着我自己的孩子普林斯、帕里斯，还有我希望他们长大后怎样看我。我肯定的是，我希望他们想起我的时候，能记得我不管去哪，都要他们在我身边，想起我如何总是把他们放在一切之前。但他们的生活里总是有挑战。因为我的孩子们总是被那些八卦小报跟踪，他们也不能和我经常去公园或者影院。

所以如果他们长大了之后怨恨我，那又怎么样呢?我的选择给他们的童年带来了多大的影响?他们也许会问，为什么我们没有和其他孩子一样的童年呢?在那一刻，我祈祷，我的孩子能够理解我。他们会对自己说："我们的爸爸已经尽了他最大努力，考虑到他面对的是独特的状况。他或许不完美，但他却是个温和正派的人，想把这世上所有的爱都给我们。"

我希望他们能总是把焦点放在那些积极的方面，比如我心甘情愿为他们做出的牺牲；而不是那些他们不得不放弃的事情，或我在抚养他们的过程中犯过的或不能避免犯下的错误。因为我们都曾是他人的孩子，而且我们都清楚，尽管计划很周密也很努力，但错误总是在所难免。因为人非圣贤，孰能无过?

每当我想到这时，想到我是多么希望我的孩子不会无情地批判我并原谅我的缺点时，我不得不想起我自己的父亲，不管我之前是多么地否定他，我必须承认他一定是爱我的。

他的确爱我,我知道的。

　　从一件小事就可以看出来,在我小的时候,非常喜欢吃甜食——孩子们都这样。我父亲知道我最喜欢吃炸面包圈。于是每隔几个星期,当我早上从楼上下来时,我都会在厨房的柜台上发现一整袋面包圈——没有字条、没有说明。就像是圣诞老人送来的礼物。

　　有时我曾经想通宵不睡觉,以便能够看到他把它们藏在哪里。但就像对待圣诞老人的传说那样,我不想破坏掉这种神奇幻想,更害怕他再也不会继续。父亲晚上不得不悄悄地把它们留在那里,并不让任何人知道。他害怕提及人类的情感,他不懂也不知道怎么处理。但他却懂得炸面圈对我的意义。

　　当我打开记忆的洪闸时,记忆如洪潮般涌入,尽管那些关于一些微妙动作的记忆已经不太清晰,但绝对体现了他在尽力而为。于是今晚,与其专注于我父亲没有做到什么,我更愿意专注于所有他在面临自身挑战并且克服困难而做到的事情。我不想对他进行批评。

　　这让我想起了我的父亲成长于美国南方一个非常贫穷的家庭这样一个事实。他成年于大萧条时期,而他的父亲拼力养育着他的孩子们,却并没有给予他们关爱,我父亲和他的兄弟姐妹是在他父亲的铁拳头下长大的。谁能够想象一下一个贫穷黑人在南方长大是什么样的一个情形?被剥夺了尊严,失去了希望,拼命想在那个视我父亲为下等人的世界里争做一个男人。我是第一个上MTV的黑人艺术家,至今我还记得那是多么了不起的一件事情,而那已经是在20世纪80年代了!

　　我的父亲移居到了印第安纳州并且在那里有了自己的大家庭,他在钢铁厂长时间工作,他干的是一份损害肺部且不体面的工作,但这一切都是为了支撑他的家庭。如此说来,他不善表达感情,这也就不足为奇了吧?他变得铁石心肠,他筑起了情感的围墙,这还有什么神秘的吗?最重要的,他如此强烈地迫使自己的儿子们成为成功的表演家,以便让他们脱离没有尊严、贫穷的生活,这还有什么不可理解的吗?

　　我开始逐渐明白,就连父亲的严酷也是一种爱,是一种不完美的爱,但肯定是爱。他强逼我是因为他爱我,因为他不愿意有人看低他的子孙后代。

　　随着时间的流逝,我现在感到的是幸福,而非辛酸。以前的愤怒被赦免取代,以前的报复被和解取代,而我最初的狂怒也慢慢让位于宽恕。

　　差不多在十年前,我建立了一个叫"拯救世界"的慈善机构。这个名字直抒我胸臆。正如后来希墨利指出的那样,我很少知道那两个字是构成《旧约全书》预言的基石。我真的相信我们能够拯救这个被今天的战争和种族灭绝所困扰着的世界吗?

　　我真的认为我们能够拯救我们的孩子吗?能够拯救那些带着枪和仇恨进入学校并开枪射击那两个正值生命之初的孩子们吗?(如同两年之前在哥伦拜中学所发生的那样)还是能够拯救那些将手无还手之力的幼儿殴打至死的孩子们——例如杰米·布格的悲惨故事?当然我相信我们能做到,否则我今晚就不会来到这里。

　　但是这一切都始于宽恕,因为要想拯救世界我们就必须首先拯救自己。而要拯救孩子，我们首先必须要拯救我们每个人内心的那颗童心。作为一个成年人，作为一位父亲，我意识到我不能作为一个完整的人，也不能成为一个给予孩子无条件爱的父亲，除非我让我的童年的梦魇得以安息。

这就是今晚我请求大家要做的事。不辜负十大戒律中的第五条：尊重你们的父母而不评判他们。对于他们，凡事都要向好处想。我要宽恕我的父亲，因为我想要拥有一个父亲，而他是我唯一所拥有的父亲。

我想卸掉过去压在我肩膀上的包袱，我想在我的余生里自由地向前迈出一步，和我父亲建立起新的关系，不受过去阴影的阻碍。

如果世界充满仇恨，我们须依然敢于希望；如果世界充满愤怒，我们须依然敢于安慰；如果世界充满绝望，我们须依然敢于梦想；如果世界充满猜忌，我们须依然敢于信任。

对于今晚对父母失望的人们，我要你们对自己的沮丧失望；今晚感觉被父母亲欺骗的人们，我要你们不要再欺骗自己；今晚所有希望将父母踢开的人们，我要你们把手伸向他们。

我在要求你，同时我在要求自己，把无条件的爱给我们的父母，这样他们也会学会怎样爱我们，爱他们的孩子。这样，爱会最终重建这个孤寂的世界。希墨利曾向我提到过古圣经预言——当"父母的心通过孩子的心而恢复童真"的时候，一个新世界和一个新时代即将诞生。

我的朋友们，我们就是那个世界，我们就是那些孩子。

圣雄甘地曾说："弱者从不原谅别人，而宽恕是强者的品格。"今晚，坚强起来吧！让我们超越坚强去迎接最大的挑战——恢复父母与子女间的亲情关系。我们必须克服我们的童年可能给我们的生活带来的所有不利影响，用杰西·杰克逊的话说就是：彼此宽恕，彼此补偿，然后继续前行。

对宽恕的呼唤或许并不能让世界到处出现"奥普拉时刻"，让成千上万孩子和他们的父母重归于好，但它至少是一个开端，当然如果出现"奥普拉时刻"，我们将会更加幸福。

因此，女士们先生们，我带着信念、欢乐和激动来结束我今晚的讲话。 在未来的日子里，或许我们会听到一首新歌。

让这首新歌使孩子们欢笑吧。

让这首新歌使孩子们嬉闹吧。

让这首新歌成为孩子们的歌唱声吧。

让这首新歌成为父母们倾听的歌曲吧。

让我们一起创作一首心灵交汇的交响曲，惊叹于我们孩子们创造的奇迹，沐浴在美丽的爱的海洋里吧。

让我们拯救世界，让世界之殇消失吧。

愿我们一同编织最美的音乐。

愿上帝保佑你们，我爱你们。

Lesson 7

Address to Beijing University

Task 1 Questions and Answers

Directions: *Work in pairs. Read the following speech then take turns to ask and answer the following questions.*

1. When was the speech delivered? Where?
2. Who delivered the speech? Who are involved in the speech?
3. What is the theme of the speech?
4. Why is there a need for the request?
5. How can the request be achieved?

Task 2 Dictation

Directions: *Watch the authentic video of the speech. Then fill in the missing words in their appropriate forms. You may watch the video for three times.*

  Of course, these changes have also brought disruptions in _____ patterns of life and work, and have imposed enormous _____ on your environment. Once every urban Chinese was ____ employment in a state enterprise. Now you must _____ in a job market. Once a Chinese worker had only to meet the demands of a central planner in Beijing. Now the global economy means all must _____ the quality and creativity of the rest of the world. For those who ____ the right training and skills and support, this new world can be daunting. In the short-term, good, hardworking people—some, at least will find themselves _____. And, as all of you can see, there have been enormous environmental and economic and health care costs to the development pattern and the energy use pattern of the last 20 years—from air pollution to deforestation to acid rain and water _____.

Task 3 Imitation and Play

Directions: *Watch the authentic video of the speech. Then try to imitate one or two paragraphs you like with appropriate delivery techniques. First practice by yourself. Then work in groups of four to take turns to deliver the speech.*

Task 4 Discussion

Directions: *Work in groups of four and discuss the following questions. You may locate some useful information from the script.*
1. According to the speaker, what changes have come to China in comparison to three decades ago?
2. What challenges do these change bring about?
3. What is Bill Clinton's position of the spread of nuclear, chemical, and biological weapons?
4. According to Clinton, what rights are universal to all human beings?

Task 5 Speaking Practice

Directions: *Give a speech to the class for 2—3 minutes on the topic of* **Protecting the Earth, the Only Household of Human Race**.

Address to Beijing University
在北京大学的讲话
By Bill Clinton

▶ 人物简介

比尔·克林顿（英文名Bill Clinton 1946年8月19日— ），美国政治家，美国民主党成员，第42任美国总统（任期为1993年至2001年），是继富兰克林·罗斯福之后，美国第一位出生于二战之后的民主党总统。克林顿的早期政治生涯并不顺利，但他下台后反思

英语演讲名篇赏析
Appreciation of Masterpiece English Speeches

了自己政治生涯上的失败与孤独，与强大的商业利益集团建立起了新的关系，并修补了与州内政府部门的关系。1982年，克林顿再度当选州长，连续执政10年，于1992年竞选总统。在外交方面，克林顿强调取消关税壁垒实现全球自由贸易，1993年在国会通过北美自由贸易协议（North American Free Trade Agreement），次年通过另一个全球范围的自由贸易协议创建世界贸易组织（World Trade Organization）。1998年至2005年期间，克林顿曾三次访华，在北大、清华和郑州大学发表演说。另外，克林顿著有个人自传《我的一生》。

▶ 名篇导读

1998年6月29日，克林顿总统怀着和平友好的心情来到北京大学发表他在中国的第一次演讲。演讲中，克林顿谈到中国在文化、宗教、哲学和艺术方面对世界作出的重大贡献。并对中国政府在亚洲金融风暴中所采取的积极政策给予了高度评价。另外，克林顿还谈到了当前中美在亚洲安全、核扩散、犯罪和毒品、环境、金融安全等方面面临的挑战，并表示希望美中两国在这些方面加强合作。

百年形成的爱国、进步、民主、科学是北京大学的优良传统，是北京大学迈向下一个世纪的精神支柱。然而中国的未来不仅仅在北大。中国的未来，中美关系的未来将寄托在全中国千千万万个有志青年身上。未来，中美两国的青年一代应有更多的了解，增进合作，为创造人类更美好的未来，为推动中美关系的健康发展共同努力。

本篇演讲稿是一篇反映国际合作的演讲稿，克林顿的风格沉稳而不乏激情，充分显示出在新世纪中，美国愿意同中国携手合作，共同发展维护世界和平的强烈愿望。他的"为了个人自由而奋斗就是为了国家的自由而奋斗。为了个性而奋斗就是为了国民性而奋斗"充分显示出美国220年来主张的自由人权和立国相结合的核心理念。"中国的年轻人必须享有心灵上的自由，以便最充分地开发自己的潜力，你们必须重新想象新世纪的中国，你们这一代必然处于中国复兴的中心。"这给予了无数中国青年为祖国发展而奋斗的强大动力。

▶ 英文原文

Thank you. Thank you, President Chen, Chairmen Ren, Vice President Chi, Vice Minister Wei.

We are delighted to be here today with a very large American delegation, including the First Lady and our daughter, who is a student at Stanford, one of the schools with which Beijing University has a relationship.

We have six members of the United States Congress; the Secretary of State; Secretary of Commerce; the Secretary of Agriculture; the Chairman of our Council of Economic Advisors;

Senator Sasser, our Ambassador; the National Security Advisor and my Chief of Staff, among others. I say that to illustrate the importance that the United States places on our relationship with China. I would like to begin by congratulating all of you, the students, the faculty, the administrators, on celebrating the **centennial**[1] year of your university. Gongxi, Beida.

As I'm sure all of you know, this campus was once home to Yenching University which was founded by American **missionaries**[2]. Many of its wonderful buildings were designed by an American architect. Thousands of Americans students and professors have come here to study and teach. We feel a special kinship with you.

I am, however, grateful that this day is different in one important respect from another important occasion 79 years ago. In June of 1919, the first president of Yenching University, **John Leighton Stuart**, was set to deliver the very first commencement address on these very grounds. At the appointed hour, he appeared, but no students appeared. They were all out leading the May 4th Movement for China's political and cultural renewal. When I read this, I hoped that when I walked into the **auditorium**[3] today, someone would be sitting here. And I thank you for being here, very much.

Over the last 100 years, this university has grown to more than 20,000 students. Your graduates are spread throughout China and around the world. You have built the largest university library in all of Asia. Last year, 20 percent of your graduates went abroad to study, including half of your math and science majors. And in this anniversary year, more than a million people in China, Asia, and beyond have logged on to your web site. At the dawn of a new century, this university is leading China into the future. I come here today to talk to you, the next generation of China's leaders, about the critical importance to your future of building a strong partnership between China and the United States.

The American people deeply admire China for its thousands of years of contributions to culture and religion, to philosophy and the arts, to science and technology. We remember well our strong partnership in World War II. Now we see China at a moment in history when your glorious past is matched by your present **sweeping**[4] transformation and the even greater promise of your future. Just three decades ago, China was virtually shut off from the world.

Now, China is a member of more than 1,000 international organizations—enterprises that affect everything from air travel to agricultural development. You have opened your nation to trade and investment on a large scale. Today, 40,000 young Chinese study in the United States, with hundreds of thousands more learning in Asia, Africa, Europe, and Latin America. Your social and economic transformation has been even more remarkable, moving from a closed command economic system to a driving, increasingly market-based and driven economy, generating two decades of unprecedented growth, giving people greater freedom to travel within and outside

---

1 centennial 一百年的
2 missionaries 传教士
3 auditorium 大礼堂
4 sweeping 彻底的；影响广泛的

China, to vote in village elections, to own a home, choose a job, attend a better school. As a result you have lifted literally hundreds of millions of people from poverty. **Per capita income**[1] has more than doubled in the last decade. Most Chinese people are leading lives they could not have imagined just 20 years ago.

Of course, these changes have also brought **disruptions**[2] in settled patterns of life and work, and have imposed enormous strains on your environment. Once every urban Chinese was guaranteed employment in a state enterprise. Now you must compete in a job market. Once a Chinese worker had only to meet the demands of a central planner in Beijing. Now the global economy means all must match the quality and creativity of the rest of the world. For those who lack the right training and skills and support, this new world can be **daunting**[3]. In the short-term, good, hardworking people—some, at least will find themselves unemployed. And, as all of you can see, there have been enormous environmental and economic and health care costs to the development pattern and the energy use pattern of the last 20 years—from air pollution to **deforestation**[4] to acid rain and water shortage.

In the face of these challenges, new systems of training and social security will have to be devised, and new environmental policies and technologies will have to be introduced with the goal of growing your economy while improving the environment. Everything I know about the intelligence, the **ingenuity**[5], the enterprise of the Chinese people and everything I have heard these last few days in my discussions with President Jiang, Prime Minister Zhu and others give me confidence that you will succeed. As you build a new China, America wants to build a new relationship with you.

We want China to be successful, secure and open, working with us for a more peaceful and prosperous world. I know there are those in China and the United States who question whether closer relations between our countries is a good thing. But everything all of us know about the way the world is changing and the challenges your generation will face tell us that our two nations will be far better off working together than apart. The late Deng Xiaoping counseled us to seek truth from facts. At the dawn of the new century, the facts are clear.

The distance between our two nations, indeed, between any nations, is shrinking. Where once an American **clipper**[6] ship took months to cross from China to the United States. Today, technology has made us all virtual neighbors. From laptops to lasers, from **microchips**[7] to **megabytes**[8], an information revolution is lighting the landscape of human knowledge, bringing us all closer together. Ideas, information, and money cross the planet at the stroke of a computer key, bringing with them extraordinary opportunities to create wealth, to prevent and conquer disease,

---

1　Per capita income 个人平均所得;人均国民收入
2　disruption 破坏
3　daunting 使人畏缩的
4　deforestation 森林砍伐
5　ingenuity 心灵手巧
6　clipper 快速帆船
7　microchips 微芯片
8　megabytes 兆字节

to foster greater understanding among peoples of different histories and different cultures.

But we also know that this greater openness and faster change mean that problems which start beyond one nations borders can quickly move inside them—the spread of weapons of mass destruction, the threats of organized crime and drug **trafficking**[1], of environmental degradation, and severe economic **dislocation**[2]. No nation can isolate itself from these problems, and no nation can solve them alone. We, especially the younger generations of China and the United States, must make common cause of our common challenges, so that we can, together, shape a new century of brilliant possibilities. In the 21st century—your century—China and the United States will face the challenge of security in Asia.

On the Korean Peninsula, where once we were adversaries, today we are working together for a permanent peace and a future **freer**[3] of nuclear weapons. On the Indian **subcontinent**[4], just as most of the rest of the world is moving away from nuclear danger, India and Pakistan risk sparking a new arms race. We are now pursuing a common strategy to move India and Pakistan away from further testing and toward a dialogue to resolve their differences.

In the 21st century, your generation must face the challenge of stopping the spread of **deadlier**[5] nuclear, chemical, and biological weapons. In the wrong hands or the wrong places, these weapons can threaten the peace of nations large and small. Increasingly, China and the United States agree on the importance of stopping **proliferation**[6]. That is why we are beginning to act in concert to control the world's most dangerous weapons. In the 21st century, your generation will have to reverse the international tide of crime and drugs. Around the world, organized crime robs people of billions of dollars every year and undermines trust in government.

America knows all about the devastation and despair that drugs can bring to schools and neighborhoods. With borders on more than a dozen countries, China has become a crossroad for **smugglers**[7] of all kinds. Last year, President Jiang and I asked senior Chinese and American law enforcement officials to step up our cooperation against these **predators**[8], to stop money from being laundered, to stop aliens from being cruelly smuggled, to stop currencies from being undermined by **counterfeiting**[9]. Just this month, our drug enforcement agency opened an office in Beijing, and soon Chinese **counternarcotics**[10] experts will be working out of Washington.

In the 21st century, your generation must make it your mission to ensure that today's progress does not come at tomorrow's expense. China's remarkable growth in the last two decades has come with a toxic cost, pollutants that **foul**[11] the water you drink and the air you

---

1　trafficking 非法交易
2　dislocation 混乱
3　freer 给与自由的人或事
4　subcontinent 次大陆
5　deadly 致命的
6　proliferation 扩散
7　smuggler 走私贩
8　predator 掠夺者
9　counterfeiting 造假
10　counternarcotics 反对独裁
11　foul 污染，弄脏

breathe—the cost is not only environmental, it is also serious in terms of the health consequences of your people and in terms of the drag on economic growth. Environmental problems are also increasingly global as well as national. For example, in the near future, if present energy use patterns persist, China will overtake the United States as the world's largest **emitter**[1] of greenhouse gases, the gases which are the principal cause of global warming.

If the nations of the world do not reduce the gases which are causing global warming, sometime in the next century there is a serious risk of dramatic changes in climate which will change the way we live and the way we work, which could literally bury some island nations under mountains of water and undermine the economic and social **fabric**[2] of nations. We must work together. We Americans know from our own experience that it is possible to grow an economy while improving the environment. We must do that together for ourselves and for the world. Building on the work that our Vice President, Al Gore, has done previously with the Chinese government, President Jiang and I are working together on ways to bring American clean energy technology to help improve air quality and grow the Chinese economy at the same time.

But I will say this again—this is not on my remarks—your generation must do more about this. This is a huge challenge for you, for the American people and for the future of the world. And it must be addressed at the university level, because political leaders will never be willing to adopt environmental measures if they believe it will lead to large-scale unemployment or more poverty. The evidence is clear that does not have to happen. You will actually have more rapid economic growth and better paying jobs, leading to higher levels of education and technology if we do this in the proper way. But you and the university, communities in China, the United States and throughout the world will have to lead the way.

In the 21st century your generation must also lead the challenge of an international financial system that has no respect for national borders. When stock markets fall in Hong Kong or Jakarta, the effects are no longer local; they are global. The vibrant growth of your own economy is tied closely, therefore, to the **restoration**[3] of stability and growth in the Asia Pacific region. China has **steadfastly**[4] shouldered its responsibilities to the region and the world in this latest **financial crisis**—helping to prevent another cycle of dangerous **devaluations**[5]. We must continue to work together to counter this threat to the global financial system and to the growth and prosperity which should be embracing all of this region.

In the 21st century, your generation will have a remarkable opportunity to bring together the talents of our scientists, doctors, engineers into a shared quest for progress. Already the breakthroughs we have achieved in our areas of joint cooperation—in challenges from dealing with **spina bifida**[6] to dealing with extreme weather conditions and earthquakes—have proved

---

1　emitter 排放体
2　fabric 结构，构造
3　restoration 恢复
4　steadfastly 坚定地
5　devaluation 货币贬值
6　spina bifida 脊柱裂

what we can do together to change the lives of millions of people in China and the United States and around the world. Expanding our cooperation in science and technology can be one of our greatest gifts to the future.

In each of these vital areas that I have mentioned, we can clearly accomplish so much more by walking together rather than standing apart. That is why we should work to see that the productive relationship we now enjoy blossoms into a fuller partnership in the new century. If that is to happen, it is very important that we understand each other better, that we understand both our common interest and our shared aspirations and our honest differences. I believe the kind of open, direct exchange that President Jiang and I had on Saturday at our press conference—which I know many of you watched on television—can both clarify and narrow our differences, and, more important, by allowing people to understand and debate and discuss these things can give a greater sense of confidence to our people that we can make a better future.

From the windows of the White House, where I live in Washington, D.C., the monument to our first President, George Washington, dominates the skyline. It is a very tall **obelisk**[1]. But very near this large monument there is a small stone which contains these words: The United States neither established titles of nobility and royalty, nor created a **hereditary**[2] system. State affairs are put to the vote of public opinion. This created a new political situation, unprecedented from ancient times to the present. How wonderful it is. Those words were not written by an American. They were written by Xu Jiyu, governor of Fujian Province, **inscribed**[3] as a gift from the government of China to our nation in 1853.

I am very grateful for that gift from China. It goes to the heart of who we are as a people—the right to life, liberty, and the pursuit of happiness, the freedom to debate, to **dissent**[4], to associate, to worship without interference from the state. These are the ideals that were at the core of our founding over 220 years ago. These are the ideas that led us across our continent and onto the world stage. These are the ideals that Americans cherish today. As I said in my press conference with President Jiang, we have an **ongoing**[5] quest ourselves to live up to those ideals. The people who framed our Constitution understood that we would never achieve perfection.

They said that the mission of America would always be to form a more perfect union—in other words, that we would never be perfect, but we had to keep trying to do better. The darkest moments in our history have come when we abandoned the effort to do better, when we denied freedom to our people because of their race or their religion, because there were new immigrants or because they held unpopular opinions. The best moments in our history have come when we protected the freedom of people who held unpopular opinion, or extended rights enjoyed by the many to the few who had previously been denied them, making, therefore, the promises of our

---

1 obelisk 方尖碑
2 hereditary 世袭的
3 inscribed 雕刻
4 dissent 不同的
5 ongoing 前进的

Declaration of Independence and Constitution more than faded words on old **parchment**[1].

Today we do not seek to impose our vision on others, but we are convinced that certain rights are universal—not American rights or European rights or rights for developed nations, but the birthrights of people everywhere, now **enshrined**[2] in *the United Nations Declaration on Human Rights*—the right to be treated with dignity; the right to express ones opinions, to choose one's own leaders, to associate freely with others, and to worship, or not, freely, however one chooses. In the last letter of his life, the author of our *Declaration of Independence* and our third President, Thomas Jefferson, said then that all eyes are opening to the rights of man. I believe that in this time, at long last, 172 years after Jefferson wrote those words, all eyes are opening to the rights of men and women everywhere.

Over the past two decades, a rising tide of freedom has lifted the lives of millions around the world, sweeping away failed **dictatorial**[3] systems in the Former Soviet Union, throughout Central Europe; ending a vicious cycle of military coups and civil wars in Latin America; giving more people in Africa the chance to make the most of their **hard-won**[4] independence. And from the Philippines to South Korea, from Thailand to Mongolia, freedom has reached Asian shores, powering a surge of growth and **productivity**[5]. Economic security also can be an essential element of freedom. It is recognized in *the United Nations* **Covenant**[6] *on Economic, Social, and Cultural Rights*. In China, you have made extraordinary strides in nurturing that liberty, and spreading freedom from want, to be a source of strength to your people. Incomes are up, poverty is down; people do have more choices of jobs, and the ability to travel—the ability to make a better life. But true freedom includes more than economic freedom.

In America, we believe it is a concept which is **indivisible**[7]. Over the past four days, I have seen freedom in many **manifestations**[8] in China. I have seen the fresh shoots of democracy growing in the villages of your heartland. I have visited a village that chose its own leaders in free elections. I have also seen the cell phones, the video players, the fax machines carrying ideas, information and images from all over the world. I've heard people speak their minds and I have joined people in prayer in the faith of my own choosing. In all these ways I felt a steady breeze of freedom. The question is, where do we go from here? How do we work together to be on the right side of history together? More than 50 years ago, Hu Shi, one of your great political thinkers and a teacher at this university, said these words: Now some people say to me you must sacrifice your individual freedom so that the nation may be free. But I reply, the struggle for individual freedom is the struggle for the nation's freedom. The struggle for your own character is the struggle for the nation's character.

---

1 parchment 羊皮纸；仿羊皮纸
2 enshrine 铭记
3 dictatorial 独裁的
4 hard-won 来之不易的
5 productivity 生产力
6 Covenant 契约
7 indivisible 不可分割的
8 manifestation 表现

We Americans believe Hu Shi was right. We believe and our experience demonstrates that freedom strengthens stability and helps nations to change. One of our founding fathers, Benjamin Franklin, once said, our critics are our friends, for they show us our faults. Now, if that is true, there are many days in the United States when the President has more friends than anyone else in America.

But it is so. In the world we live in, this global information age, constant improvement and change is necessary to economic opportunity and to national strength. Therefore, the freest possible flow of information, ideas, and opinions, and a greater respect for **divergent**[1] political and religious convictions will actually breed strength and stability going forward.

It is, therefore, profoundly in your interest, and the worlds, that young Chinese minds be free to reach the fullness of their potential. That is the message of our time and the **mandate**[2] of the new century and the new millennium. I hope China will more fully embrace this mandate. For all the grandeur of your history, I believe your greatest days are still ahead. Against great odds in the 20th century China has not only survived, it is moving forward dramatically. Other ancient cultures failed because they failed to change. China has constantly proven the capacity to change and grow. Now, you must re-imagine China again for a new century, and your generation must be at the heart of China's regeneration. The new century is upon us.

All our sights are turned toward the future. Now your country has known more millennia than the United States has known centuries. Today, however, China is as young as any nation on Earth. This new century can be the dawn of a new China, proud of your ancient greatness, proud of what you are doing, prouder still of the tomorrows to come. It can be a time when the world again looks to China for the vigor of its culture, the freshness of its thinking, the elevation of human dignity that is apparent in its works. It can be a time when the oldest of nations helps to make a new world. The United States wants to work with you to make that time a reality.

Thank you very much.

文化快递

1. John Leighton Stuart（司徒雷登）

司徒雷登（John Leighton Stuart，1876年生于中国杭州，1962年9月19日逝于美国华盛顿）美国基督教传教士、教育家、外交官。其父母皆为美国在华传教士，司徒雷登在美国大学毕业后，于1904年底携妻返华，开始在中国传教，并钻研汉文。1919年，他筹集资金创办燕京大学并任校长。主要著作有《启示录注释》、《在华五十年——司徒雷登回忆录》等。

2. this latest financial crisis 1998（亚洲金融危机）

这里"最近的金融危机"指的是亚洲金融危机。危机的发展过程十分复杂。危机发生

1　divergent 相异的
2　mandate 命令；指令

于1997年7月至10月，由泰国开始，之后进一步影响了邻近亚洲国家的货币、股票市场和其它的资产价值。1997年7月2日，泰国宣布放弃固定汇率制，实行浮动汇率制，引发了一场遍及东南亚的金融风暴。

3. Declaration of Independence（美国《独立宣言》）

美国《独立宣言》（The Declaration of Independence）为北美洲十三个英属殖民地宣告自大不列颠王国独立，并宣明此举正当性之文告。其中美国总统托马斯·杰斐逊起草了很大一部分。1776年7月4日，本宣言由第二次大陆会议于费城批准，当日之后7月4日成为美国独立纪念日。《独立宣言》包括三个部分：第一部分阐明政治哲学——民主与自由的哲学，内容深刻动人；第二部分列举若干具体的不平等事例，以证明乔治三世破坏了美国的自由；第三部分郑重宣布独立，并宣誓支持该项宣言。

《独立宣言》的中心思想是宣布美国独立，它深刻地阐述了资产阶级民主主义原则。《独立宣言》是一个伟大的政治文件，代表了广大殖民地人民的心声。它在人类历史上第一次以政治纲领的形式提出了如下原则：人人生而平等、人具有不可剥夺的生命、自由和追求幸福的权利，以及政府必须经人民的同意而组成，应为人民幸福和保障人民权利而存在，人民有权起来革命以推翻不履行职责的政府。这些原则成为以后美国的意识形态，为美国此后200多年的发展奠定了思想基础。它也直接影响了法国大革命，对亚洲、拉丁美洲的民族独立运动起了一定的推动作用。

4. Over the past two decades, a rising tide of freedom （1978年的自由潮流）

20世纪80—90年代民族主义浪潮发生的最为突出的表现是地方分离主义运动，广泛地表现为中东、西亚和南部非洲的经久不息的民族战争，世界范围内的汹涌不止的难民浪潮，再度复苏的种族歧视和种族排外等都刺激着世界的神经。而拉丁美洲国家在结束1950—1980年30年持续的经济增长之后陷入严重的经济危机和政治危机，但其进行了两场相应的改革。恢复国内政局的相对稳定，克服经济危机。而这些动荡在20世纪末都得到了较好的解决。

参考译文

谢谢。陈校长、任书记、迟副校长、韦副部长，谢谢你们。

今天，我很高兴率领一个庞大的美国代表团来到这里，代表团中包括第一夫人和我们的女儿，她是斯坦福大学的学生，该校是和北大具有交流关系的学校之一。

此外，我们的代表团中还包括六位美国国会议员、国务卿、商务部长、农业部长、经济顾问理事会理事长、我国驻华大使参议员尚慕杰、国家安全顾问和我的办公厅主任等。我提到这些人是为了说明美国极为重视对华关系。在北大百年校庆之际，我首先要向你们全体师生员工、管理人员祝贺。恭喜了，北大！

各位知道，这个校园曾经一度是由美国传教士建立的燕京大学。学校许多美丽的建筑物由美国建筑师设计。成千上万的美国学生和教授来到北大求学和教课。我们对你们有一种特殊的亲近感。

我很庆幸，今天和79年前的一个重要的日子大不相同。1919年6月，就在这里，燕京大学首任校长司徒雷登准备发表第一个毕业典礼致辞。他准时出场，但学生一个未到。学生们为了振兴中国的政治文化，全部走上街头领导"五四"运动去了。我读到这个故事后，希望今天当我走进这个礼堂时，会有人坐在这里。非常感谢大家前来听我演讲。

一百年以来，北大已经发展到两万多学生。贵校的毕业生遍及中国和全世界。贵校建成了亚洲最大的大学图书馆。去年贵校有20%的毕业生去国外深造，其中包括一半的数理专业学生。在这个百年校庆之年，中国、亚洲和全世界有100多万人登录贵校的网址。在新世纪黎明之际，北大正在率领中国奔向未来。你们是中国下一代的领导者。我今天要跟你们讲的是，建立中美两国牢固的伙伴关系，对于你们的未来至关重要。

在几千年的历史长河中，中国为人类文化、宗教、哲学、艺术和科技作出了贡献，美国人民深深钦佩你们。我们铭记着第二次世界大战期间两国的牢固伙伴关系。现在我们看到，中国处于历史性时刻：能和你们光辉灿烂的过去相提并论的，只有贵国目前气势磅礴的改革和更加美好的未来。仅仅在30年前，中国还与世界隔绝。

现在，中国参加了从航空旅行到农业开发等领域的1000多个国际组织。贵国为大规模贸易和投资敞开了大门。今天有40,000多年轻的中国学生在美国留学，还有数十万中国学生在亚洲、非洲、欧洲和拉美国家留学。贵国在社会和经济领域的变革更为显著，从一个封闭的指令性经济体制向一个日显生机、日趋注重市场性的经济转变，产生了连续20年史无前例的增长，赋予人民更大的自由，如到国内外旅游、进行村委会选举、拥有住房、选择职业以及上更好学校。因此，贵国帮助成千上百万的人们摆脱了贫困。在过去的10年中人均收入翻了一番以上。大多数中国人民过上了20年前还难以想象的美好生活。

当然，这些变化也打乱了固有的生活和工作格局，给贵国的环境造成了巨大压力。以前，每个城市居民到国有企业就业都有保障。现在，你们必须到就业市场上去竞争。以前，每个中国工人只要满足北京中央计划人员的要求，现在，全球性经济意味着人人必须跟上世界其他地区的质量和创造力。对于缺乏适当训练、技能和支持的人们来说，这个新世界的确令人生畏。在短期内，一些诚实勤快的人会失业。正如你们所见，过去20年的开发模式和能源使用模式，造成了空气污染、滥伐森林、酸雨和缺水，在环境、经济和医疗保健方面付出了巨大代价。

面对这些挑战，必须制定出培训和社会保障的新体系，推出保护环境的新政策和新技术，以便在促进经济增长的同时改进环境。我对中国人民智慧、独创性和开发精神的所见所闻，过去几天我和江主席和朱总理及其他人会谈中的所见所闻，给了我信心，相信你们定能成功。在你们建设新中国的同时，美国希望同你们建立新关系。

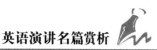

我们要看到一个成就非凡、安全开放的中国，和我们携手为一个和平繁荣的世界而努力。我知道，无论在中国还是在美国，都有人怀疑两国之间的紧密关系是否是好事。但是，世界在变化，我们面临着种种挑战，我们了解的这一切告诉我们，我们两国携手合作比分道扬镳要有利得多。已故的邓小平告诫我们要实事求是。新世纪来临之际，事实显而易见。

我们两国间的距离在缩短，实际上是所有国家间的距离在缩短。以前，美国的快速帆船开到中国要花几个月。今天，高科技使我们天涯若比邻。从笔记本电脑到激光技术、从微芯片到兆字节储存器，信息革命正在照亮人类知识领域，将我们更紧密地联结起来。人们只要敲一下电脑的键盘，观念、信息和资金就能跨越全球，为人们创造财富、预防和征服疾病、加深具有不同历史和文化背景人民之间的了解，带来了极大的机会。

但我们也知道，更大的开放和更快的变革也意味着，别国产生的问题会很快蔓延到本国境内，如大规模毁灭性武器的扩散、有组织的犯罪和贩卖毒品的威胁、环境的恶化和严重的经济混乱等问题。没有哪个国家能避免这些问题，没有那个国家能独自解决这些问题。我们，特别是中美两国的年轻一代必须以迎接这些共同的挑战为共同的事业，共创一个光辉灿烂的新世纪。21世纪是你们的世纪。中美两国将面临亚洲安全的挑战。

我们两国曾在朝鲜半岛为敌，现在我们携手合作，为一个永久和平和无核武器的未来而努力。世界各国正在摆脱核威胁，而在印度次大陆，印度和巴基斯坦却甘冒挑起新一轮军备竞赛的风险。我们正在谋求一个共同的策略，以使印巴两国停止进一步的核试验，并为解决分歧进行对话。

在21世纪，你们年轻一代必须承担制止更加致命的核武器、化学武器和生物武器扩散的重任。如果这种武器落入坏人之手或流入不适当的场所，无论大小国家，其安全都会受到威胁。中美两国日益认识到制止这类武器扩散的重要性，因此我们已开始齐心协力，控制世界上最危险的武器。在21世纪，你们年轻一代一定要扭转犯罪和毒品的国际逆流。全世界有组织的犯罪分子每年从人民手中抢走的财产达数十亿美元，破坏了人们对政府的信任。

美国人民深知毒品给学校师生和社区居民造成的破坏和绝望。中国的边境和十几个国家相邻，已成了各种走私分子的通道。 去年，我和江主席请求中美双方的高级执法官员加强合作，打击这些犯罪分子，防止洗钱，防止在残酷条件下偷渡，防止伪币破坏货币的信用。就在本月，我们的缉毒署在北京开设了办事处。不久，中国的缉毒专家也将在华盛顿开展工作。

在21世纪，你们年轻一代的使命是必须保证今天的进步发展不以明天为代价。中国过去20年来的快速增长以遭受毒害为代价，即贵国人民的饮用水和呼吸的空气都已遭受污染。这种代价不仅仅体现在环境方面，对人民的健康也造成了严重的危害，而且还会阻碍经济的发展。环境问题正在变得日趋全球化和全国化。例如，在不久的将来，如果目前的能源使用模式不改变，中国将超过美国成为世界最大的温室气体的排放国。温室气体是全球性升温的主要原因。

如果世界各国不减少排放造成全球性升温的气体，下世纪的某个时候就会出现气候急剧变化的严重威胁，这将改变我们的生活和工作方式，某些岛国就会被大水淹没，某些国家的经济社会结构就会遭到破坏。我们必须大力合作。经验告诉我们美国人，可以在促使经济增长的同时保护环境。为了我们自己也为了世界，我们必须做到这一点。我国副总统戈尔已同中国政府合作开展了不少工作。在此基础上，我和江主席正一同探讨方法，在中国推出美国的清洁能源技术，促进中国经济发展的同时提高中国的大气质量。

但我还要重申——这话不在我的讲稿上——在这一点上你们这一代还要有更多的作为。这对你们、对美国人民和世界的未来都是一个巨大的挑战。这个问题必须在大学里提出，因为如果政治领导人认为采取环保措施会导致大规模的失业或严重的贫困，他们就不愿意这样做。事实证明环保不会造成失业和贫困。如果我们的方法得当，人们将取得更快的经济增长，拥有薪水更高的工作，促进教育和科技向更高水平发展。但是，你们大学生和你们的大学，中美两国以及全世界的人民都必须带这个头。

在21世纪，你们必须承担不分国界的国际金融系统的重任。当香港和雅加达的股票市场下跌时，其影响再也不是局部性，而是全球性的。因此，贵国充满生机的经济增长同整个亚太地区恢复稳定和经济发展紧密相连。在最近一次的金融危机中，中国坚定不移地承担了对本地区和全世界的责任，帮助避免了又一个危险的货币贬值周期。我们必须继续携手合作，对付全球金融系统面临的威胁以及对整个亚太地区本应有的发展和繁荣的威胁。

在21世纪，你们这一代将有极大的机会，将我们科学家、医生、工程师的各种才能结合起来，用于追求共同的发展。我们早就在一些合作领域中取得了突破，包括从医治脊柱对裂到预报恶劣天气和地震等。这些突破证明，只要我们合作，就能改变中美乃至全世界数以百万计人口的生活。扩大我们在科技领域的合作是我们给未来奉献的厚礼之一。

在我以上列举的每一个关键领域，显然，只要我们相互合作而不是互不往来，我们就能取得更大的成就。因此，我们应该努力，确保双方之间目前的建设性关系在下个世纪结出圆满的协作果实。要做到这一点，我们就必须更好地相互了解，了解各自的共同利益、共有的期望和真诚的分歧。我相信大家在电视上都看到了，我和江主席星期六在联合记者招待会上公开直接的交流，有助于澄清和缩小我们的分歧。更为重要的是，允许人们理解、辩论和探讨这些问题，能使他们对我们建设美好的未来更加充满信心。

从我居住的华盛顿特区白宫的窗口向外眺望，我们第一任总统乔治·华盛顿的纪念碑俯视全城。那是一座高耸的方形尖塔。在这个庞大的纪念碑旁，有一块很小的石碑，上面刻着的碑文是：美国决不设置贵族和皇室头衔，也不建立世袭制度。国家事务由舆论公决。美国就是这样建立了一个从古至今史无前例的崭新政治体系。这是最奇妙的事物。这

些话不是美国人写的，而出自福建省巡抚徐继玉之手，并于1853年由中国政府刻成碑文，作为礼物送给美国。

我很感激中国送的这份礼物。它道出了我们全体美国人民的心声，即人人有生命和自由的权利、追求幸福的权利，有不受国家的干涉，辩论和持不同政见的自由、结社的自由和宗教信仰的自由。这些就是220年前美国立国的核心理想。这些理想指引我们跨越美洲大陆，走向世界舞台。这些仍然是美国人民今天珍视的理想。正如我在和江主席举行的记者招待会上所说，我们美国人民正在不断寻求实现这些理想。美国宪法的制定者了解，我们不可能做到尽善尽美。

他们说，美国的使命始终是要"建设一个更为完美的联邦"。换言之，我们永远不可能尽善尽美，但我们必须不断改进。每当我们放弃不断改进的努力，每当我们由于种族或宗教原因、由于新移民，或者由于有人持不受欢迎的意见，而剥夺我们人民的自由，我们的历史就出现最黑暗的时刻。每当我们保护持不受欢迎的意见者的自由，或者将大多数人享受的权利给予以前被剥夺权利的人们，从而实践《独立宣言》和《宪法》的诺言，而不是使其成为一纸空文，我们的历史就出现最光明的时刻。

今天，我们没有谋求将自己的见解强加于人，但我们深信，某种权利具有普遍性，它们不是美国的权利或者欧洲的权利或者是发达国家的权利，而是所有的人们与生俱来的权利。这些权利现在载于《联合国人权宣言》。这些就是待人以尊严、各抒己见、选举领袖、自由结社、自由选择信教或不信教的权利。《独立宣言》的作者、我国第三任总统托马斯·杰克逊在他一生的最后一封信中写道："人们正在睁开眼睛关注人权。"在杰克逊写了这句话172年之后，我相信，人们现在终于睁开眼睛关注着世界各地男男女女应享受的人权。

过去20年以来，一个高涨的自由浪潮解放了成千上百万的生灵，扫除了前苏联和中欧那种失败的独裁统治，结束了拉美国家军事政变和内战的恶性循环，使更多的非洲人民有机会享受来之不易的独立。从菲律宾到韩国，从泰国到蒙古，自由之浪已冲到亚洲的海岸，给发展和生产力注入了动力。经济保障也应该是自由的要素。这在《联合国经济社会文化权益公约》中获得承认。在中国，你们为培育这种自由已迈出了大步，保证不遭受匮乏，并成为贵国人民的力量源泉。中国人的收入提高了，贫困现象减轻了；人们有了更多的选择就业的机会和外出旅游的机会，有了创造更好生活的机会。但真正的自由不仅仅是经济的自由。

我们美国人民认为这是一个不可分割的概念。在过去的4天中，我在中国看到了自由的许多表现形式。我在贵国内地的一个村庄看到民主的萌芽正在迸发。我访问了一个自由选举村委领导的村庄。我也看到了手机、录像机和带来全世界观念、信息和图像的传真机。我听到人们抒发自己的想法，我还同当地的人们一起为我选择的宗教信仰祈祷。在所有这些方面，我感觉到自由的微风在吹拂。但人们不禁要问，我们的发展方向是什么？

我们怎样相互合作走上历史的正确一面？贵校伟大的政治思想家之一、胡适教授在50多年前说过："有些人对我说，为了国家的自由你必须牺牲自己的个人自由。但我回答，为了个人自由而奋斗就是为了国家的自由而奋斗。为了个性而奋斗就是为了国民性而奋斗。"

我们美国人认为胡适是对的。我们相信，并且我们的经验表明，自由加强稳定，自由有助于国家的变革。我国的一位开国先贤本杰明·富兰克林曾经说过："我们的批评者是我们的朋友，因为他们指出我们的缺点。"如果这话正确，在美国很多时候，总统的朋友比其他任何人都多。

但确实如此。在我们生活的世界，全球性的信息时代、不断的改进和变革是增加经济机会和国力的必要条件。因此，让信息、观念和看法最自由地流通，更多地尊重不同的政治和宗教信仰，实际上将增加实力，推动稳定。

因此，为了贵国和世界的根本利益，中国的年轻人必须享有心灵上的自由，以便最充份地开发自己的潜力。这是我们时代的信息，也是新的世纪和新的千年的要求。我希望中国能更充份地赞同这个要求。尽管贵国历史上有过辉煌的功绩，我认为，贵国最伟大的时光仍在前头。中国不仅顶着20世纪的种种艰难险阻生存了下来，而且正在迅速向前迈进。其它的古老文化消亡了，因为他们没有进行变革。中国始终显示出变革和成长的能力。你们必须重新想象新世纪的中国，你们这一代必然处于中国复兴的中心。我们即将进入新世纪。

我们所有的目光瞄向未来。贵国以千年计算历史，美国以百年计算历史，相比之下，贵国的历史更加悠久。然而，今天的中国和任何一个国家一样年轻。新世纪将是新中国的黎明，贵国为其在历史上的伟大而自豪，为你们进行的事业而自豪，为明天的到来更加自豪。在新世纪中，世界可能再次转向中国寻求她文化的活力、思想的新颖、人类尊严的升华，这在中国的成就中已显而易见。在新世纪中，最古老的国家有可能帮助建设一个新世界。美国希望与贵国合作，使那个时刻成为现实。

非常感谢。

Chapter 3

Communication of Hearts
（礼仪演讲篇——心灵的交流）

Lesson 1

Beautiful Smile and Love

Task 1　Questions and Answers

Directions: Work in pairs. Read the following speech then take turns to ask and answer the following questions.
1. When was the speech delivered? Where?
2. Who delivered the speech? Who are involved in the speech?
3. What is the theme of the speech?
4. Why is there a need for the request?
5. How can the request be achieved?

Task 2　Brainstorming and Paper Talk

Directions: Work in groups of six. Each group selects one topic among the three words "love, beauty and happiness". Put the word in the middle of a piece of paper, then each member brainstorms and puts any ideas, questions, answers or comments on the topic using a mind map. Then one representative from the group summarizes and reports to the class.

Task 3　Dictation

Directions: Watch the authentic video of the speech. Then fill in the missing words in their appropriate forms. You may watch the video for three times.

　　I could not help but _____ my conscience before her and I asked what would I say if I was in her _____. And my answer was very simple. I would have tried to _____ a little attention to myself. I would have said I am hungry, that I am _____, I am cold, I am in pain, or something, but she gave me much more—she gave me her _____ love. And she died with a smile on her face. So did that man whom we picked up from the drain, half eaten with worms, and we brought him to the home. "I have lived like an _____ in the street, but I am going to die like an _____, loved and cared for."

Task 4 Imitation and Play

Directions: *Watch the authentic video of the speech. Then try to imitate the whole speech appropriate delivery techniques. First practice by yourself. Then work in groups of four to take turns to deliver the speech.*

Task 5 Speaking Practice

Directions: *Suppose you were one person who had been helped by Mother Teresa. What would say to her on her funeral in 1997? Please deliver a speech to your fellow students for 2-3 minutes.*

Beautiful Smile and Love
美丽的微笑与爱心
*Nobel Prize Reception Lecture
By Mother Teresa*

▶ 人物简介

特雷莎修女（1910—1997），生于南斯拉夫，37岁正式成为修女，1948年远赴印度加尔各答，两年后正式创立仁爱传教修女会，在世界范围内建立了一个庞大的慈善机构网，竭力服侍贫困中的人们，赢得了国际社会的广泛尊敬。1979年，她被授予诺贝尔和平奖。

1997年病逝，葬于加尔各答。

1997年9月，当她去世时，印度政府为她举行国葬，全国哀悼两天。成千上万的人冒着倾盆大雨走上街头，为她的离去流下哀伤的眼泪。1979年授予她的诺贝尔和平奖的颁奖词说："她的事业的一个特征就是对单个人的尊重。最孤独的人、最悲惨的人、濒临死亡的人，都从她的手中接受到了不含施舍意味的同情，接受到了建立在对人的尊重之上的同情。"本文所选即她在领取该奖项时的演讲词，语言简洁质朴而感人至深。

▶ 名篇导读

《美丽的微笑与爱心》是特蕾莎嬷嬷于1979年领取诺贝尔和平奖时所做的演讲词，行文简洁质朴，随意自然，感人至深。诺贝尔奖领奖台上响起的声音往往都是热烈激昂、文采飞扬的。而特蕾莎修女的演说朴实无华，其所举事例听来似平凡之至，然而其中所蕴含的伟大而神圣的爱感人至深。平凡中孕育伟大，真情才能动人。

▶ 英文原文

The poor are very wonderful people. One evening we went out and we picked up four people from the street. And one of them was in a most terrible condition—and I told the sisters: You take care of the other three. I take care of this one who looked worse. So I did for her all that my love can do. I put her in bed, and there was such a beautiful smile on her face. She took hold of my hand as she said just the words "Thank you." and she died.

I could not help but examine my **conscience**[1] before her and I asked what would I say if I was in her place. And my answer was very simple. I would have tried to draw a little attention to myself. I would have said I am hungry, that I am dying, I am cold, I am in pain, or something, but she gave me much more—she gave me her grateful love. And she died with a smile on her face. So did that man whom we picked up from the drain, half eaten with worms, and we brought him to the home. "I have lived like an animal in the street, but I am going to die like an angel, loved and cared for." And it was so wonderful to see the greatness of that man who could speak like that, who could die like that without blaming anybody, without **cursing**[2] anybody, without comparing anything. Like an angel—this is the greatness of our people. And that is why we believe what Jesus had said: I was hungry—I was naked…I was homeless…I was unwanted, unloved, uncared for…and you did it to me.

I believe that we are not real social workers. We may be doing social work in the eyes of the people, but we are really **contemplatives**[3], in the heart of the world. For we are touching the body of Christ twenty-four hours… And I think that in our family we don't need bombs and guns,

---

1　conscience 良心
2　curse 咒骂
3　contemplative 修行者

to destroy, to bring peace—just get together, love one another, bring that peace, that joy, that strength of presence of each other in the home. And we will be able to overcome all the evil that is in the world.

And with this prize that I received as a **Prize of Peace**, I am going to try to make the home for many people who have no home, because I believe that love begins at home, and if we can create a home for the poor, I think that more and more love will spread. And we will be able through this understanding love to bring peace, be the good news to the poor. The poor in our own family first, then in our country and in the world. To be able to do this, our Sisters, our lives have to be woven with prayer. They have to be woven with Christ to be able to understand, to be able to share, because to be woven with Christ is to be able to understand, to be able to share, because today there is so much suffering. When I pick up a person from the street, hungry, I give him a plate of rice, a piece of bread, I have satisfied. I have removed that hungry. But a person who is shut out, who feels unwanted, unloved, terrified, the person who has been thrown out from society—that poverty is so full of hurt and so **unbearable**[1]. And so let us always meet each other with a smile, for the smile is the beginning of love, and once we begin to love each other naturally we want to do something.

文化快递

1. "I was hungry. I was naked. I was homeless. I was unwanted, unloved, uncared for, and you did it to me."

选自圣经《马太福音》，原文是"Come, you blessed of My Father, inherit the kingdom prepared for you from the foundation of the world: for I was hungry and you gave Me food; I was thirsty and you gave Me drink; I was a stranger and you took Me in; I was naked and you clothed Me; I was homeless and you took me in."

2. Prize of Peace（诺贝尔和平奖）

诺贝尔和平奖是由瑞典发明家阿尔弗雷德·诺贝尔（Alfred Bernhard Nobel，1833—1896）所创立的五个诺贝尔奖中的一个。根据诺贝尔的遗嘱，诺贝尔和平奖不应该与其他四个奖项一起在瑞典颁发，而是应该在挪威首都奥斯陆。和平奖的评奖委员会是由5人组成的挪威诺贝尔委员会，其成员由挪威议会任命。

根据诺贝尔的遗嘱，和平奖应该奖给"为促进民族团结友好、取消或裁减常备军队以及为和平会议的组织和宣传尽到最大努力或作出最大贡献的人"。但评选委员会逐渐拓宽了和平奖所涵盖的范围，而且也开始将该奖授予符合获奖条件的机构与组织。从1901年至2013年，共颁发94个诺贝尔和平奖。

---

1 unbearable 无法忍受的

> **参考译文**

穷人是非常了不起的人。一天晚上，我们外出，从街上带回了四个人，其中一个生命岌岌可危。于是我告诉修女们说："你们照料其他三个，这个濒危的人就由我来照顾了。"这样，我为她做了我的爱所能做的一切。我将她放在床上，看到她脸上绽露出如此美丽的微笑。她握着我的手，只说了句"谢谢您"就死了。

我情不自禁地在她面前审视起自己的良知来。我问自己，如果我是她的话，会说些什么呢？答案很简单，我会尽量引起旁人对我的关注，我会说我饥饿难忍，冷得发抖，奄奄一息，痛苦不堪，诸如此类的话。但是她给我的却更多更多——她给了我她的感激之情。她死了，脸上却带着微笑。我们从排水道带回的那个男子也是如此。他几乎全身都快被虫子吃掉了，我们把他带回了家。"在街上，我一直像个动物一样地活着，但我将像个天使一样地死去，有人爱，有人关心。"真是太好了，我看到他的伟大之处，他竟然能说出那样的话。他那样地死去，不责怪任何人，不诅咒任何人，无欲无求。像天使一样——这便是我们的人民的伟大之所在。因此我们相信耶稣所说的话——"我饥肠辘辘……我衣不蔽体……我无家可归……我不为人所要，不为人所爱，也不为人所关心……然而，你却为我做了这一切。"

我想，我们算不上真正的社会工作者。在人们的眼中，或许我们是在做社会工作，但实际上，我们真的只是世界心中的修行者。因为一天24小时，我们都在触摸基督的圣体。我想，在我们的大家庭里，我们不需要枪支和炮弹来破坏和平，或带来和平——我们只需要团结起来，彼此相爱，将和平、欢乐以及每一个家庭成员灵魂的活力都带回世界。这样，我们就能战胜世界上现存的一切邪恶。

我准备以我所获得的诺贝尔和平奖奖金为那些无家可归的人们建立自己的家园。因为我相信，爱源自家庭，如果我们能为穷人建立家园，我想爱便会传播得更广。而且，我们将通过这种宽容博大的爱而带来和平，成为穷人的福音。首先为我们自己家里的穷人，其次为我们国家，为全世界的穷人。为了做到这一点，姐妹们，我们的生活就必须与祷告紧紧相连，必须同基督结合一体才能互相体谅，共同分享，因为同基督结合一体就意味着相互体谅，共同分享。因为在今天的世界上仍然有如此多的苦难存在。当我从街上带回一个饥肠辘辘的人时，给他一盘米饭，一片面包，我就能使他心满意足了，我就能驱除他的饥饿。但是，如果一个人露宿街头，感到不为人所要，不为人所爱，惶恐不安，被社会抛弃——这样的贫困让人心痛，如此令人无法忍受。因此，让我们总使微笑相见，因为微笑就是爱的开端，一旦我们开始彼此自然地相爱，我们就会想着为对方做点什么了。

Lesson 2

Unconscious Plagiarism

Task 1 Questions and Answers

Directions: *Work in pairs. Read the following speech then take turns to ask and answer the following questions.*
1. To whom was the speech delivered? Where?
2. What is the background of the speech delivered?
3. Which style does the speech belong to according to the text?
4. Does the style of speech match the identity of the speaker?

Task 2 Translation

Directions: *Translate the following poem into Chinese.*

    Holmes successfully concentrated his verse upon concrete objects with which he was long familiar, or had studied at length, such as the one-horse shay or a seashell. Some of his works also deal with his personal or family history; for example, the poem "Dorothy Q" is a portrait of his maternal great-grandmother. The poem combines pride, humor and tenderness in short rhyming couplets:

    O Damsel Dorothy! Dorothy Q!
    Strange is the gift that I owe to you;
    Such a gift as never a king
    Save to daughter or son might bring,—
    All my tenure of heart and hand,
    All my title to house and land;
    Mother and sister and child and wife
    And joy and sorrow and death and life!

Task 3 Role Play

Directions: *Work in group of six. Suppose it's the birthday party of Dr. Holmes. People at present were Dr. Holmes, his family, and friends. An anchor announced the commencement of the party, then guests including Mark Twain started to deliver speeches.*

Task 4 Discussion

Directions: *Work in groups of four and discuss the following questions. You may locate some useful information from the script.*

1. How did Mark Twain feel when he first received a letter from Dr. Holmes?
2. Why did Mark Twain write the letter?
3. What's Dr. Holmes' reaction to this letter?
4. What kind of person is Dr. Holmes? Use specific details or examples to share your understanding his character?
5. Dr. Holmes believed, "We all unconsciously worked over ideas gathered in reading and hearing, imagining they were original with ourselves". Do you have similar experiences?

Task 5 Writing Practice

Directions: *What would Mark Twain include in his apology letter to Dr. Holmes? Please write a letter in the name of Mark Twain, with any rational imagination to build up the information gap.*

Unconscious Plagiarism[1]
无意的剽窃

Lecture on Dr. Holmes Seventith Birthday
By Mark Twain

▶ 人物简介

马克·吐温（Mark Twain）（1835—1910），原名塞姆·朗赫恩·克列门斯（Samuel Langhorne Clemens）；是美国的幽默大师、小说家、作家，亦是著名演说家。

---

1 plagiarism 剽窃

40年的创作生涯中，马克·吐温写出了10多部长篇小说、几十部短篇小说及其他体裁的大量作品，其中著名的有短篇小说《竞选州长》、《哥尔斯密的朋友再度出洋》和《百万英镑》等，长篇小说《镀金时代》、《汤姆·索亚历险记》、《王子与贫儿》等。《哈克贝利·费恩历险记》是他最优秀的作品，曾被美国小说家海明威誉为是"第一部真正的美国文学"。

名篇导读

这是霍姆斯七十寿辰（1879年12月3日）时，马克·吐温在波士顿为他祝寿的致词。霍姆斯（1809~1894），美国著名作家、诗人，是美国杂志《大西洋月刊》的创始人。

马克·吐温的这篇演讲词写得既真切又幽默，既坦诚又真诚。祝寿词中既有发自肺腑的祝福——祝福对自己有帮助、支持、理解的长者的七十高龄，又在坦陈自己曾经有过的"无意间的剽窃"——借用名人诗作中的诗句而使自己功成名就，还有对长辈豁达大度成人之美的高尚德行的赞美。字里行间，既有幽默的调侃又有真诚的自辩；既表现出无比的自豪，又充满了无限的感激。"任何一个有茶匙那么点脑子的人都会有一点尊严，决不会有意地去剽窃别人的思想。"由此可以说，这是一篇独具特色的祝寿演讲词。

英文原文

Mr. Chairman, Ladies and Gentlemen:

I would have traveled a much greater distance than I have come to witness the paying of honors to **Dr. Holmes.** For my feeling toward him has always been one of peculiar warmth. When one receives a letter from a great man for the first time in his life, it is a large event to him, as all of you know by your own experience. You never can receive letters enough from famous men afterward to **obliterate**[1] that one, or dim the memory of the pleasant surprise it was, and the **gratification**[2] it gave you. **Lapse**[3] of time cannot make it **commonplace**[4] or cheap.

Well, the first great man who ever wrote me a letter was our guest—Oliver Wendell Holmes. He was also the first great literary man I ever stole anything from (laughter), and that is how I came to write to him and he to me. When my first book was new a friend of mine said to me, "The **dedication**[5] is very neat." "Yes," I said, "I thought it was." My friend said: "I always admired it, even before I saw it in the '*Innocents Abroad*'." I naturally said, "What do you mean? Where did you ever see it before?" "Well, I saw it first some year ago as Dr. Holmes's dedication to his '*Songs in Many Keys*'." Of course, my first impulse was to prepare this man's remains for burial (laughter), but upon reflection I said I would **reprieve**[6] him for a moment or two, and give him a

---

1 obliterate 擦掉；使消失；忘掉
2 gratification 满足；满意；喜悦；使人满意之事
3 lapse 流逝
4 commonplace 普普通通的
5 dedication （书等作品上的）题词
6 reprieve 对……缓期执行

chance to prove his assertion if he could. We stepped into a bookstore, and he did prove it. I had really stolen that dedication, almost word for word. I could not imagine how this curious thing had happened; for I knew one thing, for a dead certainty—that a certain amount of pride always goes along with a **teaspoonful**[1] of brains, and that this pride protects a man from deliberately stealing other people's ideas. That is what a teaspoonful of brains will do for a man, —and admirers had often told me I had nearly a basketful, though they were rather reserved as to the size of the basket. (Laughter)

However, I thought the thing out and solved the mystery. Two years before I have been laid up a couple of weeks in the Sandwich Islands, and had read and reread Dr .Holmes's poems until my mental **reservoir**[2] was filled up with them to the **brim**[3]. The dedication lay on top and handy (laughter), so by and by I unconsciously stole it. Perhaps I unconsciously stole the rest of the volume, too, for many people have told me that my book was pretty poetical, in one way or another. Well, of course, I wrote Dr. Holmes and told him I hadn't meant to steal, and he wrote back and said in the kindest way that it was all right and no harm done; and added that he believed we all unconsciously worked over ideas gathered in reading and hearing, imagining they were original with ourselves. He stated a truth, and did it in such a pleasant way, and **salved**[4] over my sore spot so gently and so **healingly**[5], that I was rather glad I had committed the crime, for the sake of the letter. I afterward called on him and told him to make perfectly free with any ideas of mine that struck him as being good **protoplasm**[6] for poetry. (Laughter) He could see by that that there wasn't anything mean about me; so we got along right from the start.

I have met Dr. Holmes many times since; and lately he said, —however, I am wandering wildly away from the one thing which I got on my feet to do: that is, to make my compliments to you, my fellow teachers of the great public, and likewise to say I am right glad to see that Dr. Holmes is still in his prime and full of generous life; and as age is not determined by years, but by trouble and **infirmities**[7] of mind and body, I hope it may be a very long time yet before any can truthfully say, " He is growing old". (Applause)

文化快递

1. Dr. Holmes（霍姆斯博士）

老奥利弗·温德尔·霍姆斯（Oliver Wendell Holmes, Sr., 1809年8月29日—1894年10月7日）是美国医生，著名作家，美国杂志《大西洋月刊》的创始人，被誉为美国19世纪最佳诗人之一。他的儿子是美国著名法学家小奥利弗·温德尔·霍姆斯。

2. The Innocents Abroad（《傻子国外旅行记》）

马克·吐温的早期著作，发表于1869年。主人公是一个美国游客，讲述途中在欧洲

1　teaspoonful 一茶匙满的
2　reservoir 蓄水池；贮液器；储藏；蓄积
3　brim 充盈，满；溢出
4　salved 使良心得到宽慰，减轻内疚感
5　healingly 有治疗功用地
6　protoplasm 原生质，细胞质
7　infirmities 体弱；虚弱；疾病；病症

大陆和中东的所见所闻。虽然所到之处都是有名的博物馆或者圣地，但叙述者抛开崇拜心态，直抒己见，而且不乏幽默和调侃。此书一年内发行近7万册，奠定了马克·吐温幽默作家的地位。本书献词为"To my most patient reader and most charitable critic, my aged mother, this volume is affectionately inscribed."

3. Songs in Many Keys（《多调之歌》）

霍姆斯所著诗歌集，发表于1862年。

参考译文

主席先生、各位女士、先生：

为了亲临为霍姆斯博士祝寿，再远的路程我也要前来。因为我一直对他怀有特别亲切的感情。你们所有的人都会有这样的体验，一个人一生中初次接到一位大人物的信时，总是把这当成一件大事。不管你后来接到多少名人的来信，都不会使这第一封失色，也不会使你淡忘当时那种又惊又喜又感激的心情。流逝的时光也不会湮灭它在你心底的价值。

第一次给我写信的伟大人物正是我们的贵客——奥列弗·温德尔·霍姆斯。这也是第一位被我从他那里偷得了一点东西的大文学家。（笑声。）这正是我给他写信以及他给我回信的原因。我的第一本书出版不久，一位朋友对我说："你的卷首献词写得漂亮简洁。"我说："是的，我认为是这样。"我的朋友说："我一直很欣赏这篇献词，甚至在你的《傻子国外旅行记》出版前，我就很欣赏这篇献词了。"我当然感到吃惊，便问："你这话什么意思？你以前在什么地方看到这篇献词？""唔，几年前我读霍姆斯博士《多调之歌》一书的献词时就看过了。"当然啦，我一听之下，第一个念头就是要了这小子的命（笑声），但是想了一想之后，我说可以先饶他一两分钟，给他个机会，看看他能不能拿出证据证实他的话。我们走进一间书店，他果真证实了他的话。我确确实实偷了那篇献词，几乎一字未改。我当时简直想象不出怎么会发生这种怪事；因为我知道一点，绝对无庸置疑的一点，那就是，一个人若有一茶匙头脑，便会有一份傲气。这份傲气保护着他，使他不致有意剽窃别人的思想。那就是一茶匙头脑对一个人的作用——可有些崇拜我的人常常说我的头脑几乎有一只篮子那么大，不过他们不肯说这只篮子的尺寸罢了（笑声）。

后来我到底把这事想清楚了，揭开了这谜。在那以前的两年，我有两三个星期在桑威奇岛休养。这期间，我反复阅读了霍姆斯博士的诗集，直到这些诗句填满我的脑子，快要溢了出来。那献词浮在最上面，信手就可拈来（笑声），于是不知不觉地，我就把它偷来了。说不定我还偷了那集子的其余内容呢，因为不少人对我说，我那本书在有些方面颇有点诗意。当然啦，我给霍姆斯博士写了封信，告诉他我并非有意偷窃。他给我回了信，十分体谅地对我说，那没有关系，不碍事；他还相信我们所有的人都会不知不觉地运用读到的或听来的思想，还以为这些思想是自己的创见呢。他说出了一个真理，而且说得那么令人愉快，帮我顺顺当当地下了台阶，使我甚至庆幸自己亏得犯了这剽窃罪，因而得到了这封信。后来我拜访他，告诉他以后如果看到我有什么可供他作诗的思想原料，他尽管随意取用好了。（笑声）那样他可以看到我是一点也不小气的；于是我们从一开始就很合得来。

从那以后，我多次见过霍姆斯博士；最近，他说——噢，我离题太远了。我本该向你们，我的同行、广大公众和教师们说出我对霍姆斯的祝词。我应该说，我非常高兴地看到霍姆斯博士的风采依然不减当年。一个人之所以年迈，非因年岁而是由于身心的衰弱。我希望许多许多年之后，人们还不能真正他说："他已经老了。"（鼓掌）

Lesson 3

Cultural Programs and the 2008 Olympic Games

Task 1　Questions and Answers

Directions: *Work in pairs. Read the following speech then take turns to ask and answer the following questions.*

1. When was the speech delivered? Where?
2. Who delivered the speech? Who are involved in the speech?
3. What is the theme of the speech?
4. Why is there a need for the request?
5. How can the request be achieved?

Task 2　Dictation

Directions: *Watch the authentic video of the speech. Then fill in the blank the missing words in their appropriate forms. You may watch the video for three times.*

　　But _____ that, it is a place of millions of friendly people who love to meet people from around the world. People of Beijing believe that the 2008 Olympic Games in Beijing will help to enhance the _____ between our culture and the _____ cultures of the world. Their gratitude will _____ out in open expressions of _____ for you and the great Movement that you guide.

　　Within our cultural programs, education and communication will receive the highest _____. We seek to create an intellectual and sporting legacy by _____ the understanding of the Olympic Ideals throughout the country.

Task 3　Imitation and Performance

Directions: *Watch the authentic video of the speech. Then try to imitate this speech with appropriate delivery techniques. First practice by yourself. Then work in groups* *of four to take turns to deliver the speech.*

Task 4 Role Play

Directions: *Suppose you were representatives of different cities to bid for World Expo in 2022. Work in groups of six. Each group first selects a city they like most, then prepares a bid speech as a group, and finally chooses one member to deliver the speech in class. The group getting the most support wins.*

Task 5 Writing Practice

Directions: *Write a speech for about 300 words. You may choose one topic which interests most from the following:*

1. Fair Play
2. Where Real Power Comes From
3. Does the NBA need China more than China need the NBA?
4. Olympic Spirit: Faster, Higher, Stronger

Cultural Programs and the 2008 Olympic Games
文化活动与2008年奥运会

A speech in helping Beijing bid for the 2008 Olympics
By Yang Lan

▶ 人物简介

杨澜,女,生于北京。中国著名电视节目主持人及企业家。从1990年起曾与赵忠祥一同主持中国中央电视台《正大综艺》节目并为大家熟知。现主持多档谈话节目,如采访

英语演讲名篇赏析
Appreciation of Masterpiece English Speeches

类节目《杨澜访谈录》及女性类节目《天下女人》。曾被评选为"亚洲二十位社会与文化领袖"、"能推动中国前进、重塑中国形象的十二位代表人物"、"《中国妇女》时代人物"。现在她是阳光媒体投资控股有限公司主席。

▶ 名篇导读

2001年7月13日,在中国申奥的最关键时刻,赴莫斯科的中国申奥大使杨澜,代表中国在莫斯科作4分钟的最后陈述。杨澜陈述的具体内容有:北京特殊的文化和奥林匹克运动的关系、北京的教育计划,闭幕式的设计以及火炬接力的设计等因素。

杨澜的英文演说极具演讲风采、东方魅力。杨澜以亲和的微笑、宁静自信的眼神和流畅的英文,讲述北京的悠久历史文化和北京举办奥运会的文化意义。为了与评委和世界观众的沟通,杨澜的论述很有西方技巧:杨澜上场第一句话是"你们将会在北京享受一个愉快的夏天!"拉近了与西方的心理距离,很平淡的一句话但有技巧。借用好莱坞李安的电影和西方人马可波罗两个元素,拉近与西方文化的距离。杨澜的演说还生动阐述了奥运火炬传递壮观景象设想,把东方的雄浑大气、厚重底蕴和西方的浪漫精神、挑战理想融合为一,富有想象力和浪漫感,感染和震动评委和观众。

杨澜4分钟的英文演说成为一次经典演说。杨澜的演说打动评委、感动世界。杨澜以她的东方魅力嫁接起沟通世界的桥梁。

▶ 英文原文

Mr. President, Ladies and Gentlemen, Good afternoon!

Before I introduce our cultural programs, I want to tell you one thing first about 2008. You're going to have a great time in Beijing.

China has its own sport legends. Back to Song Dynasty, about the 11th century, people started to play a game called Cuju, which is regarded as the origin of ancient football. The game was very popular and women were also participating. Now, you will understand why our women football team is so good today.

There are a lot more wonderful and exciting things waiting for you in New Beijing, a **dynamic**[1] modern **metropolis**[2] with 3,000 years of cultural treasures woven into the urban **tapestry**[3]. Along with the **iconic**[4] imagery of the Forbidden City, the Temple of Heaven and the Great Wall, the city offers an endless mixture of theatres, museums, discos, all kinds of

---

1　dynamic 充满活力的
2　metropolis 大都会;首都;大城市
3　tapestry 挂毯;绣帷;织锦
4　iconic 标志性的;偶像的

restaurants and shopping malls that will amaze and delight you.

But beyond that, it is a place of millions of friendly people who love to meet people from around the world. People of Beijing believe that the 2008 Olympic Games in Beijing will help to **enhance**[1] the harmony between our culture and the diverse cultures of the world. Their gratitude will pour out in open expressions of affection for you and the great Movement that you guide.

Within our cultural programs, education and communication will receive the highest priority. We seek to create an **intellectual**[2] and sporting **legacy**[3] by broadening the understanding of the Olympic Ideals throughout the country.

Cultural events will **unfold**[4] each year, from 2005 to 2008. We will stage **multi-disciplined**[5] cultural programs, such as concerts, exhibitions, art competitions and camps which will involve young people from around the world. During the Olympics, they will be staged in the Olympic Village and the city for the benefit of the athletes.

Our Ceremonies will give China's greatest—and the world's greatest artists a stage for celebrating the common aspirations of humanity and the unique **heritage**[6] of our culture and the Olympic Movement.

With a concept inspired by the famed Silk Road, our Torch Relay will break new ground, traveling from Olympia through some of the oldest civilizations known to man—Greek, Roman, Egyptian, **Byzantine, Mesopotamian, Persian**, Arabian, Indian and Chinese. Carrying the message "Share the Peace, Share the Olympics", the **eternal**[7] flame will reach new heights as it crosses the Himalayas over the world's highest summit—Mount Qomolangma, which is known to many of you as Mt. Everest. In China, the flame will pass through Tibet, cross Yangtze and Yellow Rivers, travel the Great Wall and visit Hong Kong, Macau, Taiwan and the 56 ethnic communities who make up our society. On its journey, the flame will be seen by and inspire more human beings than any previous relay.

I am afraid I can not present the whole picture of our cultural programs within such a short period of time. Before I end, let me share with you one story. Seven hundred years ago, amazed by his incredible descriptions of a far away land of great beauty, people asked Marco Polo whether his stories about China were true. He answered, "What I have told you was not even half of what I saw." Actually, what we have shown you here today is only a **fraction**[8] of Beijing that **awaits**[9] you.

1　enhance 提升，促进
2　intellectual 智力的
3　legacy 遗产；遗赠
4　unfold 展开
5　multi-disciplined 多种多样的；多才多艺的；多学科的
6　heritage 遗产；继承物；传统；文化遗产
7　eternal 永恒的；不朽的
8　fraction 分数；一小部分，些微
9　await 等待

文化快递

1. Cuju（蹴鞠）

蹴鞠，《战国策》和《史记》是最早记录蹴鞠的文献典籍，前者描述了2300多年前的春秋时期，齐国都城临淄流行蹴鞠活动，后者则记载，蹴鞠是当时训练士兵、考察兵将体格的方式（"蹹鞠，兵势也，所以练武士，知有材也"）。《史记·苏秦列传》，苏秦游说齐宣王时形容临苗："临苗甚富而实，其民无不吹竽、鼓瑟、蹋鞠者"。蹴鞠又名"蹋鞠"、"蹴球"、"蹴圆"、"筑球"、"踢圆"等，"蹴"即用脚踢，"鞠"系皮制的球，"蹴鞠"就是用脚踢球，它是中国一项古老的体育运动，有直接对抗、间接对抗和白打三种形式。2004年初，国际足联确认足球起源于中国，"蹴鞠"是有史料记载的最早足球活动。

2. Byzantine（拜占庭）

拜占庭帝国（395年—1453年），即东罗马帝国，是一个信奉东正教的君主专制国家。位于欧洲东部，领土曾包括亚洲西部和非洲北部，极盛时领土还包括意大利、叙利亚、巴勒斯坦、埃及和北非地中海沿岸。是古代和中世纪欧洲最悠久的君主制国家。在其上千年的存在期内它一般被人简单地称为"罗马帝国"。拜占庭帝国共历经12个朝代；93位皇帝。帝国的首都为新罗马（拉丁语：Nova Roma，即君士坦丁堡，Constantinople）。1453年，被奥斯曼土耳其攻入君士坦丁堡而灭亡。

3. Mesopotamian（美索不达米亚）

Mesopotamia，希腊语的意思是两河之间的土地。美索不达米亚是世界最早的文明（又称两河文明）。发源于底格里斯河（Tigris）和幼发拉底河（Euphrates）之间的流域——苏美尔（Sumer）中下游地区。美索不达亚是古巴比伦（Babylon）的所在，在今伊拉克（Iraq）共和国境内。

参考译文

主席先生，各位来宾，大家午安！

在介绍我们的文化节目之前，我想先告诉大家，2008年你们将在北京渡过愉快的时光。

中国有自己的体育传奇。回到宋代，大约11世纪，人们开始玩一个叫"蹴鞠"的游戏，这被看作是足球古老的起源。这个游戏很受欢迎，妇女也会参加。现在，你就会明白，为什么我们的女子足球队这么厉害了。

还有更多精彩的事物在等着你。北京是一座充满活力的现代都市，三千年的历史文化与都市的繁荣相呼应，除了紫禁城、天坛和万里长城这几个标志性的建筑，北京拥有无数的影院、博物馆、舞厅、各种各样的餐厅和购物中心，这一切的一切都会令您感到惊奇和高兴。

除此之外，北京城里还有千千万万友善的人民，热爱与世界各地的人民相处。北京人民相信，2008年北京奥运会将有助于促进我国与世界多元文化的和谐交融。他们对此心怀感激，并会不吝表达对各位和随各位而来的奥运盛会的喜爱之情。

在我们的文化发展中，教育和交流将得到优先发展，我们想通过在全国范围内扩宽对奥运精神的理解，来创造一笔智力和体育的宝贵财富。

文化活动也将因之而每一年开展，从2005年至2008年，我们将举办多元化的文化节目，如音乐会、展览会、美术比赛和夏令营，将涉及来自世界各地的青少年。奥运会期间，他们将分别在奥运村和北京与所有受惠的运动员一起活动。

我们的开闭幕式，将是展现中国杰出艺术家的舞台，讴歌人类共同理想，以及我们独特的奥林匹克运动。

基于丝绸之路带来的灵感，我们的火炬接力，将途经希腊、罗马、埃及、美索布达米亚、波斯、印度和中国，以"共享和平、共享奥运"为主题，永恒不熄的火炬，将跨越世界最高峰——珠穆朗玛峰，从而达到最高的高度。在中国，圣火还将穿过西藏，穿越长江与黄河，游历长城，途经香港、澳门、台湾，在组成我们国家的56个民族中传递。通过这样的路线，我们保证目睹这次火炬接力的人们，会比任何一次都多。

恕我不能在这么短的时间里介绍我们的文化活动的全貌。在我结束前，让我跟大家分享这样一个故事：七百年前，由于不相信马可波罗对一个遥远国度的种种令人难以置信的描绘，人们问，他在中国的故事是不是真的。他回答道："我告诉你的连我看到的一半都没有达到。"而实际上，我们今天在这里介绍的也只是一小部分，更多的精彩在北京正等待着你！

Lesson 4

Shall We Choose Death

Task 1 Questions and Answers

Directions: *Work in pairs. Read the following speech then take turns to ask and answer the following questions.*

1. When was the speech delivered? Where?
2. Who delivered the speech? Who are involved in the speech?
3. What is the theme of the speech?
4. Why is there a need for the request?
5. How can the request be achieved?

Task 2 Vocabulary Learning

Directions: *Translate the following phrases into Chinese.* Then *try to learn by heart the cultural connotations of these phrases.*

set aside _____   appeal to _____

put an end to _____   reach agreements _____

renounce war _____   in terms of _____

at the most _____   in the course of _____

be incapable of _____   be acquainted with _____

military contest _____   illusory hope _____

Task 3 Writing Practice

Directions: *Read through the script. Then abbreviate it into a piece of speech for about 100 words with the main claims and supports from the original speech remained.*

Task 4 Discussion

Directions: *Work in groups of four and discuss the following questions. You may locate some useful information from the script.*

1. What do you know about the speaker?
2. What is his main claim in this speech?
3. How did he support himself?
4. Can you use specific details or examples to share your understanding of the statement that "I appeal, as a human being to human beings: remember your humanity, and forget the rest. If you can do so, the way lies open to a new Paradise; if you cannot, nothing lies before you but universal death."?

Task 5 Debate

Directions: *Work in groups of six. Debate on the topic "This House Believes Our Government Should Enlarge Military Investment".*

Shall We Choose Death
我们是否该选择死亡?

By Bertrand Russell
December 30, 1954

▶ 人物简介

伯特兰·罗素（Bertrand Russell，1872年5月18日—1970年2月2日），英国哲学家、数学家和逻辑学家，同时也是活跃的政治活动家，出生于英国威尔士的一个贵族家庭。1890年罗素进入剑桥大学三一学院学习哲学、逻辑学和数学，1908年成为学院的研究员并获选为英国皇家学会院士。1920年罗素访问俄国和中国，并在北京讲学一年。1939年罗素搬到美国，到加利福尼亚大学洛杉矶分校讲学，并很快被任命为纽约城市大学教授，1944年回到英国，并重新执教于三一学院。1950年罗素获得诺贝尔文学奖，以表彰其"多样且重要的作品，持续不断的追求人道主义理想和思想自由"。1970年伯特兰·罗素去世，骨灰被撒在威尔士的群山之中。

▶ 名篇导读

伯特兰·罗素被誉为二十世纪西方最有影响的哲学家之一，为我们留下了许多值得品味的作品和无数的经典语录。他一生兼有学者和社会活动家的双重身份，以追求真理和正义为终生职志。罗素是一个具有强烈社会关怀的人道主义者、和平主义者，他的胸怀充满正义、良知、睿智、温情，多姿多彩，博大精深。上世纪40至50年代间，罗素在英国BBC广播发表了一系列演讲，这是在1954年12月30日所做的。当时正值美国和前苏联冷战期，

英语演讲名篇赏析
Appreciation of Masterpiece English Speeches

　　双方为争夺军事优势展开了疯狂的核军备竞赛。1952年11月1日，美国进行了首次氢弹爆炸试验，苏联不甘示弱，于1953年8月12日宣布，成功地试爆了100万吨当量的氢弹。其后美苏又先后于1954年和1955年分别制造出可供飞机携载用于实战的氢弹。核武器威胁的不仅是两国的安危，还直接关系着全球人类的生死存亡。罗素正是在这样的背景下，发表了这篇演讲。

　　演说以严肃的生死问题为题，以核战或不战的不同未来命运选择结束，很好的突出了其人道主义立场和反战的主题。贯穿整篇的是罗素博大的人道主义精神，超越意识形态差异的对全人类未来命运的担忧。演说中不乏反诘、举例、引用等论证方式；他缜密、严谨的逻辑推导和细致入微的语言刻画值得我们回味。

◉ 英文原文

　　I am speaking not as a Briton, not as a European, not as a member of a western democracy, but as a human being, a member of the species Man, whose continued existence is in doubt. The world is full of conflicts: Jews and Arabs; Indians and Pakistanis; white men and Negroes in Africa; and, overshadowing all minor conflicts, the **titanic**[1] struggle between communism and anticommunism.

　　Almost everybody who is politically conscious has strong feelings about one or more of these issues; but I want you, if you can, to <u>set aside</u> such feelings for the moment and consider yourself only as a member of a biological species which has had a remarkable history and whose disappearance none of us can desire. I shall try to say no single word which should appeal to one group rather than to another. All, equally, are in **peril**[2], and, if the peril is understood, there is hope that they may collectively **avert**[3] it. We have to learn to think in a new way. We have to learn to ask ourselves not what steps can be taken to give military victory to whatever group we prefer, for there no longer are such steps. The question we have to ask ourselves is: What steps can be taken to prevent a <u>military contest</u> of which the issue must be disastrous to all sides?

　　The general public, and even many men in positions of authority, have not realized what would be involved in a war with **hydrogen bombs**[4]. The general public still thinks <u>in terms of</u> the **obliteration**[5] of cities. It is understood that the new bombs are more powerful than the old and that, while one atomic bomb could obliterate Hiroshima, one hydrogen bomb could obliterate the largest cities such as London, New York, and Moscow. No doubt in a hydrogen-bomb war great cities would be obliterated. But this is one of the minor disasters that would have to be faced. If everybody in London, New York, and Moscow were **exterminated**[6], the world might, <u>in the</u>

1　titanic 十分巨大的；非常庞大的
2　peril 危险
3　avert 避免
4　hydrogen bomb 氢弹
5　obliteration 消除
6　exterminate 灭绝

course of a few centuries, recover from the blow. But we now know, especially since the Bikini test, that hydrogen bombs can gradually spread destruction over a much wider area than had been supposed. It is stated on very good authority that a bomb can now be manufactured which will be 25,000 times as powerful as that which destroyed Hiroshima. Such a bomb, if exploded near the ground or under water, sends **radioactive particles**[1] into the upper air. They sink gradually and reach the surface of the earth in the form of a deadly dust or rain. It was this dust which infected the Japanese fishermen and their catch of fish although they were outside what American experts believed to be the danger zone. No one knows how widely such **lethal**[2] radioactive particles might be **diffused**[3], but the best authorities are **unanimous**[4] in saying that a war with hydrogen bombs is quite likely to put an end to the human race. It is feared that if many hydrogen bombs are used there will be universal death—sudden only for a fortunate minority, but for the majority a slow torture of disease and **disintegration**[5].

Many warnings have uttered by **eminent**[6] men of science and by authorities in military strategy. None of them will say that the worst results are certain. What they do say is that these results are possible and no one can be sure that this will not be realized. We have not yet found that the views of experts depend in any degree upon their politics or prejudice. They depend only, so far as our researches have revealed, upon the extent of the particular expert's knowledge. We have found that the men who know most are the most gloomy.

Here, then, is the problem which I present to you, **stark**[7] and dreadful and inescapable: Shall we put an end to the human race; or shall mankind **renounce**[8] war? People will not face this alternative because it is so difficult to abolish war. The abolition of war will demand distasteful limitations of national sovereignty. But what perhaps **impedes**[9] understanding of the situation more than anything else is that the term "mankind" feels vague and abstract. People scarcely realize in imagination that the danger is to themselves and their children and their grandchildren, and not only to a **dimly**[10] apprehended humanity. And so they hope that perhaps war may be allowed to continue provided modern weapons are prohibited. I am afraid this hope is **illusory**[11]. Whatever agreements not to use hydrogen bombs had been reached in time of peace, they would no longer be considered binding in time of war, and both sides would set to work to manufacture hydrogen bombs as soon as war broke out, for if one side manufactured the bombs and the other did not, the side that manufactured them would inevitably be victorious.

As geological time is reckoned, Man has so far existed only for a very short period one

---

1. radioactive particle 放射性粒子
2. lethal 致命的
3. diffuse 扩散
4. unanimous 一致的
5. disintegration 瓦解
6. eminent 知名的，杰出的
7. stark 严酷的
8. renounce 放弃
9. impede 阻碍
10. dimly 模糊地
11. illusory 虚幻的；虚无缥缈

million years <u>at the most</u>. What he has achieved, especially during the last 6,000 years, is something utterly new in the history of the **Cosmos**[1], so far at least as we <u>are acquainted with it</u>. For countless ages the sun rose and set, the moon **waxed**[2] and **waned**[3], the stars shone in the night, but it was only with the coming of Man that these things were understood. In the great world of astronomy and in the little world of the atom, Man has unveiled secrets which might have been thought undiscoverable. In art and literature and religion, some men have shown a **sublimity**[4] of feeling which makes the species worth preserving. Is all this to end in trivial horror because so few are able to think of Man rather than of this or that group of men? Is our race so **destitute**[5] of wisdom, so <u>incapable of</u> impartial love, so blind even to the simplest dictates of self-preservation, which the last proof of its silly cleverness is to be the extermination of all life on our planet?—For it will be not only men who will perish, but also the animals, whom no one can accuse of communism or anticommunism.

I cannot believe that this is to be the end. I would have men forget their quarrels for a moment and reflect that, if they will allow themselves to survive, there is every reason to expect the triumphs of the future to exceed immeasurably the triumphs of the past. There lies before us, if we choose continual progress in happiness, knowledge, and wisdom. Shall we, instead, choose death, because we cannot forget our quarrels? <u>I appeal, as a human being to human beings: remember your humanity, and forget the rest. If you can do so, the way lies open to a new Paradise; if you cannot, nothing lies before you but universal death.</u>

▶ 文化快递

The Bikini Test（比基尼实验）

比基尼岛（Bikini Island），是一个位于马绍尔群岛北端的堡礁，为比基尼环礁（Bikini Atoll）中最大的一个岛。1946年到1958年间，美国共在比基尼岛进行了23次核试验，使马绍尔群岛的比基尼等岛上的居民受到严重的放射性污染被迫迁居。1946年7月25日，在比基尼群岛附近平静的太平洋海面上爆炸了一枚原子弹。这是历史上由美国军方实施的第一次水下核爆炸。被曼哈顿工程的工程师们称为"比基尼·海伦"的这枚原子弹爆炸的威力相当惊人，炸沉了11艘巨型军舰，炸伤6艘。

▶ 参考译文

我不是作为一个英国人、一个欧洲人、一个西方民主国家的一员，而是作为一个人，作为不知是否还能继续生存下去的人类的一员在讲演。世界充满了争斗：犹太人和阿拉伯

---

1. Cosmos 宇宙
2. wax（月）渐圆，渐盈
3. wane（月）亏，缺
4. sublimity 崇高
5. destitute 缺少

人；印度人和巴勒斯坦人；非洲的白人和黑人；以及使所有的小冲突都相形见绌的共产主义和反共产主义之间的大搏斗。

差不多每个有政治意识的人都对这类问题怀有强烈的感受；但是我希望你们，如果你们能够的话，把这份感受暂搁一边，并把自己只看作一种具有非凡历史、谁也不希望它灭亡的生物的一员。可能会迎合一群人而冷落另一群人的词语，我将努力一个字都不说。所有的人，不分彼此，都处在危险之中；如果大家都看到了这种危险，那么就有希望联合起来避开它。我们必须学习新的思维方法。我们必须学会自问的不是能采取什么措施来使我们所喜欢的人群获得军事上的胜利，因为不再有这样的措施。我们必须自问的问题是：能采取什么措施来避免必然会给各方造成灾难的军事竞赛？

普通群众，甚至许多当权人士，不清楚一场氢弹战所包含的会是什么。普通群众仍旧从城市的毁灭上思考问题。不言而喻，新炸弹比旧炸弹更具威力——一颗原弹能毁灭广岛，而一颗氢弹能毁灭像伦敦、纽约和莫斯科这样的大都市。毫无疑问，一场氢弹战将会毁灭大城市。但这只是世界必须面对的小灾难中的一个。假如伦敦人、纽约人和莫斯科人都灭绝了，世界可能要经过几个世纪才能从这场灾难中恢复过来。而我们现在，尤其是从比基尼核试验以来很清楚：氢弹能够逐渐把破坏力扩散到一个比预料要广大得多的地区。据非常权威的人士说，现在能够制造出一种炸弹，其威力比毁灭广岛的炸弹大2.5万倍。这种炸弹如果在近地或水下爆炸，会把放射性微粒送入高层大气。这些微粒逐渐降落，呈有毒灰尘或毒雨的状态到达地球表面。正是这种灰尘使日本渔民和他们所捕获的鱼受到了感染，尽管他们并不在美国专家所确认的危险区之内。没有人知道这种致命的放射性微粒怎么会传播得这么广，但是这个领域的最高权威一致表示：一场氢弹战差不多就是灭绝人类的代名词。如果许多氢弹被使用，死神恐怕就会降临全球——只有少数幸运者才会突然死亡，大多数人却须忍受疾病和解体的慢性折磨。

许多杰出的科学家和军事战略家都做出过警告，但没有人说最坏的结果会是必然。他们说的是这些会有可能但没人确信这不会发生。我们还没有发现专家们的这些观点出于政治立场或人为偏见。就我们的研究表明，这只基于个别专家的认知。我们发现，知之越多者越悲观。

这里，我要向你提起一个直率的、令人不快而又无法回避的问题：我们该消灭人类，还是人类该抛弃战争？人们不愿面对这个抉择，因为消灭战争太难了。消灭战争要求限制国家主权，这令人反感。然而"人类"这个专门名词给人们的感觉是模糊、抽象的，它可能比任何其他东西都更容易妨碍认识这种形势。人们几乎没有用自己的想象力去认识这种危险不仅指向他们所模模糊糊理解的人类，而且指向他们自己和他们的子子孙孙。于是他们相信只要禁止使用现代武器，也许可以允许战争继续下去。恐怕这个愿望只是幻想。任何不使用氢弹的协定是在和平时期达成的，在战争时期这种协定就被认为是没有约束力的，一旦战争爆发，双方就会着手制造氢弹，因为如果一方制造氢弹而另一方不造的话，造氢弹的一方必然会取胜……

按照地质年代来计算，人类到目前为止只存在了一个极短的时期——最多100万年。在至少就我们所了解的宇宙而言，特别是最近6000年里人类所达到的认识，在宇宙史上是一些全新的东西。太阳升升落落，月亮盈盈亏亏，夜空星光闪烁，无数岁月就这样过去了，只是到人类出现以后，这些才被理解。在天文学的宏观世界和原子的微观世界，人类揭示了原先可能认为无法揭示的秘密。在艺术、文学和宗教领域里，一些人显示了一种崇高的感情，它使人们懂得人类是值得保全的。难道因为很少有人能考虑整个人类而不是这个或那个人群，这一切就会在毫无价值的恐怖行动中结束吗？人类是否如此缺少智慧，如此缺少无私的爱，如此盲目，甚至连自我保存的最简单命令都听不见，以致要用灭绝地球上的所有生命来最后证明它那缺乏理智的小聪明？——因为不只人会被消灭，而且动物也会被消灭，没有人能指责它们是共产主义或反共产主义。

我无法相信结局会是这样。人们如果想让自己生存下去，他们就应暂时忘掉争吵，进行反省，人们有千万条理由期待未来的成就极大地超过以往的成就，如果让我们选择，那么摆在我们面前的有幸福、知识和智慧的持续增长。我们能因为无法忘掉争吵而舍此去选择死亡吗？作为一个人，我向所有的人呼吁：记住你们的人性，忘掉其余的一切。如果你们能这样做，通向一个新的天堂的路就畅通无阻；如果你们做不到这一点，摆在你们面前的就只有全世界的毁灭。

Lesson 5

Every Home in Scotland Keeps His Fame Bright

Task 1 Questions and Answers

Directions: Work in pairs. Read the following speech then take turns to ask and answer the following questions.

1. To whom was the speech delivered? Where?
2. What is the background of the speech delivered?
3. Which style does the speech belong to according to the text?
4. Does the style of speech match the identity of the speaker?

Task 2 Co-Operative Study

Directions: Work in pairs. Go through the script and locate the lines that confuse you. Underline these places. Then discuss with your partner to seek for their *understanding of these lines. Then bring the unsolved questions to a larger group of six, and finally to the whole class.*

Task 3 **Translation**

Directions: *Translate the following poem into Chinese with the help of a dictionary or other necessary facilities.*

A Red, Red Rose
by Robert Burns
O my luve's like a red, red rose.
That's newly sprung in June;
O my luve's like a melodie
That's sweetly play'd in tune.
As fair art thou, my bonnie lass,
So deep in luve am I;
And I will luve thee still, my Dear,
Till a'the seas gang dry.
Till a' the seas gang dry, my Dear,
And the rocks melt wi' the sun:
I will luve thee still, my Dear,
While the sands o'life shall run.
And fare thee weel my only Luve!
And fare thee weel a while!
And I will come again, my Luve,
Tho' it were ten thousand mile!

Task 4 **Paraphrasing**

Directions: *Work in groups of four and paraphrase the following sentences into simple English. Use specific details and examples to support yourself. You may locate some useful information from the script.*

1. I do not know by what untoward accident it has chanced, and I forbear to inquire, that, in this accomplished circle, it should fall to me, the worst Scotsman of all, to receive your commands, and which indeed makes the occasion.
2. I can only explain this singular unanimity in a race which rarely acts together, but rather after their watch-world, each for himself.
3. No man existed who could look down on him. They that looked into his eyes saw that they might look down the sky as easily.
4. And, as he was thus the poet of the poor, anxious cheerful, working humanity, so had he the language of low life.

Task 5 Reading Practice

Directions: *Work in groups of four. Take turns to read the whole speech sentence by sentence with due emotion and techniques. Help each other to improve their phonetic errors.*

Every Home in Scotland Keeps His Fame Bright
英格兰广袤的大地上闪耀着他的英名
Celebration of the Hundredth Anniversary of the Birth of Robert Burns
By Ralph Emerson

🔊 人物简介

拉尔夫·爱默生（Ralph Emerson, 1803—1882）美国散文作家、思想家、诗人、超验主义创始人。1803年5月出生于马萨诸塞州波士顿附近的康考德村，1882年4月27日在波士顿逝世。1837年爱默生以《美国学者》为题发表了一篇著名的演讲词，宣告美国文学已脱离英国文学而独立，告诫美国学者不要让学究习气蔓延，不要盲目地追随传统，不要进行纯粹的摹仿。另外这篇讲词还抨击了美国社会的拜金主义，强调人的价值。被誉为美国思想文化领域的"独立宣言"。一年之后，爱默生在《神学院献辞》中批评了基督教唯一神教派死气沉沉的局面，竭力推崇人的至高无尚，提倡靠直觉认识真理。"相信你自己的思想，相信你内心深处认为对你合适的东西对一切人都适用。"文学批评家劳伦斯·布尔在《爱默生传》中评论，爱默生与他的学说，是美国最重要的世俗宗教。

爱默生的哲学思想中保持了唯一神教派强调人的价值的积极成分，又吸收了欧洲唯心主义先验论的思想，发展成为超验主义观点。其基本出发点是反对权威，崇尚直觉；其核心是主张人能超越感觉和理性而直接认识真理。这一观点有助于打破当时神学和外国的教条的束缚，建立民族文化，集中体现了时代精神，为美国政治上的民主主义和经济上的资本主义发展提供了理论根据。

名篇导读

拉尔夫·爱默生酷爱演讲，面对人群令他兴奋不已，他说他感觉到一种伟大的情感在召唤，他的主要声誉和成就建立于此。爱默生说过："演讲就是力量,演讲的目的是说服别人、传递信息、征服思想。"他通过自己的论文和演说成为美国超验主义的领袖，并且成为非正式哲学家中最重要的一个。

爱默生当时被视为欧洲和美洲最伟大的演说家之一，以低沉的声音令听众着迷，他相当具有热忱，并以平等的态度对待且重视听众。他发表激进的废除黑奴演讲。他努力试着不加入任何公开的政治运动或团体，并迫切地要独立自主，这反映了他的个人主义立场。他常常坚持不要拥护者，要成为一个只靠自己的人。后来他把自己的演讲汇编成书，这就是著名的《论文集》。这部著作为爱默生赢得了巨大的声誉，他的思想被称为超验主义的核心，他本人则被冠以"美国的文艺复兴领袖"之美誉。

本篇演讲是1859年1月25日爱默生为纪念罗伯特·彭斯诞辰100周年而作，感情真挚、言辞恳切、辞藻华丽、意向优美，是抒情性演讲的经典之作。

英文原文

Mr. President and Gentlemen,

I do not know by what **untoward**[1] accident it has chanced, and I **forbear**[2] to inquire, that, in this accomplished circle, it should fall to me, the worst Scotsman of all, to receive your commands, and which indeed makes the occasion. But I am told there is no appeal, and I must trust to the inspirations of the theme to make a fitness which does not otherwise exist.

Yet, Sir, I heartily feel the singular claims of the occasion. At the first announcement, from I know not **whence**[3], that the 25th of January was the hundredth anniversary of the birth of ***Robert Burns***, a sudden **consent**[4] warmed the great English case, in all its kingdoms, colonies, and states, all over the world, to keep the festival. We are here to hold our parliaments with love and **poesy**[5], as men were not to do in the Middle Ages. Those famous parliaments might or might not have had more **stateliness**[6] and better singers than we——though that is yet to be known——but they could not have better reason.

---

1 untoward 意外的；不顺利的；难对付的
2 forbear 克制，忍耐，容忍
3 whence 来源，来处，根源
4 consent 准许，赞同；同意；（意见等的）一致
5 poesy 诗歌，韵文
6 stateliness 威严，庄严

I can only explain this singular **unanimity**[1] in a race which rarely acts together, but rather after their watch-world, each for himself—by the fact that Robert Burns, the poet of the middle class, represents in the mind of men today that great **uprising**[2] of the middle class against the armed and privileged minorities, that uprising which worked politically in the American and French Revolutions, and which, not in governments so much as in education and social order, has changed the face of the world. In order for this destiny, his birth, breeding and fortunes were low. His organic sentiment was absolute independence, and resting as it should on a life of labor. No man existed who could look down on him. They that looked into his eyes saw that they might look down the sky as easily. His **muse**[3] and teaching was common sense, joyful, aggressive, irresistible. Not Latimer, nor Luther struck more telling blows against false **theology**[4] than did this brave singer. *The Confession of Augsburg, the Declaration of Independence, the French Rights of Man,* and *the Marseillaise,* are not more weighty documents in the history of freedom than the songs of Burns. His **satire**[5] has lost none of its edge. His musical arrows yet sing through the air. He is so substantially a reformer that I find his grand plain sense in close chain with the greatest masters—Rabelais, Shakespeare in comedy, Cervantes, Butler, and Burns. He is an exceptional genius. The people who care nothing for literature and poetry care for Burns. It was indifferent they thought who saw him whether he wrote verse or not: he could have done anything else as well.

Yet how true a poet is he! And the poet, too, of poor men, of **hodden-gray**[6] and the **Guernsey-coat**[7] and the blouse. He has given voice to all the experiences of common life; he has **endeared**[8] the farmhouse and cottages, patches and poverty, beans and barley; ale, the poor man's wine; hardship; the fear of debt; the dear society of weans and wife, of brothers and sisters, proud of each other, knowing so few and finding **amends**[9] for want and **obscurity**[10] in books and thoughts. What a love of nature, and—shall I say?—of middle-class nature. Not great, like Goethe, in the stars, or like Byron, on the ocean, or Moore, in the luxurious East, but in the homely landscape which the poor see around them—**bleak**[11] leagues of **pasture**[12] and stubble, ice and **sleet**[13] and rain and snow-choked brooks; birds, hares, field-mice, **thistles**[14] and heather, which he daily knew. How many *Bonny Doons* and *John Anderson, my joes* and *Auld Lang Synes* all around the earth have his verses been applied to! And his love songs still woo and melt the youths

---

1 unanimity 全体一致
2 uprising 起义
3 muse 沉思；冥想
4 theology 神学
5 satire 讽刺
6 hodden-gray 黑白羊毛混织粗灰呢
7 Guernsey-coat 格恩西的外套
8 endear 使受喜爱
9 amend 补偿
10 obscurity 朦胧；晦涩；不分明；身份低微
11 bleak 萧瑟的
12 pasture 牧场
13 sleet 雨夹雪
14 thistle 蓟

and maids; the farm work, the country holiday, the fishing **cobble**[1] are still his **debtors**[2] today.

And, as he was thus the poet of the poor, anxious cheerful, working humanity, so had he the language of low life. He grew up in a rural district, speaking a **patois**[3] unintelligible to all but natives, and he has made that Lowland Scotch a Doric dialect of fame. It is the only example in history of a language made classic by the genius of a single man. But more than this. He had that secret of genius to draw from the bottom of society the strength of its speech, and astonish the ears of the polite with these artless words, better than art, and filtered of all offense through his beauty. It seemed **odious**[4] to Luther that the devil should have all the best tunes; he would bring them into the churches; and Burns knew how to take from fairs and **gypsies**,[5] black-smiths and **drovers**[6], the speech of the market and street, and clothe it with melody.

But I am **detaining**[7] you too long. The memory of Burns—I am afraid heaven and earth have taken too good care of it to leave us anything to say. The west winds are murmuring it. Open the windows behind you, and **hearken**[8] for the incoming tide, what the waves say of it. The doves, perching always on the eaves of the Stone Chapel (King's Chapel) opposite, may know something about it. Every home in broad Scotland keeps his fame bright. The memory of Burns——every man's and boy's, and girl's head carried **snatches**[9] of his songs, and can say them by heart, and, what is strangest of all, never learned them from a book, but from mouth to mouth. The wind whispers them the birds whistle them, the corn, **barley**[10], and **bulrushes**[11] **brassily**[12] **rustle**[13] them; nay, the music boxes at Geneva are framed and toothed to play them; the hand organs of the Sao yards in all cities repeat them, and the chimes of bells ring them in the **spires**[14]. They are the property and the **solace**[15] of mankind.

文化快递

1. Robert Burns（罗伯特·彭斯）

罗伯特·彭斯（Robert Burns, 1759—1796）苏格兰农民诗人，在英国文学史上占有重要的地位。他复活并丰富了苏格兰民歌；他的诗歌富有音乐性，可以歌唱。彭斯生于苏格兰民族面临被异族征服的时代，因此，他的诗歌充满了激进的民主、自由的思想。诗人

1　cobble 鹅卵石
2　debtor 债务人，借方
3　patois 方言
4　odious 可憎的
5　gypsy 吉普赛人
6　drover 把家畜赶到市集的人
7　detain 耽搁
8　hearken 倾听
9　snatch 一阵子，一下工夫；很小的数量
10　barley 大麦
11　bulrush 芦苇，香蒲，纸草；菖蒲
12　brassily 似黄铜地，低廉而华丽地
13　rustle 发出沙沙声
14　spire （教堂的）尖塔
15　solace 慰藉

生活在破产的农村，和贫苦的农民血肉相连。他的诗歌歌颂了故国家乡的秀美，抒写了劳动者纯朴的友谊和爱情。

2. the Guernsey-coat（格恩西外套）

格恩西外套起源于英国同名的河间岛，是当地渔民穿着的由羊毛通过特殊工艺编制的毛衣，质地厚实耐穿、防水而且保暖、有助于渔民抵御海水的泼溅。19世纪曾被用作英国皇家海军的统一制服。格恩西传统上由渔民的妻子手工编制而成，然后由母亲传授给女儿，其图案代代相传，至今不衰。

参考译文

主席先生及在座的各位先生们：

作为苏格兰中最不才者，不知因了怎样阴差阳错的缘故——也无意在此冒昧探究——竟于在座诸位俊贤中被临时选中对刚才的完美演说发表感言，我既已被告知无法请辞，便唯有借今日之主题，尽我所能，以不负使命。

一点不错，我完全能够感受到这是一个难得的时刻。1月25日罗伯特·彭斯百年诞辰的消息在某地一经宣布，整个大英民族，包括她在世界各地的王国、殖民地和城邦立即就举行纪念活动一事达成了一致。在这里，我们像中世纪的人们惯常所做的一样以爱与诗为题集会。尽管我们无从知晓那些更著名的集会是否比今日更庄严，那些歌咏者是否比今日更出色，但我们的集会却有着更好的理由。

大英民族绝少行动一致，各行其是乃是人人恪守的格言。我对于他们此次罕见的一致性的唯一解释便是：作为中产阶级杰出人士的罗伯特·彭斯在今天人们的心目中代表了中产者对拥有武器与特权的少数人的重大反叛。这一反叛在美国革命和法国革命中发挥了政治影响，与其说是从体制上，倒不如说是从教育和社会秩序上改变了整个世界的面貌。彭斯卑微的出身、教育和命运正是让他来完成这个使命的。他天性纯朴，独立不羁，恰如其分地植根于劳动者的生活。世上无人能藐视他，那些曾与他目光相遇的人都知道藐视他比藐视天空还难。他的诗歌与说教都是常识——欢乐、自由、强劲、不可抗拒的常识。和拉蒂莫与路德相比，这位勇敢的歌手对于虚假神学与虚假神学的痛击更加有力。在书写自由的历史上，彭斯的诗歌与《奥格斯堡自白书》、美国的《独立宣言》、法国的《人权宣言》以及《马赛曲》的分量一样重。他讽刺的锋芒依然尖利，他音乐的利箭依然穿破天空，他是一位不折不扣的革新家，我发现他伟大而朴素的智慧与拉伯雷、写喜剧的莎士比亚、塞万提斯和勃特勒等最杰出的大师一脉相承。他是一位罕见的天才。不喜欢文学与诗歌的人对彭斯却情有独钟。见过他的人觉得他是否写诗无关紧要，他做任何其他事情都会同样出类拔萃。

然而，他是一位何等纯粹的诗人！他还是一位贫苦人的诗人，一位穿着粗灰呢衣服和格恩西外套的布衣诗人。他的诗歌唱出了普通人生活的所有体验，农舍草屋、补丁贫困、青豆大麦、穷汉的麦芽酒、生活的艰难、举债的恐惧以及妻子稚儿、兄弟姐妹之间的亲密交往在他笔下都变得亲切可爱。他诗歌中的人物尽管孤陋寡闻，却以彼此为荣；尽管贫寒微贱，却有书为伴、思想充实，他如此热爱自然——姑且说是中产者眼里的自然吧，因为它不似歌德的星空、拜伦的海洋、穆尔的绮丽的东方那般宏伟。他所爱的是穷人举目可见的平常风景：大片荒凉的草地和庄家茬，冰霜雨雪和冰封的小溪，还有小鸟、野兔、田鼠和蓟草灌木。他对这一切了如指掌。世上有太多首《波尼·杜恩》、《我的心上人约翰·安德森》和《友谊地久天长》用的都是他写的诗句，少男少女们的心弦依然被他的情诗拨动，而农家活计、乡村节日、水上渔舟仍旧因为他的诗歌而受惠。

作为代表穷愁困顿而又兴高采烈的劳动大众的诗人，他的语言也是底层生活的语言。他在乡村长大，说一口只有当地人听得懂的土话，而他却让这种苏格兰低地的方言变得举世闻名。他凭借个人的天才将一种语言变为经典，这种例子在历史上绝无仅有。不仅如此，他拥有一种从底层社会的话语中汲取力量的非凡能力，用那些未经雕琢却比艺术更加美妙的语言震撼着高雅人士的耳朵，他的美滤去了其中所有刺耳的声音。路德不能容忍魔鬼拥有最美妙的音乐，于是把那些乐曲引进了教堂；而彭斯却懂得如何为从集市、吉普赛人、铁匠和牲口贩子那里获得的市井俚语披上旋律的彩衣。

我已经耽搁在座各位太多时间。对彭斯的怀念自有天地的眷顾，而我辈唯有缄口。对他的怀念在西风的低语里；打开你们身后的窗户，听那涨起的潮声中波浪如何述说；长停在对面石头教堂屋檐上的燕子可能也在怀念他。苏格兰广袤的土地上的每一户人家都让他的英名闪耀。对于彭斯的怀念属于所有人。每一个小男孩和小女孩的脑海里都有他的诗句片段可以随口念出，奇怪的是，他们并非学自书本，而是来自人们的口耳相传。他的诗歌被风轻吟着，被鸟儿鸣唱着，在玉米、大麦和宽叶香蒲中粗犷地沙沙作响。不仅如此，装有齿轮的日内瓦八音盒演奏着他的歌；所有城市的萨伏依管风琴重复着他的歌；尖塔顶、端的钟铃奏响着他的歌。彭斯的诗歌是全人类的财产和慰藉。

Lesson 6

Oscar Best Actress Speech

Task 1 Questions and Answers

Directions: *Work in pairs. Read the following speech then take turns to ask and answer the following questions.*

1. When was the speech delivered? Where?

2. Who delivered the speech? Who are involved in the speech?
3. What is the theme of the speech?
4. Why is there a need for the request?
5. How can the request be achieved?

Task 2 Co-Operative Study

Directions: *Work in pairs. Go through the script and locate the lines that confuse you. Underline these places. Then discuss with your partner to seek for their understanding of these lines. Then bring the unsolved questions to a larger group of six, and finally to the whole class.*

Task 3 Imitation and Play

Directions: *Watch the authentic video of the speech. Then try to imitate the passage with appropriate delivery techniques. First practice by yourself. Then work in groups of four to take turns to deliver the speech.*

Task 4 Discussion

Directions: *Work in groups of four and discuss the following questions. You may locate some useful information from the script.*

1. What do you know about the Speaker?
2. Has she won Oscar Prize before?
3. How did Kate Winslet feel when delivering this speech?
4. What are the linguistic features of this speech?

Task 5 Speaking Practice

Directions: *Give a speech to the class for 2-3 minutes on a topic which you are interested in. You may choose from the following:*

1. An Apology Speech for Improper Behavior
2. A Farewell Speech at Retirement
3. A Thank-You Speech at Your Birthday Party

Oscar Best Actress Speech
奥斯卡最佳女主角获奖演说
Address at Oscar Acceptance on February 22, 2009
By Kate Winslet

🔵 人物简介

凯特·温斯莱特（Kate Winslet）生于英国，是美国的好莱坞著名女演员，国际巨星，奥斯卡影后，曾五次获得奥斯卡提名，被誉为"英伦玫瑰"。从小在一个戏剧之家长大，1997年凭借《泰坦尼克号》中的女主角"Rose"一角迅速红遍全球，并以此片获奥斯卡金像奖最佳女主角提名和金球奖最佳女主角提名。2008年凭借在影片《生死朗读》中出色表现问鼎第81届奥斯卡最佳女主角奖殊荣。这是她第六次获得奥斯卡奖提名，第四次获最佳女主角提名。2011年因《欲海情魔》获得电视剧界最高奖艾美奖最佳女主角奖。

🔵 名篇导读

从影13年间，凯特·温丝莱特5次与小金人失之交臂。"先前一直被误解我不在乎奥斯卡奖，其实每次提名我都很想得奖，我讨厌每次宣读得奖结果时自己要挤出笑容以免被别人嘲笑输不起，第6次获奥斯卡表演奖提名，这次我不想输。"颁奖夜之前，温丝莱特情不自已。终于，她凭借《生死朗读》赢下了人生中的第一座小金人。走上颁奖台的那一刻，她的眼中含着泪光，挤出笑容的换成了别人。

温斯莱特是个神奇的女演员，她只拍能打动她的电影，而且为了角色不惜扮丑。对自己时常被批评的过于丰腴的身材，温斯莱特也一直保持着我行我素的做派。在家里，她甚至把时尚杂志都藏起来，不让女儿看见杂志上骨瘦如柴的模特。这个不走寻常路的女演员，用了14年终于问鼎影后宝座。凯特以自己多年的坚持得到了更大的礼遇。在《乱世佳人》的背景音乐下，妮可·基德曼等五大影后共同揭晓影后殊荣。

凯特·温斯莱特在发表获奖感言时，万分激动，语句断断续续，身体不断地抖动，其间，还高举奖杯，大吼一声，为自己鼓气，引起现场一阵赞美的掌声。世界级的演员站在世界级的舞台，凯特的演讲诙谐幽默、真情流露，从中可以一窥凯特率真、坚韧的个性。

英文原文

I'd be lying if I have not made a **version**[1] of this speech before, I think I was probably 8 years old and staring into the bathroom mirror. And this (holding up her statuette) would've been a shampoo bottle.

Well, it's not a shampoo bottle now!

I feel very fortunate to have made it all the way from there to here.

And I'd like to thank some of the people along the way who had faith in me, my friends and my family, especially my mum and dad, who are in this room somewhere.

Dad, whistle or something, 'cause then I'll know where you are. (He whistles.) Yeah! (Waving to him.) I love you.

And I also want to thank Hylda Queally, Dallas Smith and the late, much loved, much missed Robert Garlock.

And from Peter Jackson and Emma Thompson to my very own Sam and Stephen Daldry.

I'm very lucky to have been given Hanna Schmitz by Bernhard Schlink and David Hare and Stephen and working with you is an experience I will never forget.

There was no division between **the cast**[2] and **the crew**[3] on this film, and that's what made it so special.

So, to have been surrounded by a remarkable group of people who provided an unbroken chain of support from David Kross to Ralph Fiennes, Bruno Ganz, Lena Olin, from hair and makeup to **cinematography**[4], from the art department to the ADs, and from New York to Berlin.

And I am so lucky to have a wonderful husband and two beautiful children who let me do what I love and who love me just the way that I am.

Anthony and Sidney, this is for you. This is for both of you.

And I want to acknowledge my fellow **nominees**[5], these goddesses. I think we all can't believe we're in a category with *Meryl Streep* at all.

I'm sorry, Meryl, but you have to just suck that up! And, just to the Academy, thank you so much, my God! Thank you!

---

1 version 版本；译文，译本；说法；倒转术
2 the cast 演员们
3 the crew 职员们
4 cinematography 电影摄影术；电影制作方法
5 nominee 被提名者

文化快递

1. Oscar（奥斯卡奖）

奥斯卡奖，也称奥斯卡金像奖，原名学院奖（Academy Award），正式名称是"电影艺术与科学学院奖"，设立于1927年，每年一次在美国洛杉矶举行。该奖是由美国电影艺术与科学学院颁发，旨在鼓励优秀电影的创作与发展，半个多世纪来一直享有盛誉。第86届奥斯卡颁奖典礼于2014年3月2日（周日）举行。

2. Meryl Streep（梅丽尔·斯特里普）

梅丽尔·斯特里普（1949年6月22日—　），美国著名女演员，很多观众与评论家评价她为电影史上最伟大的女演员，她迄今为止获得过17项奥斯卡提名，为史上最多。分别获得第52届（1979年度）奥斯卡最佳女配角奖与第55届（1982年度）奥斯卡最佳女主角奖以及第84届（2012年度）奥斯卡最佳女主角奖。她善于塑造各种各样的女性角色。女儿、母亲、妻子、恋人，一切女性的社会角色她都游刃有余；坚强、软弱、乐观、迷茫，女人所有的品质和情绪她都展现得淋漓尽致。梅丽尔·斯特里普的银幕魅力早已超越了国界和种族，她的表演受到全世界观众的认同，成为"一代只出一个"的世界影坛常青树。17次奥斯卡提名，3樽小金人、戛纳影后、柏林影后、26次金球提名、8次获奖、3次艾美提名、2次获奖……无数的奖项与赞誉，为后继者树起一座难以逾越的"梅丽尔·斯特里普屏障"，以至于在发表获奖感言时提及梅丽尔，已经成为很多获奖影人向前辈致敬的标准动作。

参考译文

如果说此前我没有为这次感言排演，那么我是在撒谎。我想象着自己可能是个八岁大的孩子，痴痴地盯着盥洗室的镜子，而这东西（凯特举着小金人）是一个香波瓶。

不过，现在它可不是一个香波瓶。

我觉得我一路走来，取得了成就，非常幸运。

我要谢谢那些在我前进的路上对我充满信心的人们，我的朋友和我的家庭，特别是我的妈妈和爸爸，他们正待在这个会场的某个地方。

爸爸，吹个口哨或表示点什么，那样的话我就知道你在哪儿了。（凯特的父亲吹口哨，凯特向父亲招手）我爱你。

我还想谢谢希尔达·科尔里，达拉斯·史密斯和故去的、我十分敬爱和怀念的罗伯特·卡洛克。

以及皮特·杰克逊和艾玛·汤普森，还有我的山姆和史蒂芬·戴尔垂。

伯恩哈德·施林克，大卫·海尔和斯蒂芬将汉娜·史密茨这个角色给我，我深感幸运。而和你们一道工作则是我永远难忘的经历。

在这部电影中，演职人员和工作人员没有隔阂，而这也造就了这部电影的卓越非凡。

我被围绕在一群为影片提供持续服务的非凡人物当中，这些人从大卫·克洛斯到拉尔夫·菲尼斯、布鲁诺·甘孜、勒娜·奥林，从发型师、化妆师到摄影师，从艺术指导到广告人员。

我很幸运地拥有一个出色的丈夫和两个漂亮的孩子,他们由着我去做我爱做的事,并且深爱着本色的我。

安东尼和西德尼,这是献给你们的,献给你们两个的。

我还想感谢其他的被提名者,那些女神们。我想我们都不会相信我们居然能够和梅丽尔·斯特里普比肩。

抱歉,梅丽尔,你必须承认这一点。此外,我想对电影学院说,真谢谢你们,天哪。谢谢。

Lesson 7

On not Winning the Nobel Prize

Task 1 Questions and Answers

Directions: Work in pairs. Read the following speech then take turns to ask and answer the following questions.

1. When was the speech delivered? Where?
2. Who delivered the speech? Who are involved in the speech?
3. What is the theme of the speech?
4. Why is there a need for the request?
5. How can the request be achieved?

Task 2 Vocabulary Learning

Directions: First translate the following phrases into Chinese. Then try to make up a story by using these phrases as much as possible.

blowing dust _____   uncut forest _____
range from _____   grass roots _____
brown paper _____   fragmenting culture _____

Task 3 Co-Operative Study

Directions: Work in pairs. Go through the script and locate the lines that confuse you. Underline these places. Then discuss with your partner to seek for their understanding of these lines. Then bring the unsolved questions to a larger group of six, and finally to the whole class.

Task 4 **Discussion**

Directions: *Work in groups of four and discuss the following questions. Do you agree or disagree to the following statement. Use specific details or examples to support yourself. You may also locate some useful information from the script.*
1. How will our lives, our way of thinking, be changed by this Internet?
1. Please use specific details and examples to share with us your understanding of the statement "Reading maketh a full man".
3. What is the most important for a writer, talent, aspiration or hard work?

Task 5 **Speaking Practice**

Directions: *Give a speech to the class for 2-3 minutes on a topic which you are interested in. You may choose from the following:*
1. TV Eats Family Relationship
2. Network Addiction
3. Stop Phubbing

On not Winning the Nobel Prize
未获奖者致词
Nobel Literature Prize Acceptance Lecture on December 7, 2007
By Doris Lessing

◉ 人物简介

多丽丝·莱辛（Doris Lessing，1919年10月22日—2013年11月17日），英国女作家，

笔名简·萨默斯，代表作有《金色笔记》等，被誉为继伍尔芙之后最伟大的女性作家，并几次获得诺贝尔文学奖提名以及多个世界级文学奖项。十三岁辍学,十五岁离家出走,结过两次婚也离过两次婚。质疑男人有什么用,却否认自己是女性主义作家。诺贝尔文学奖得主多丽丝·莱辛，一直努力从各种标签桎梏中脱逃。她在国际文坛赫赫有名，但在中国却鲜为人知。

在2007年10月11日，瑞典皇家科学院诺贝尔奖委员会宣布将2007年度诺贝尔文学奖授予这位英国女作家。她是迄今为止获奖时最年长的女性诺贝尔获奖者。此外她是历史上第三十四位女性诺贝尔奖得主。

名篇导读

本文是莱辛获得2007年度诺贝尔文学奖时的获奖致辞。

由于多丽丝·莱辛缺席颁奖典礼，诺奖官方网站全文刊载了她的获奖致词。在这篇名为《未获奖者致词》的文章中，莱辛呼吁人们不要沉溺于电视和网络，因为作家"不会从没有书的房子里突然冒出"。

致词中，莱辛对比了津巴布韦简陋教室里的孩子对书本的渴求，和英国北部一所贵族男生学校糟糕的阅读状况。她认为，在有条件读书的发达国家，电脑、电视和网络给人们的思考能力带来了极大的影响。"因特网用其虚无引诱了整整一代人，理性的人们即使承认他们为此而上钩，但却难以再得到自由。比如，他们可能发现一整天都在阅览博客中过去了。"

莱辛说，"阅读成就完人，阅读令男人或女人充满信息、历史和其他所有的知识。"当一些人写信给她，表示"我也要成为作家，因为我和你出身的房子一样贫穷"时，莱辛的回答是："这很难。写作，作家，不会从没有书的房子里突然冒出。"

英文原文

I am standing in a doorway looking through clouds of <u>blowing dust</u> to where I am told there is still **uncut**[1] <u>forest</u>. Yesterday I drove through miles of **stumps**[2], and **charred**[3] remains of fires where, in '56, there was the most wonderful forest I have ever seen, all now destroyed. People have to eat. They have to get fuel for fires.

This is north-west Zimbabwe in the early eighties, and I am visiting a friend who was a teacher in a school in London. He is here "to help Africa", as we put it. He is a gently idealistic soul and what he found in this school shocked him into a depression, from which it was hard to recover. This school is like every other built after Independence. It consists of four large brick

---

1　uncut 未雕琢的；人迹罕至的
2　stump 树桩；残肢；残余部分
3　char 把……烧成炭；烧焦

rooms side by side, put straight into the dust, one two three four, with a half room at one end, which is the library. In these classrooms are blackboards, but my friend keeps the chalks in his pocket, as otherwise they would be stolen. There is no **atlas**[1] or globe in the school, no textbooks, no exercise books, or **biros**[2]. In the library there are no books of the kind the pupils would like to read, but only **tomes**[3] from American universities, hard even to lift, rejects from white libraries, or novels with titles like *Weekend in Paris* and *Felicity Finds Love*.

There is a goat trying to find **sustenance**[4] in some aged grass. The headmaster has **embezzled**[5] the school funds and is suspended, arousing the question familiar to all of us but usually in more **august**[6] contexts: How is it these people behave like this when they must know everyone is watching them?

My friend doesn't have any money because everyone, pupils and teachers, borrow from him when he is paid and will probably never pay him back. The pupils range from six to twenty-six, because some who did not get schooling as children are here to make it up. Some pupils walk many miles every morning, rain or shine and across rivers. They cannot do homework because there is no electricity in the villages, and you can't study easily by the light of a burning log. The girls have to fetch water and cook before they set off for school and when they get back.

As I sit with my friend in his room, people drop in shyly, and everyone begs for books. "Please send us books when you get back to London," one man says. "They taught us to read but we have no books." Everybody I met, everyone, begged for books.

I was there some days. The dust blew. The pumps had broken and the women were having to fetch water from the river. Another idealistic teacher from England was rather ill after seeing what this "school" was like.

On the last day they slaughtered the goat. They cut it into bits and cooked it in a great tin. This was the much anticipated end-of-term feast: boiled goat and porridge. I drove away while it was still going on, back through the charred remains and stumps of the forest.

I do not think many of the pupils of this school will get prizes.

The next day I am to give a talk at a school in North London, a very good school, whose name we all know. It is a school for boys, with beautiful buildings and gardens.

These children here have a visit from some well known person every week, and it is in the nature of things that these may be fathers, relatives, even mothers of the pupils. A visit from a celebrity is not unusual for them.

As I talk to them, the school in the blowing dust of north-west Zimbabwe is in my mind, and I look at the mildly **expectant**[7] English faces in front of me and try to tell them about what I

1　atlas 地图集
2　biros 伯罗牌圆珠笔
3　tome 大而重的书
4　sustenance 食物，营养，养料
5　embezzle 贪污，盗用
6　august 令人敬畏的，威严的
7　expectant 期待的，预期的

have seen in the last week. Classrooms without books, without textbooks, or an atlas, or even a map pinned to a wall. A school where the teachers beg to be sent books to tell them how to teach, they being only eighteen or nineteen themselves. I tell these English boys how everybody begs for books: "Please send us books." I am sure that anyone who has ever given a speech will know that moment when the faces you are looking at are blank. Your listeners cannot hear what you are saying, there are no images in their minds to match what you are telling them—in this case the story of a school standing in dust clouds, where water is short, and where the end of term treat is a just-killed goat cooked in a great pot.

Is it really so impossible for these privileged students to imagine such bare poverty?

I do my best. They are polite.

I'm sure that some of them will one day win prizes.

Then, the talk is over. Afterwards I ask the teachers how the library is, and if the pupils read. In this privileged school, I hear what I always hear when I go to such schools and even universities.

"You know how it is," one of the teacher's says. "A lot of the boys have never read at all, and the library is only half used."

Yes, indeed we do know how it is. All of us.

We are in a <u>fragmenting culture</u>, where our certainties of even a few decades ago are questioned and where it is common for young men and women, who have had years of education, to know nothing of the world, to have read nothing, knowing only some **speciality**[1] or other, for instance, computers.

What has happened to us is an amazing invention—computers and the internet and TV. It is a revolution. This is not the first revolution the human race has dealt with. The printing revolution, which did not take place in a matter of a few decades, but took much longer, transformed our minds and ways of thinking. A **foolhardy**[2] lot, we accepted it all, as we always do, never asked, "What is going to happen to us now, with this invention of print?" In the same way, we never thought to ask. How will our lives, our way of thinking, be changed by this internet, which has seduced a whole generation with its **inanities**[3] so that even quite reasonable people will confess that once they are hooked, it is hard to cut free, and they may find a whole day has passed in blogging etc..

Very recently, anyone even mildly educated would respect learning, education, and our great store of literature. Of course, we all know that when this happy state was with us, people would pretend to read, would pretend respect for learning. But it is on record that working men and women longed for books, and this is evidenced by the founding of working men's libraries and institutes, the colleges of the 18th and 19th centuries.

Reading, books, used to be part of a general education.

1　speciality 专业；特性；特制品；（英）同specialty
2　foolhardy 莽撞的，有勇无谋的
3　inanity 空洞；浅薄；愚蠢；空洞的言行

Older people, talking to young ones, must understand just how much of an education reading was, because the young ones know so much less. And if children cannot read, it is because they have not read.

We all know this sad story.

But we do not know the end of it.

We think of the old **adage**[1], "Reading **maketh**[2] a full man"—and forgetting about jokes to do with over-eating-reading makes a woman and a man full of information, of history, of all kinds of knowledge.

But we in the West are not the only people in the world. Not long ago a friend who had been in Zimbabwe told me about a village where people had not eaten for three days, but they were still talking about books and how to get them, about education.

I belong to an organisation which started out with the intention of getting books into the villages. There was a group of people who in another connection had travelled Zimbabwe at its grass roots. They told me that the villages, unlike what is reported, are full of intelligent people, teachers retired, teachers on leave, children on holidays, old people. I myself paid for a little survey to discover what people in Zimbabwe want to read, and found the results were the same as those of a Swedish survey I had not known about. People want to read the same kinds of books that we in Europe want to read—novels of all kinds, science fiction, poetry, detective stories, plays, and do-it-yourself books, like how to open a bank account. All of Shakespeare too. A problem with finding books for villagers is that they don't know what is available, so a set book, like the *Mayor of Casterbridge*, becomes popular simply because it just happens to be there. *Animal Farm*, for obvious reasons, is the most popular of all novels.

Our organisation was helped from the very start by Norway, and then by Sweden. Without this kind of support our supplies of books would have dried up. We got books from wherever we could. Remember, a good **paperback**[3] from England costs a month's wages in Zimbabwe: that was before *Mugabe's* reign of terror. Now with inflation, it would cost several years' wages. But having taken a box of books out to a village—and remember there is a terrible shortage of petrol—I can tell you that the box was greeted with tears. The library may be a **plank**[4] on bricks under a tree. And within a week there will be literacy classes—people who can read teaching those who can't, citizenship classes—and in one remote village, since there were no novels written in the language *Tonga*, a couple of lads sat down to write novels in Tonga. There are six or so main languages in Zimbabwe and there are novels in all of them: violent, **incestuous**[5], full of crime and murder.

It is said that a people gets the government it deserves, but I do not think it is true of Zimbabwe. And we must remember that this respect and hunger for books comes, not from

---

1 adage 格言，谚语；箴言
2 maketh make 的古语
3 paperback 平装本，平装书
4 plank （厚）木板；支持物；政纲条目
5 incestuous 乱伦的

Mugabe's **regime**[1], but from the one before it, the whites. It is an astonishing phenomenon, this hunger for books, and it can be seen everywhere from Kenya down to the Cape of Good Hope.

This links improbably with a fact: I was brought up in what was virtually a mud hut, **thatched**[2]. This kind of house has been built always, everywhere there are reeds or grass, suitable mud, poles for walls. Saxon England for example. The one I was brought up in had four rooms, one beside another, and it was full of books. Not only did my parents take books from England to Africa, but my mother ordered books by post from England for her children. Books arrived in great brown paper **parcels**[3], and they were the joy of my young life. A mud hut, but full of books.

Even today I get letters from people living in a village that might not have electricity or running water, just like our family in our **elongated**[4] mud hut. "I shall be a writer too," they say, "because I've the same kind of house you lived in."

But here is the difficulty, no?

Writing, writers, do not come out of houses without books.

There is the gap. There is the difficulty.

I have been looking at the speeches by some of your recent prizewinners. Take the magnificent Pamuk. He said his father had 500 books. His talent did not come out of the air, he was connected with the great tradition.

Take *V.S. Naipaul.* He mentions that the Indian Vedas were close behind the memory of his family. His father encouraged him to write, and when he got to England he would visit the British Library. So he was close to the great tradition.

Let us take *John Coetzee.* He was not only close to the great tradition, he was the tradition: he taught literature in Cape Town. And how sorry I am that I was never in one of his classes, taught by that wonderfully brave, bold mind.

In order to write, in order to make literature, there must be a close connection with libraries, books, with the Tradition.

I have a friend from Zimbabwe, a Black writer. He taught himself to read from the labels on jam jars, the labels on preserved fruit cans. He was brought up in an area I have driven through, an area for rural blacks. The earth is **grit**[5] and **gravel**[6], there are low **sparse**[7] bushes. The huts are poor, nothing like the well cared-for huts of the better off. A school—but like one I have described. He found a discarded children's encyclopedia on a rubbish heap and taught himself from that.

On Independence in 1980 there was a group of good writers in Zimbabwe, truly a nest of

---

1 regime 政治制度，政权，政体
2 thatched 茅草覆盖的；浓密的，毛茸茸的
3 parcel 包裹
4 elongate 延长，加长
5 grit 细沙，沙砾
6 gravel 沙砾，碎石；砾石
7 sparse 稀疏的；稀少的

singing birds. They were bred in old Southern Rhodesia, under the whites—the mission schools, the better schools. Writers are not made in Zimbabwe. Not easily, not under Mugabe.

All the writers travelled a difficult road to literacy, let alone to becoming writers. I would say learning to read from the printed labels on jam jars and discarded encyclopedias was not uncommon. And we are talking about people hungering for standards of education beyond them, living in huts with many children—an overworked mother, a fight for food and clothing.

Yet despite these difficulties, writers came into being. And we should also remember that this was Zimbabwe, conquered less than a hundred years before. The grandparents of these people might have been storytellers working in the oral tradition. In one or two generations there was the transition from stories remembered and passed on, to print, to books. What an achievement.

Books, literally **wrested**[1] from rubbish heaps and the **detritus**[2] of the white man's world. But a sheaf of paper is one thing, a published book quite another. I have had several accounts sent to me of the publishing scene in Africa. Even in more privileged places like North Africa, with its different tradition, to talk of a publishing scene is a dream of possibilities.

Here I am talking about books never written, writers that could not make it because the publishers are not there. Voices unheard. It is not possible to estimate this great waste of talent, of potential. But even before that stage of a book's creation which demands a publisher, an advance, encouragement, there is something else lacking.

Writers are often asked, How do you write? With a word-processor? An electric typewriter? A **quill**[3]? **Longhand**[4]? But the essential question is, "Have you found a space, that empty space, which should surround you when you write?" Into that space, which is like a form of listening, of attention, will come the words, the words your characters will speak, ideas—inspiration.

If a writer cannot find this space, then poems and stories may be stillborn.

When writers talk to each other, what they discuss is always to do with this imaginative space, this other time. "Have you found it? Are you holding it fast?"

Let us now jump to an apparently very different scene. We are in London, one of the big cities. There is a new writer. We **cynically**[5] enquire, Is she good-looking? If this is a man, **charismatic**[6]? Handsome? We joke but it is not a joke.

This new find is **acclaimed**[7], possibly given a lot of money. The buzzing of **paparazzi**[8] begins in their poor ears. They are **feted**[9], **lauded**[10], **whisked**[11] about the world. Us old ones, who

---

1 wrest 费力取得；攫取
2 detritus 岩屑；碎石；瓦砾；风化物
3 quill 羽毛笔；翎；刺
4 longhand 普通书写；手写
5 cynically 爱嘲笑地，冷笑地
6 charismatic 有魅力的；神赐能力的；神授
7 acclaim 向……欢呼；向……喝彩；称赞
8 paparazzi 专门追逐名人的摄影记者(paparazzo的名词复数)
9 fete 宴请（某人），款待；向……致敬
10 laud 称赞，赞美
11 whisk 搅拌；挥动；拂，掸

have seen it all, are sorry for this **neophyte**[1], who has no idea of what is really happening.

He, she, is flattered, pleased.

But ask in a year's time what he or she is thinking—I've heard them: "This is the worst thing that could have happened to me," they say.

Some much publicised new writers haven't written again, or haven't written what they wanted to, meant to.

And we, the old ones, want to whisper into those innocent ears. "Have you still got your space? Your soul, your own and necessary place where your own voices may speak to you, you alone, where you may dream. Oh, hold onto it, don't let it go."

My mind is full of splendid memories of Africa which I can revive and look at whenever I want. How about those sunsets, gold and purple and orange, spreading across the sky at evening. How about butterflies and moths and bees on the aromatic bushes of the Kalahari? Or, sitting on the pale grassy banks of the Zambesi, the water dark and glossy, with all the birds of Africa darting about. Yes, elephants, giraffes, lions and the rest, there were plenty of those, but how about the sky at night, still unpolluted, black and wonderful, full of restless stars.

There are other memories too. A young African man, eighteen perhaps, in tears, standing in what he hopes will be his "library". A visiting American seeing that his library had no books, had sent a **crate**[2] of them. The young man had taken each one out, reverently, and wrapped them in plastic. "But," we say, "these books were sent to be read, surely?" "No," he replies, "they will get dirty, and where will I get any more?"

This young man wants us to send him books from England to use as teaching guides.

"I only did four years in senior school," he says, "but they never taught me to teach."

I have seen a teacher in a school where there were no textbooks, not even a chalk for the blackboard. He taught his class of six to eighteen-year-olds by moving stones in the dust, **chanting**[3] "Two times two is..." and so on. I have seen a girl, perhaps not more than twenty, also lacking textbooks, exercise books, **Biros**[4], seen her teach the A B C by scratching the letters in the dirt with a stick, while the sun beat down and the dust swirled.

We are witnessing here that great hunger for education in Africa, anywhere in the Third World, or whatever we call parts of the world where parents long to get an education for their children which will take them out of poverty.

I would like you to imagine yourselves somewhere in Southern Africa, standing in an Indian store, in a poor area, in a time of bad drought. There is a line of people, mostly women, with every kind of container for water. This store gets a **bowser**[5] of precious water every afternoon from the town, and here the people wait.

The Indian is standing with the heels of his hands pressed down on the counter, and he is

---

1 neophyte 初学者，新手；新近皈依某宗教的人
2 crate 板条箱，柳条箱；装货箱
3 chant 吟颂，咏唱
4 Biros 必洛斯圆珠笔
5 bowser 加油车；加油站油泵

watching a black woman, who is bending over a **wadge**[1] of paper that looks as if it has been torn from a book. She is reading *Anna Karenin*.

She is reading slowly, mouthing the words. It looks a difficult book. This is a young woman with two little children clutching at her legs. She is pregnant. The Indian is distressed, because the young woman's headscarf, which should be white, is yellow with dust. Dust lies between her breasts and on her arms. This man is distressed because of the lines of people, all thirsty. He doesn't have enough water for them. He is angry because he knows there are people dying out there, beyond the dust clouds. His older brother had been here holding the **fort**[2], but he had said he needed a break, had gone into town, really rather ill, because of the drought.

This man is curious. He says to the young woman, "What are you reading?"

"It is about Russia," says the girl.

"Do you know where Russia is?" He hardly knows himself.

The young woman looks straight at him, full of dignity, though her eyes are red from dust, "I was best in the class. My teacher said I was best."

The young woman resumes her reading. She wants to get to the end of the paragraph.

The Indian looks at the two little children and reaches for some **Fanta**[3], but the mother says, "Fanta makes them thirstier."

The Indian knows he shouldn't do this but he reaches down to a great plastic container beside him, behind the counter, and pours out two mugs of water, which he hands to the children. He watches while the girl looks at her children drinking, her mouth moving. He gives her a mug of water. It hurts him to see her drinking it, so painfully thirsty is she.

Now she hands him her own plastic water container, which he fills. The young woman and the children watch him closely so that he doesn't spill any.

She is bending again over the book. She reads slowly. The paragraph fascinates her and she reads it again.

"*Varenka, with her white kerchief over her black hair, surrounded by the children and gaily and **good-humouredly**[4] busy with them, and at the same visibly excited at the possibility of an offer of marriage from a man she cared for, looked very attractive. Koznyshev walked by her side and kept casting admiring glances at her. Looking at her, he recalled all the delightful things he had heard from her lips, all the good he knew about her, and became more and more conscious that the feeling he had for her was something rare, something he had felt but once before, long, long ago, in his early youth. The joy of being near her increased step by step, and at last reached such a point that, as he put a huge **birch**[5] mushroom with a slender **stalk**[6] and up-curling top into*

---

1 wadge 一卷，一沓
2 fort 堡垒，要塞
3 Fanta 芬达（饮料）
4 good-humouredly 和气地
5 birch 桦树，桦木
6 stalk 茎，秆；叶柄，花梗

*her basket, he looked into her eyes and, noting the flush of glad and frightened **agitation**[1] that **suffused**[2] her face, he was confused himself, and in silence gave her a smile that said too much."*

This lump of print is lying on the counter, together with some old copies of magazines, some pages of newspapers with pictures of girls in bikinis.

It is time for the woman to leave the **haven**[3] of the Indian store, and set off back along the four miles to her village. Outside, the lines of waiting women **clamour**[4] and complain. But still the Indian lingers. He knows what it will cost this girl—going back home, with the two clinging children. He would give her the piece of prose that so fascinates her, but he cannot really believe this **splinter**[5] of a girl with her great belly can really understand it.

Why is perhaps a third of *Anna Karenin* here on this counter in a remote Indian store? It is like this.

A certain high official, from the United Nations as it happens, bought a copy of this novel in a bookshop before he set out on his journey to cross several oceans and seas. On the plane, settled in his business class seat, he tore the book into three parts. He looked around his fellow passengers as he did this, knowing he would see looks of shock, curiosity, but some of amusement. When he was settled, his seat belt tight, he said aloud to whomever could hear, "I always do this when I've a long trip. You don't want to have to hold up some heavy great book." The novel was a paperback, but, true, it is a long book. This man is well used to people listening when he spoke. "*I always do this, travelling,*" he **confided**[6]. "Travelling at all these days, is hard enough." And as soon as people were settling down, he opened his part of Anna Karenin, and read. When people looked his way, curiously or not, he confided in them. "No, it really is the only way to travel." He knew the novel, liked it, and this original mode of reading did add spice to what was after all a well known book.

When he reached the end of a section of the book, he called the air hostess, and sent the chapters back to his secretary, travelling in the cheaper seats. This caused much interest, **condemnation**[7], certainly curiosity, every time a section of the great Russian novel arrived, **mutilated**[8] but readable, in the back part of the plane. Altogether, this clever way of reading *Anna Karenin* makes an impression, and probably no one there would forget it.

Meanwhile, in the Indian store, the young woman is holding on to the counter, her little children clinging to her skirts. She wears jeans, since she is a modern woman, but over them she has put on the heavy woollen skirt, part of the traditional dress of her people: her children can easily cling onto its thick folds.

---

1 agitation 搅动，搅拌；煽动
2 suffuse 弥漫于，布满
3 haven 港口；避难所，安息所
4 clamour 喧哗，吵闹；大声抗议
5 splinter 尖片；碎片；微不足道的事情；〈美俚〉极瘦的人
6 confide （向某人）吐露（隐私、秘密等）
7 condemnation 谴责；定罪；征用
8 mutilate 切断（手足等）；毁坏，毁伤；使……支离破碎

She sends a thankful look to the Indian, whom she knew liked her and was sorry for her, and she steps out into the blowing clouds.

The children are past crying, and their throats are full of dust.

This was hard, oh yes, it was hard, this stepping, one foot after another, through the dust that lay in soft deceiving **mounds**[1] under her feet. Hard, but she was used to hardship, was she not? Her mind was on the story she had been reading. She was thinking, She is just like me, in her white headscarf, and she is looking after children, too. I could be her, that Russian girl. And the man there, he loves her and will ask her to marry him. She had not finished more than that one paragraph. Yes, she thinks, a man will come for me, and take me away from all this, take me and the children, yes, he will love me and look after me.

She steps on. The can of water is heavy on her shoulders. On she goes. The children can hear the water **slopping**[2] about. Half way she stops, sets down the can. Her children are **whimpering**[3] and touching it. She thinks that she cannot open it, because dust would blow in. There is no way she can open the can until she gets home.

"Wait," she tells her children, "wait."

She has to pull herself together and go on.

She thinks, My teacher said there is a library, bigger than the supermarket, a big building and it is full of books. The young woman is smiling as she moves on, the dust blowing in her face. I am clever, she thinks. Teacher said I am clever. The cleverest in the school—she said I was. My children will be clever, like me. I will take them to the library, the place full of books, and they will go to school, and they will be teachers—my teacher told me I could be a teacher. My children will live far from here, earning money. They will live near the big library and enjoy a good life.

You may ask how that piece of the Russian novel ever ended up on that counter in the Indian store?

It would make a pretty story. Perhaps someone will tell it.

On goes that poor girl, held upright by thoughts of the water she will give her children once home, and drink a little of herself. On she goes, through the **dreaded**[4] dusts of an African drought.

We are a **jaded**[5] lot, in our threatened world. We are good for irony and even cynicism. Some words and ideas we hardly use, so worn out have they become. But we may want to restore some words that have lost their **potency**[6].

We have a treasure-house of literature, going back to the Egyptians, the Greeks, the Romans. It is all there, this wealth of literature, to be discovered again and again by whoever is lucky

---

1 mound 土堆，土丘；坟墩
2 slop 晃出；使溢出
3 whimper 啜泣，呜咽；抱怨
4 dreaded 令人畏惧的；害怕的
5 jaded 精疲力竭的；厌倦的；腻烦的；迟钝的
6 potency 效力；潜能；权势

enough to come upon it. A treasure. Suppose it did not exist. How **impoverished**[1], how empty we would be.

We own a legacy of languages, poems, histories, and it is not one that will ever be exhausted. It is there, always.

We have a **bequest**[2] of stories, tales from the old storytellers, some of whose names we know, but some not. The storytellers go back and back, to a clearing in the forest where a great fire burns, and the old **shamans**[3] dance and sing, for our heritage of stories began in fire, magic, the spirit world. And that is where it is held, today.

Ask any modern storyteller and they will say there is always a moment when they are touched with fire, with what we like to call inspiration, and this goes back and back to the beginning of our race, to the great winds that shaped us and our world.

The storyteller is deep inside every one of us. The story-maker is always with us. Let us suppose our world is **ravaged**[4] by war, by the horrors that we all of us easily imagine. Let us suppose floods wash through our cities, the seas rise. But the storyteller will be there, for it is our imaginations which shape us, keep us, create us—for good and for ill. It is our stories that will recreate us, when we are torn, hurt, even destroyed. It is the storyteller, the dream-maker, the myth-maker, that is our **phoenix**[5], that represents us at our best, and at our most creative.

That poor girl **trudging**[6] through the dust, dreaming of an education for her children, do we think that we are better than she is—we, stuffed full of food, our cupboards full of clothes, **stifling**[7] in our **superfluities**[8]?

I think it is that girl, and the women who were talking about books and an education when they had not eaten for three days, that may yet define us.

文化快递

1. Mayor of Casterbridge（《卡斯特桥市长》）

《卡斯特桥市长》是英国著名小说家、诗人哈代的重要代表作之一。在哈代的十四部长篇小说中，《卡斯特桥市长》既体现了哈代创作的一贯风格，又独创了别具一格的艺术特色，由此也显现了一位大艺术家与平庸的多产作家本质的不同。至于这部小说的内容，不论是在历史的和现实的社会认知方面，至今都有鲜活的意义。

2. Animal Farm（《动物庄园》）

《动物庄园》（Animal Farm）亦译作《动物农场》、《动物农庄》，英国著名作家乔

---

1 impoverished 穷困的，无力的，用尽了的
2 bequest 遗赠；遗产
3 shaman 萨满教的道士，僧人或巫师
4 ravage 破坏；蹂躏
5 Phoenix 凤凰
6 trudge 跋涉，吃力地走
7 stifle （使）窒息；（使）窒闷；扼杀
8 superfluity 过多；过剩；多余物；过剩品

治·奥威尔的一个重要作品。本故事描述了一场"动物主义"革命的酝酿、兴起和最终蜕变。本书于1945年首次出版。

3. V.S. Naipaul（V·S·奈保尔）

V·S·奈保尔（V. S. Naipaul,1932年—　）西印度作家、游记作者和社会评论家。他的小说描写各种文化中那些疏离于社会、一生都在寻找自我身份认同的个体。

4. John Coetzee

约翰·马克斯韦尔·库切（John Maxwell Coetzee），南非白人小说家、文学评论家、翻译家、大学教授。是第一位两度获得英国文学最高奖"布克奖"的作家。于2003年获得诺贝尔文学奖，是非洲第五位、南非第三位诺贝尔文学奖得主。

参考译文

我站在门口，远远望去，穿过风卷黄沙的云层，眼光落在一片树丛中，听说那里还有未被砍伐的森林。昨天，我驱车好几英里，一路经过那砍伐过后留下的树桩和林火过后的焦土。1956年，我目睹那里的奇妙森林几乎砍伐殆尽，因为人们既缺少吃的，也缺少柴火。

转眼到了80年代初期津巴布韦西北部，我在拜访一位朋友——伦敦一所学校的教师。他在那里"援助非洲"，如我们所说的那样。他是一位有理想的人，可是，在非洲那所学校发现的一切都令他震惊，从此以后，他陷入一种难以自拔的消沉之中。这所学校与津巴布韦独立后建立的所有学校没有什么两样。它有四间大砖房，一间靠一间，整整齐齐，坐落在蒙蒙灰尘里，一、二、三、四，最后一间以半间房子作图书馆。教室里有黑板，可我的这位朋友经常把粉笔放在口袋里，要不就会被偷窃。学校里没有地图或地球仪，甚至连教科书都没有，更没有练习本或圆珠笔。图书馆的书，不是学生要读的那种：大多是来自美国各大学的大部头书，甚至很难捧起来，被白人图书馆弃置的，还有一些小说如《巴黎周末》或《费丽西蒂找到了爱情》之类的书。

一只山羊想在干枯的草丛中寻找可以吃的。校长挪用了学校资金，已经停职处理，由此引发了我们大家都很熟悉的问题，但一般在较严重的情况中才会提出来：在众目睽睽之下，这些人的行径怎么会如此大胆？

我朋友的钱包已经空了，因为不少学生和教师，在他领工资的时候都伸手向他借钱，也许从来没有人还过钱。学生小的六岁，大到二十六岁，因为早先没上过学的青年，也在这里补习。有些学生每天清早要走好几英里，无论天晴下雨，都得穿越几条河流赶到学校。他们无法做家庭作业，因为村庄里没有电，靠柴火照明，不方便学习。女孩子在放学回家后和上学之前，还必须去打水和煮饭。

当我和这位朋友坐在他的房间里，顺道而来的人们害羞地走进来，所有的来客，个个

向我们讨要书本。"你回到伦敦后，请给我们寄书吧。"一名男子说，"他们教我们读书，可我们没有书。"我遇见的每一个人，都讨要书本。

我在那里呆了几天。风卷沙尘掠过黄土，水泵坏了，更缺水了，妇女们来来回回从河里取水。另一位来自英国怀抱理想的教师，看到这个"学校"的样子后，病了一场。

最后一天，即期末结束的那一天，他们宰了一只羊，剁成肉片放进一个大罐子里煮。这是师生期待很久的期末宴会：清水煮羊肉片和麦片粥。"宴会"进行时我驾车离开了，经由那片焦土和森林留下的树桩，一路回程。

我不认为这个学校的许多学生会获什么奖。

次日，我应邀到伦敦北部的一所学校，那是一所非常好的知名学校。它是专为男孩开办的，有漂亮的楼房和花园。

这些学生每周有一次会见来访名人的机会。实际上，应邀的访客往往是学生们的父母、亲戚。英国名人来访，对于他们已经不是什么了不起的大事情了。

津巴布韦西北部风沙尘土中那所学校盘旋在我心里。我盯着（伦敦的）那些温和的充满期待的面孔，想把上一周看到的情形告诉他们。那是没有教科书，没有地图集，连贴在墙上的地图都没有的教室。学校的教师请求我给他们寄书，要我教他们如何教学。他们自己只有十八九岁。我告诉伦敦的孩子们：他们每个人都讨要图书："求求你，请寄书给我们吧。"在这里发表过演讲的每一个名人，都难免经历这样的时刻：看到了一张张没有表情的脸。他们不明白你在说什么。因为，他们心里没有与你告诉他们的情形相对应的画面。那样的情形：尘土中的学校，缺水的土地，期末的羊肉片"宴会"，这一切，对于他们都是多么陌生啊。

他们真的无法想象那种赤贫吗？

我尽力而为。他们毕竟是懂得礼貌的。

我敢肯定，他们中间，将来总会有人会得什么奖的。

然后，到此为止吧。我遇见的那些教师，总是问：图书馆怎么样？学生读些什么书？在那里，在那所得天独厚的学校，我听到的是我访问中学甚至访问大学时经常听到的事情。

"你知道学校的情况吧。许多孩子连一本书也没有读过，图书馆不少书都没有人借过。"

是的，我们的确了解它的真实状况。我们所有的人都有所了解。

我们处在一种断裂的文化中，在这里，我们所知的确切事实，甚至几十年前不言自明的事情，现在也成了一个有疑问的话题。受过多年教育的年轻人，竟然对这个世界近乎一无所知，几乎没有读过什么文学作品，仅仅知道计算机之类极少的几个专业。这样的情况，对于受过现代教育的青年男女来说，是一个共同的问题。

在我们周围发生的，是令人惊异的发明创造——电视，计算机和互联网。这是一场革命。这并不是人类遭遇的第一次革命。印刷术革命，不是发生在几十年前的事情，而是发生在很久以前，改变了我们的意识和思维方式。我们糊里糊涂接受了这一切，如我们经常所做的那样，从来不问："随着印刷术的发明，我们身边将发生怎样的变化？"正如我们从来没有自我约束，从来没有问过的那样：我们，我们的心灵，随着新的互联网发生了怎样的变化。整个一代人已经被诱惑到一种虚拟的生活中，甚至很理性的人也承认，一旦他们上钩了，就很难摆脱出来，他们可能一整天泡在博客里，泡在网虫堆里。

不久以前，任何稍微念过书上过学的人都会尊重知识和教育，对我们伟大文学宝库心怀崇敬。当然，大家都知道，在养尊处优的情况下，人们会假装在读书，假装尊重知识。但是，历史告诉我们，贫苦的劳工和妇女才真正渴望读书，这是由十八世纪和十九世纪的工人图书馆，各种学会和学校证明了的事实。

阅读，书籍，通常是普及教育的一部分。

年长者在和年轻人谈话时一定能体会到，读书对人起到了何等重要的教育作用，因为，年轻人懂得的东西太有限了。如果儿童不会读书，那是因为他们还没有读过书。

我们都知道这个辛酸的故事。

可是，我们并不知道故事的结尾。

我们记得一句名言："读书使人充实"——但我们忘记了有关饱食过量的这句戏言：读书使得男人和女人胀饱了信息、历史和各种各样的知识。

但是，我们并不是这个世界与众不同的人。不久以前，一位朋友打电话给我说，她到过津巴布韦，看到一个村庄，村民们三天没有吃的了，可他们却谈论图书，谈论如何得到图书和教育问题。

我属于一个小组织，这个组织发起的目的在于把图书送到村庄。有一群人通过别的联系渠道去过津巴布韦，深入到草根阶层。他们报道说，不像别人报道的那样，那些村庄，有很多聪明人，有退休的教师，有休假的教师，度假的儿童，以及老人。我自己花钱做了一个小小的、关于当地人想读什么书的调查，结果与我原来不知道的瑞典的一个调查相同。那里的人们想要读的书，就是欧洲人想要读的书——各种各样的小说、科幻小说、诗歌、侦探小说、戏剧、莎士比亚，和各种实用书籍都需要，例如，教他们如何开一个银行账号的书。他们都知道莎士比亚这个名字和他的作品。为村庄找书的一个麻烦是，他们不知道可以得到什么样的书，像《卡斯特桥市长》这样的书，有读者，受欢迎，因为他们知道有这样一本书。《动物农庄》，由于显而易见的原因，是所有长篇小说中最受欢迎的。

我们的小组织开始是由挪威资助的，后来得到瑞典的资助。假如没有资助，我们的图书供给就会断流。我们的小组织想方设法从可能的地方得到图书，但请记得，从英国来的一本好的平装书，要花津巴布韦人几个月的工资：那是在穆加贝的恐怖统治之前的情况。现在随着通货膨胀，它得花几年的工资。因此，在汽油奇缺的情况下，开车把一箱书送到一个村庄，会受到热泪纵横的欢迎。那个图书馆也许只是一棵树下砖头堆起来的一个支架而已。在一周之内就会出现几个识字班——会读书的人教不会读书的人，教普通的公民学习班。在一个遥远的村庄，由于没有汤加语的小说，两个青年人坐下来开始尝试以汤加语写作。在津巴布韦有六种以上主要的语言，每一个语种都有长篇小说，暴力的、乱伦的、连篇累牍的犯罪和谋杀。

有人说，有什么的人民，就有什么样的政府。但我不认为这句话适合于津巴布韦的真实情况。我们应当记得，这种对于图书的尊重和饥渴，不是来自穆加贝的政权，而是来自在它之前的那个政权，白人的政权。这是一个令人惊异的现象，对图书的渴望，从肯尼亚一直到好望角，无处不可以发现。

这个现象难以置信地与下述事实相关：我是在一间泥墙茅屋里长大的。那样的房子到处都有，那里有芦苇和野草，有适宜造墙的泥巴和柱杆，有撒克逊时代的英格兰风格。我住过的茅屋有四个房间，一间靠一间，不仅是一个房间，重要的是，屋里藏书丰富。我父母常从英国带书到非洲来，母亲还给孩子们通过邮寄订购英国图书。一大包一大包牛皮纸包裹里的书，是我青春的欢乐。虽然是茅屋，却堆满了书。

有时我接到一些村民的来信，他们村里也许没有电，没有自来水（正如我们的泥墙茅屋的家庭一样），但有人告诉我："我也要当作家，因为我有你住过的同样的茅屋。"

这就很难说了，几乎不可能。

写作有必要的前提，作家不能出自没有书的房子。

有难以逾越的鸿沟，难以克服的困难。

我读过你们学院近几年来的几位获奖者的演讲词。拿高贵的帕穆克来说吧。他说，他父亲有500本图书。他的天才并非凭空而来，他与伟大的传统密切相联。

拿V. S. 奈保尔来说，他谈到印度的吠陀经在他家里是常备书。他父亲鼓励他写作。他到英国后，很好地利用了大不列颠图书馆。因此他是贴近伟大传统的。

让我们再看看约翰·库切的情况。他不仅仅贴近伟大传统，他自己就是传统：他在开普敦教文学。遗憾的是，我还从来没有听过他的课——那个奇妙的勇敢的天才讲授的文学课。

为了写作，为了创造文学，必须与图书馆、与书籍、与传统保持密切联系。

我有一个从津巴布韦来的朋友，一位黑人作家。黑人——那就成问题了。他告诉我：他靠什么自学呢，靠读果酱瓶子上的标签，读水果罐头上的标签。他是在我驾车经过的一个地区长大的。那是一个乡村黑人区，土地都是粗沙，有矮矮的稀疏的灌木丛。那些茅屋真可怜，一点也不像富裕人家精心筑起好生照管的茅屋。那里也有一所学校，跟我描绘过的那种学校差不多。他从一个垃圾堆里发现了一本被丢弃的儿童百科全书，然后自学这本书。

1980年津巴布韦独立时，出现了一批优秀作家，真是一窝歌唱的鸟。他们是在旧称南罗得西亚，在好得多的白人教会学校里喂养大的。作家并不是在津巴布韦造就的。在穆加贝的统治之下很难造就作家。

所有的作家都有一条困难的提高读写能力的道路，要步入创作阶段更不容易。我想说的是，靠果酱罐头的标签和被丢弃的百科全书来学习，并不是不同寻常的事情。我正在谈论的，是那些远离正规教育却渴望得到这种教育的人们。他们挤在茅屋里，有好几个孩子，一位过度操劳的母亲，为衣食奔波，甚至在拼命挣扎。

可是，尽管这些困难，作家诞生了。还有另一件事情我们应当记得。这是津巴布韦，将近一百年前被征服的土地。这些人的祖父母，也许是为部落讲故事的人，有丰富的口头文学传统。从一代人、两代人，从口耳相传的故事到印成文字，写成书本，这是多么了不起的成就啊。

书本，好不容易从白人世界的垃圾堆和碎石堆里拣起的书本，多么宝贵。你也许有了一堆纸，但是出版却是另一回事。我收到过好几个关于非洲出版业和图书行情的评估报道。甚至在北非洲这样的占优势的地方，有其不同的传统的地方，谈论图书行情，也只是一种奢侈，一个梦想而已。

我现在谈论的，是还没有写出来的书，是无法制作一本书的作家，因为出版商不在那里。那是没有人听见的声音。潜在的伟大天才埋没了，精神损失是无法估价的。他们缺乏出版商和预付金，缺乏外来的鼓励，也缺乏成书之前的许多基本条件。

经常有人问作家，你怎样写作？有电脑吗？有电动打字机吗？一支鹅毛笔？依照普通的书写方法？但最要紧的问题是，"你找到了一个地方吗，找到了便于写作的清静环境吗？"在那仿佛有人在聆听你注视你的地方，你的人物想说的话，纷纭的思绪，可能一齐涌上来，这就是灵感。

假如这个作家不能找到一个好地方，那么，难产的诗歌和故事也许一生下来就死了。

当作家们交谈切磋时，他们询问的，往往是适合写作的环境和时间。"你找到了吧？你握紧了它吗？"

让我们跳到一个截然不同的情境中吧。我们到了伦敦，大都市之一，遇到一位新作家。我们冷嘲热讽地问：她的乳房（boobs与books发音相近）怎么样？长得漂亮吗？假如是个男人，就会问：他很有魅力吗？帅哥？我们开玩笑，可这并不是玩笑。

这样的文学新星赢得一片喝彩，可能还赚了一大笔钱。最终明星摄影师开始在他们可怜的耳朵边嘀咕，骚扰他们。他们得到款待、称赞，似乎搅动了这个世界。我们这些老家伙，见的事情多了，把这一切看在眼里，不得不为这样的文坛新秀感到遗憾，因为他们对世界上发生的大事情，什么看法也没有。

他，她真会拍马屁，好高兴啊。

可是，问他或问她究竟在想些什么，问了一年之后，我才听到他们的声音："这可能

是降临在我头上的最糟糕的事情。"

某些出了不少书的新作家不再写了,或者没有他们想写的东西了,没有什么思考过的东西要写了。

我们这些老家伙需要对那些天真的耳朵悄悄耳语。"你找到了写作的地方吗?你的唯一的,属于自己的必要的地方,你可以在寂寞中自言自语的地方,你可以做梦的地方。啊,牢牢把握它吧,别让它溜走了。"

我心里充满对非洲的美好记忆,我不时回想起那里的情形,一幅幅画面浮现在眼前。夕阳西下,橘色的、金黄的、紫色的晚霞涂抹在黄昏的天边。蝴蝶。飞蛾和蜜蜂在喀拉哈里沙漠芬芳的灌木丛里飞来飞去。或者,在赞比西河岸,可以看到河水从暗绿色的两岸之间涌流而过。即使干旱的季节,也不乏绿色的点缀。环绕两岸的,有非洲的丰富的鸟类,还有大象、长颈鹿、狮子等各种动物。那时的夜空还没有受到污染,黝黑而神奇,缀满躁动的星星。

但也有另外一些记忆。一个十八岁上下的青年,含着眼泪站在他的"图书馆"里。一位来访的美国人看到一个没有书的图书馆,后来寄来一箱书,但这个青年心怀虔敬把每一本拿出来,用塑料袋把它们包好。"可是,"我们问道,"这些书寄来肯定是供人阅读的,对不对?"他回答说,"不,它们会弄脏的。我从哪里再弄得到呢?"

他要我们从英国给他寄书,教他如何教。"我在大龄儿童学校教了四年,"他恳求道,"可他们从来没有教我怎样教书。"

我在一所学校见过一位教师,那个学校没有教科书,有一块黑板,可连一支粉笔也没有,被人偷走了。他用石头在地上的灰堆里写写画画,比如"2 X 2 ="之类的算术,他教一个班,学生从六岁到十八岁。我见到一个女教师,也许不到二十岁,同样缺乏教科书、练习本、圆珠笔——什么都没有,她用一根棍子在地上写字,教 A、B、C,头上烈日当空,身边尘土飞扬。

我们在这里看到的,是在非洲,在第三世界的许多地方,或世界的偏远角落对教育的饥渴。父母渴望孩子们得到好的教育,那种可以引导他们摆脱贫困的教育。

我希望你们设身处地地想象一下,在南非的某个地方,站在一家印度人开的店铺附近,一个穷人区,干旱的季节。有人在排队,大多是妇女,带着盛水的坛坛罐罐。店铺每天下午从镇上得到一车厢饮用水,人们在等候这宝贵的水。

那个印度老板站在那里,双手撑在柜枱上,正在注视一个年轻的黑人妇女,她正躬着身子,盯着一沓纸张,看起来那是从一本书撕下来的。她开始读《安娜·卡列尼娜》。

她慢慢地读,轻声念着。看起来,这是一本难读的书。她身边有两个小孩正在扯她的腿,肚子里又怀上了。印度人感到难过,因为她的白色头巾被灰尘染黄了。灰尘扑满她的胸脯,盖满她的双手。同时使这个老板感到难过的,是排着长龙的人,口渴得要命,可他没有足够的水给他们喝。他感到很伤脑筋,因为有人在黄沙云层的另一边命在旦夕。他的哥哥，曾经在这里帮忙照看，但他不得不去城里休息，因为旱灾，他又累又病。

出于好奇，印度老板问那个年轻妇女说："你在读什么？"

"写俄罗斯的。"女子答道。

"你知道俄罗斯在哪里吗？"他自己也不大知道啊。

年轻妇女径直地看着他，尽管她的双眼被灰尘染红了，却充满自尊地说，"我是班上最好的学生。老师说，我是最好的。"

年轻妇女继续读书：她要读完这一个章节。

印度人看着那两个小孩，伸手取一瓶芬达饮料给他们，可母亲说，"芬达会使得他们更加口渴。"

印度人知道他不应当这样做，便从身边柜枱背后的一个大塑料罐里，倒了两塑料杯子的水，递给孩子们。他注意到，当这个年轻母亲看着她的孩子们喝水时，嘴唇随之颤动。他给她也倒了一杯水。看到她喝水时口渴的样子，不禁感到一阵酸楚。

这时，她把塑料水罐递给他，他灌进了水。她和孩子们，紧盯着他，他没有溅落一滴水。

她再次弯身读书。慢慢读，那个段落使她入迷了，她重读了一遍。

"瓦莲卡的黑发上包着一条白头巾，显得很迷人，身边环绕着一群孩子，她正亲昵而快活地为他们忙着。显然，由于她钟爱的男子可能向她求婚，她兴奋不已，模样儿楚楚动人。科兹内舍夫和她并肩走着，不住地向她抛过去爱慕的眼光。望着她，他回忆起她说过的一切动人的话语，他所知道的她的一切优点。他越来越意识到，他对她的感情是非常特殊的，这种感情，他在好久好久以前，在他的青年时代也只感到过一次。靠近她所产生的愉悦感不断加强，达到不同寻常的地步。当他发现一个茎秆并不粗壮伞盖却很大的桦树菌时，他采摘下来放到她的提篮里，望着她的眼睛，看到她满脸的又惊又喜的红晕，他自己也感到一阵迷乱，便默默向她微笑，这是无声胜有声的语言。"

这份读物又摆在柜枱上了，加上一些旧杂志，几张报纸，印有穿着比基尼的女郎。

时候到了，她要离开印度人开的这个店铺庇护所了，要走四英里才能走回村庄。是时候了。外面排队等候的妇女们吵吵嚷嚷，抱怨起来。但印度人仍然在拖延。他知道这个拖着两个孩子的妈妈在回家路上会多么艰难。他在犹豫，该不该把这本令她着迷的读物送给她，因为他不知道，这个身子瘦弱却挺着大肚子的女子，能不能真正读懂它。

这本读物，莫非就是《安娜.卡列尼娜》那本书撕下来的三分之一，结果摆在这偏远的印度人开的店铺的柜枱上？是这么一回事。

那是联合国的一位高官，启程跨海旅行的时候，碰巧在书店买了这本小说。坐在飞机头等舱的座位上，他把这本书撕成三部分。他一边撕，一边注意周围的乘客，他知道会看到惊异的好奇的表情，或逗笑的脸色。坐稳之后，他系好安全带，便高声叫嚷，唯恐大家听不见："我在旅途中经常这样做。你们不要携带太重的大书。"小说是平装本，但的确是一本很厚的书。这名男子习惯于向人们抱怨。"我在旅途中经常这样做,长途旅行太难受了。"周围的乘客坐下来之后,他就打开《安娜·卡列尼娜》的一部分,开始阅读。当人们或好奇或顺便瞟他一眼时,他就向他们倾诉:"难道不是这样吗?它的确是唯一可行的旅行方式。"这部小说他先前读过,喜欢它,这种独创的阅读方式给一本名著增添了一点趣味。

读完第一部分后,他就叫来空姐,请她把它送给坐在经济舱的他的秘书。每一次,当俄罗斯的这部伟大小说的一部分,虽然撕破了却可以阅读的一沓纸张抵达经济舱时,就会引起一阵关注,非议和好奇。总之,这种聪明的阅读《安娜.卡列尼娜》的方式造成了一个印象,令人难忘的印象。

另一幅画面是:在印度人开的店铺里,那个年轻妇女正靠在柜枱上,她的两个小孩贴身在她的裙子边。她穿着牛仔裤,是个现代妇女,但牛仔裤上面是厚重的羊毛裙,这是她的传统民族服装的一部分。两个孩子很容易扯住厚厚的裙子的褶边。

她对印度人报以感谢的一瞥,她知道他喜欢她,为她感到遗憾。她走出店铺,走进大风呼啸卷起的黄沙中。

孩子们不再哭了,他们的喉咙已经塞满灰尘。

多么艰难,是的,的确不容易。一步一步走去,经由脚下土墩上软绵绵的灰尘。虽然难,但她习惯了这一切,难道不是这样吗?她的心还流连在她读过的故事里。她正在想,"她,正像我一样,戴着白头巾,正在照看孩子们。我可以成为她,那个俄罗斯女郎。那个男子在那里,他爱她,要向她求婚(她还没有读完那一个章节)。是的,也许会有一个男人为我而来,把我从这里带走,把我和我的孩子都带走,是的,他会爱我的,会照顾我的。"

她走啊走啊。水罐沉重地压在她的肩膀上。她继续跋涉。孩子们听见水在罐子里荡漾。半路上,她停下来,放下水罐。两个孩子开始哭哭嚷嚷,摸着水罐。但她觉得,现在还不能打开水罐喝,因为灰尘会扑进来。要一直回到家里才能打开喝。

"等一等,"她告诉孩子,"等一等吧。"

她打起精神拖着身子一步一步往前走。

她想,老师说,那里有个图书馆,比超级市场还大呢,一座塞满了书的大楼房。青年妇女边走边笑,灰尘扑到她的脸上。我是聪明的,她想。老师说我聪明。学校里最聪明的——她说,我是最聪明的。我的孩子也会像我一样聪明。我要带他们到图书馆去,到堆满图书的地方,他们要上学,他们要当教师—— 我的老师说,我可以当教师。他们要远离这里,去挣钱。他们要住在靠近大图书馆的地方,过上美好的生活。

你们也许会问,俄罗斯小说的那个片段怎么到了那家印度店铺的柜枱上?

这是个动人的故事,将来也许会有人来讲述这个故事的。

那个可怜的妇女,一路上总是想着水,水,平安回到家里之后,她会给孩子们喝的,她自己要少喝一点。她继续走呵，走呵，穿过非洲旱季可怕的沙尘。

我们是迟钝的人。我们，处在这个面临威胁的世界。我们长于反讽，甚至长于冷嘲热讽。某些词或观念几乎不用了，已经成为陈词滥调了；但我们也许应该恢复某些已经失去其力量的词语。

我们有个宝库，文学的宝库，可以一直上溯到埃及人、希腊人，罗马人。所有的文学财富都在这里，不断被那些幸运儿发现和重新发现。一个宝库，假如没有这个宝库，生活会多么贫乏，我们将多么空虚。

我们拥有语言、诗歌和历史的遗产，取之不尽的遗产。始终在这里。

我们有丰富的故事的遗产，古老的讲故事的人传下来的，我们知道他们中的某些人的名字，但有些人的名字已经失传了。讲故事的人可以不断退回到林中的一片空地，那里一堆篝火燃烧，古老的萨满或巫师们载歌载舞，因为我们的故事的遗产始于火，始于魔法，始于精神世界。这就是今天它仍然被保留被承传的地方。

不管你询问哪一位现代讲故事的人，他都会告诉你这样的体验：当火舌贴近身边的时候，总会在刹那间爆发出我们称之为灵感的东西。这要追溯到人类的起源，追溯到造就了我们和人世的火、冰和大风。

讲故事的人，深藏在我们每个人的内心。编故事的人，始终伴随着我们。让我们展开想象吧，我们的世界正在受到战争的蹂躏，处在我们不难想象的恐怖的威胁之下。让我们展开想象吧，洪水淹没城镇，海水呼啸上涨……但是，讲故事的人会出现在那里，因为塑造了保存了创造了我们的，正是我们的想象——不管是好是坏，都是我们的想象。在我们被撕裂、被伤害甚至被摧毁的时候，将重塑我们的，是我们的故事。讲故事的人，是编造梦幻的人，编造神话的人，是我们劫后不死的长生鸟。我们的最佳状态，就是我们最具创造性的时候。

那可怜的女子一路穿越黄尘跋涉，梦见给她的孩子提供的教育。我们会觉得：我们比她要好得多吗——我们这些饱食终日的人，衣柜里塞满各种服饰的人，窒息在我们的奢侈品中的人们？

我想，那可怜的女孩，以及三天没吃东西却在谈论图书和教育的那些妇女，才可能定义我们。